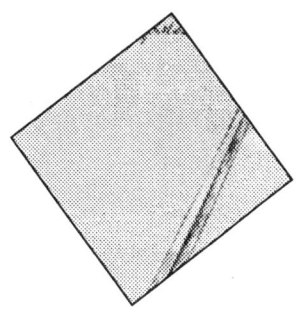

ANGELAKI

a new journal in

philosophy,

literature and

the social sciences

issue editors:
David Howarth
Aletta J. Norval

executive editors:
Charlie Blake
Pelagia Goulimari
Aletta J. Norval
Barry Stocker
Sarah Wood

general editor:
Pelagia Goulimari

managing editor:
Gerard Greenway

contributing editors:
Linnie Blake
Josep-Anton Fernández
Nick Groom
Sara Guyer
Gary Hall
Stefan Heidenreich
David Howarth
Forbes Morlock
Timothy S. Murphy
Melina Nathan
Ben Norland
Yanna Popova
Mozaffar Qizilbash
Roy Sellars
Robert Smith
Mike Whitworth

design and art direction:
Ben Norland

production and design:
John Peacock

The front cover features a portion of the frontispiece of Thomas Hobbes' *Leviathan* (1651). By courtesy of the British Library.

Printed in Great Britain
by Watkiss Studios Limited

© ANGELAKI 1994
ISBN: 1 899567 02 X
ISSN: 0969 725X

CONTENTS

ANGELAKI   1 : 3

reconsidering

the political

edited by

david howarth

and aletta j. norval

EDITORIAL INTRODUCTION

david howarth
aletta j. norval

POLITICS, ETHICS, IDENTITY
reconsidering the political

It is a strange fact, but the emergence and flourishing of post-structuralism and post-modernism has not for the most part been accompanied by a constructive rethinking of political theory and ethics. In part, this is a consequence of certain readings of post-structuralism which have embraced the increasing contingency and historicity of the present, only to deepen our incapacity to produce alternative intellectual, strategic and ethical horizons, or which appear to be complicit with political and economic currents which go contrary to the values and commitments of what is traditionally labelled 'progressive', 'socialist', 'democratic', 'radical' and so forth. In the light of these interpretations, post-modernist and post-structuralist perspectives are often seen as exacerbating the prevailing logics of decentrement, difference and abandonment, without endeavouring to transcend the pole of disintegration.

In most of the articles gathered together in this issue of *Angelaki*, another position is advanced. In these pieces, a questioning of epistemological and moral foundations does not entail a corrosive skepticism and a hastening of the retreat of the political. While these contributors accept that modern, foundational conceptions of politics and ethics are increasingly unable to make intelligible recent social and political developments, or even go as far as to suggest that they act as fetters on the production of alternative social imaginaries, there is no question of speaking of an end to politics and ethics. What is suggested is that an essential condition of possibility for thinking the present, as well as adumbrating visions for the future, is a radical engagement with those categories and assumptions which currently form our ground, so that their limitations and closures may be glimpsed, and perhaps breached.

Without wishing to impute a false paradigmatic unity, many of the arguments presented in this issue are structured according to this double imperative: an accounting for the antinomies and undecidabilities of one's own 'order of things', while endeavouring to explore and negotiate this settling of accounts without reinscribing the very closures which are being confronted. While not attempting the impossible task of 'introducing', let alone 'summarising', the articles collected in this issue, this introduction simply offers a series of notes on some of the ideas and arguments which are presented here. For presentational convenience, a threefold division of the articles is proposed: those which directly concern a reconsideration of the concept of politics and the political; those that explore the relationship between politics and ethics/philosophy; and those that examine more concrete historical conjunctures.

5

politics and the political

With respect to a rethinking of the political itself, the double injunction referred to above has centred on the displacement of politics from its usual channels of operation – witnessed in the growing popular disenchantment with formal political spaces and procedures, the failure of traditional institutions and divisions, such as the state and the state/civil society relation, to accommodate social antagonisms and representations, and the complex dialectic of politicisation and depoliticisation characteristic of contemporary social relations – and its extension into greater and greater areas of social life. Not surprisingly, a number of the articles tackle these kinds of questions directly.

In 'Tracing the Political', Benjamin Arditi seeks to account theoretically for contemporary political realities, and to assess the possibilities for political emancipation. In doing so, he draws a conceptual distinction between 'the political' and 'politics', and then articulates a relationship between them as interconnected registers. Hence 'politics', for Arditi, 'has its own public space or *locus*. It is the field of exchanges between political parties; of parliamentary and governmental affairs; of elections and representation; and in general, of the type of activity, practices and procedures that take place in the institutional ensemble of the political system'. By contrast, drawing on and extending the writings of Carl Schmitt, Arditi defines the political as a:

> [T]ype of relationship that can develop in any area of the social, regardless of whether or not it remains within the institutional closure of 'politics'. It includes but exceeds the field of 'politics'. It has no particular object, no unique actors, no necessary institutional support of its own. All that matters is the enactment of public engagements between

friends and enemies: the political is being enacted whenever and wherever these are spotted.

Plotting the interacting dimensions of these two registers, Arditi then explores the consequences of this theorisation for an understanding of contemporary political movements, and the potential emancipatory possibilities which these considerations reveal.

Arguing from similar philosophical assumptions, Michael Cholewa-Madsen's 'Enacting the Political' sets out the theoretical and ethical prerequisites for an 'anti-totalitarian political project'. Contesting attempts by French Heideggerian thinkers such as Philippe Lacoue-Labarthe and Jean-Luc Nancy to outline the essence of the political, Cholewa-Madsen draws on Derridean deconstruction, and the political theory of Ernesto Laclau and Chantal Mouffe, to insist on an 'anti-essentialist conception of the political'. In doing so, he also distinguishes between 'politics' and 'the political', in which 'politics becomes the separate subsystem 'interacting' with other subsystems, and the political becomes the very moment of openness when the structuring principle of society is questioned or reactivated by antagonizing subjective forces'. Having elaborated upon the openness of the political, grounded as he puts it on the constitutive impossibility of the social as a full positivity, Cholewa-Madsen sets out two strategies for 'enacting the political' in a non-totalitarian fashion. These include a Socratic 'strategy of suspicion' toward any actually existing situation, and the (impossible) endeavour to institutionalise a project of 'radical democracy'.

Ernesto Laclau's writings on political theory, together with Chantal Mouffe, have exhibited an unrelenting effort to articulate a political theory in a context marked by post-structuralism and post-modernism. Without giving way to a fashionable embrace of these theoretical and philosophical trends, Laclau has rigorously, and without sentiment, subjected the presuppositions and logics of radical theoretical discourse to constructive critique. A number of the contributions to this collection of articles draw explicitly on his theoretical approach. In the interview we publish here, we endeavour to locate his writings in the context of contemporary intellectual and theoretical developments, to tease out some of the productive tensions in his current theoretical work, and to examine their consequences for a rethinking of politics and ethics. Of particular interest are his remarks on the indeterminacy and undecidability of the present, which undermines any 'objective' claim to a global pessimism or optimism, and the implications of this for our experience of freedom as 'both liberating and enslaving, exhilarating and traumatic, enabling and destructive'.

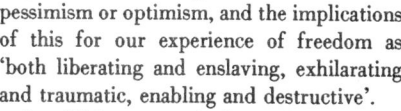

In addition to a rethinking of the concept of politics and the political, another central and contested division in contemporary political theory concerns the relationship between the state and civil society. Two articles in this issue focus on this question, both of which point to processes and conceptualisations which privilege the role of the state at the expense of civil society. In the extract we publish from their new book *Labor of Dionysus: Critique of the State-Form*, Antonio Negri and Michael Hardt argue that it is civil society, rather than the state, which has begun to whither away in the current conjuncture. Arising from their critical account of certain post-modern interpretations of John Rawls' *Theory of Justice*, they posit a coincidence of post-modern liberal theory and the neo-liberal political projects which emerged and flourished during the 1980s, pointing out the tension between the liberal notion of the minimal state, and the development of an autonomous and strong state during the same period.

Also focusing on recent theoretical discussions about civil society, Yael Shalem and David Bensusan's article 'Civil Society: The Traumatic Patient' shares to some extent Negri and Hardt's argument concerning the prioritisation of state order and organisation over pluralism and diversity, but locates this privileging in the bifurcation of the subject in the Western tradition. They argue that the state/civil society distinction, grounded as it is on a division between order and freedom, mirrors the splitting of subjectivity between reason and rationality (the disengaged self) on the one hand, and passion, desire, uneasiness (the expressive self) on the other. As they put it:

> At the social level the split self is transposed in a form of dualist agency which enforces a spatial division of functions (control v. autonomy), of tendencies (organisation v. disorder), of needs (unity v. pluralism), and of morality (public duty v. private egocentric needs). We argue that a view which represents the social in the image of split tendencies between the disengaged self as common, rational, repressive and coercive on the one hand and the expressive self as particular, impulsive, narcissistic and aggressive on the other will ultimately seek redemption in a centralist and deterministic process of socialisation.

Developing a 'traumatic' reading of Freud's 'triadic' self, they conclude that it is the unequal relationship between state and civil society which, paradoxically, produces the pluralism associated with, yet denied to, the realm of civil society.

politics contra ethics/philosophy?

Sue Golding's article 'Curiosity' tackles the question of identity and difference from a post-foundational perspective. Using ideas and arguments from writers such as Wittgenstein, Nietzsche, Foucault, Adorno, Blanchot, Derrida and Heidegger, she problematises any simple resolution of the paradox of identity/difference, whether this takes the form of an absolute negation, or the valorisation of a primordial temporality at the expense of a static spatiality. But, she asks, does the refusal of a pure identity and/or difference imply 'a kind of "chaotic meaninglessness", a kind of "radical nihilism", that "whatever is" is, *ipso facto*, good?' Refusing this alternative, her reasoning is equally unsettling in its stress on the primacy of politics in the formation of ethical and moral truths: '[b]y insisting on the radical political contingency of any social imaginary and the paradigmatic "bleeding homelands" around which they turn, it is also to say, then, that the codes of existence – and, more to the point, the moral and ethical truths implied by those codes – are only as solid as are the hegemonic expressions from whence they sprang'.

In a similar vein, Rudi Visker explores our continuing preoccupation with Foucault. In his 'Fascination with Foucault: Object and Desire of an Archaeology of Our Knowledge', he notes the fascination and irritation induced by Foucault's insistence that not only is the source of our knowledge – the 'general system of thought' – external and anonymous, but it is also denied to us.

For Visker, it is only by dwelling in this double-bind that the post-structuralist decentring of the subject – not the disappearance of the subject, 'but that which makes the subject unable to disappear' – realises its most radical and productive effects:

> By an ethos of finitude which, in depriving us of the comfort of a centre also deprives us of the comfort of a lack of centre (of a decentred *en-soi*), perhaps is meant nothing more – but also nothing less – than this: learn to linger in the 'in-between' of the decentredness, learn that we must, with our appearing ('centre'), also let go of our disappearing, and that the real message about the death of the subject consists in the subject's having to go on living until further notice.

The position of Nietzsche in contemporary philosophical and theoretical debates has become increasingly central. David Owen's article 'Agonal Thought: Reading Nietzsche as a Political Thinker' stages the different 'wars of interpretations' surrounding Nietzsche's writings as exemplary of the political itself. Contrasting the traditionally legislative and poetic interpretations of Nietzsche, and making them structurally isomorphic with the slave and master modalities of morality respectively, Owen draws out the different political implications of these opposed perspectives by counterposing Kant's political moralism (legislator/slave) with Nietzsche's political aesthetics (poet/noble). He concludes that whereas Kant 'presents us with a conception of the political as the timeless site of a single universal authority to which all are subject', Nietzsche 'offers an understanding of the political as the historically and culturally shifting site of the contest of multiple authorities'.

Michael Reid's critical reading of Richard

Rorty – 'Rorty's Pragmatism: Argument and Experience' – is not concerned explicitly with the relationship between ethics and politics, but rather with the connection, or lack thereof, between Rorty's circumvention of traditional epistemology, with its emphatic notion of truth, and the lived experiences to which it refers, and with which it ought to be involved. Though sympathising to some extent with Rorty's pragmatic critique of metaphysical realism, he draws on Adorno's critical engagement with concrete social practices to take issue with the absence in Rorty's discourse of that which calls for and orients thinking, as well as his complicity 'with a set of social practices that systematically exclude the spontaneity of the subject, handing over their guidance to topic-neutral steering mechanisms'. It is this aporia in Rorty's philosophy, argues Reid, manifest in its peculiar conception of irony, which explains Rorty's political allegiances, and his willed confinement of expressivism (which includes our most public responsibilities) to the private sphere.

democracy and identity

Jelica Sumic and Rado Riha's article 'The Reinvention of Democracy in Eastern Europe' and Aletta Norval's 'The Politics of Homecoming? Contending Identities in Contemporary South Africa or *Identité à Venir*' examine two current historical conjunctures which immediately call for and orient thinking. Both articles deal with the different logics and processes by which human beings are turned into subjects. In contrast to most critical analyses, Sumic and Riha focus on the gaze of the Western spectator to interpret and theorise the process of democratisation, and the rise of aggressive and xenophobic nationalisms, in Eastern Europe. Employing the categories of Lacanian psy-

choanalysis, and drawing on Claude Lefort's conceptualisation of democracy, they radicalise Kant and Foucault's concern with the role of the spectator in constituting the meaning of historical events. In a complex and disconcerting analysis, concentrating specifically on the case of the 'ex-Yugoslavia', they show how the progressive inversion of the role of the 'Western' onlooker and the actual social agents involved, has marked the process of democratisation in Eastern Europe by complicitly calling forth and legitimising the nationalisms rejected by Western observers. In developing their argument they simultaneously expose the irreducible void (what they refer to as the Lacanian real) manifest in particularistic identifications, at the heart of formal and universalising liberal democracy.

Norval analyses contending conceptions of identity in the wake of the April election in South Africa by deploying categories drawn from Laclau, Derrida, Lefort and Žižek. Contrasting the horizons which frame the conceptions of identity found in the discourses of the extreme Right on the one hand, and the African National Congress on the other, she argues that they are metaphorically expressed in relation to the possibility of an identity being fully 'at home with itself'. While those forms of identification expressed by the former still yearn for an identity completely coincidental with itself, those of the latter are presented as opening onto a radically different conception of identity, one in which its non-closure is thematised. This non-closure, and the consequent impurity of identity, is related to discussions in contemporary political theory on the nature of democracy as the institutionalisation of the empty place of power, as well as debates concerning the nature of the subject appropriate to it. Norval argues that democracy arises in the tension characteristic of

editorial introduction

that empty space, a tension between universality and particularity, and that this tension also characterises the discourse of non-racialism, enabling it to engage in the difficult negotiation of difference which is central to the institutionalisation of a pluralist democracy in a post-apartheid South Africa.

The interview with Jacques Rancière treats several of the concerns animating this issue of *Angelaki*. It focuses on Rancière's understanding of the relationship between politics and philosophy, and his attempt to reconceptualise the domain of politics as consisting of 'processes of subjectivation which differentiate themselves from all action in the name of a social group identifiable as a part of society', a domain which is always marked by or founded by a wrong. This emphasis on the enunciative act through which communities appear as such, leads him to interpret contemporary forms of racism as a 'striving to remove from the people its character of *appearance*', and this, for Rancière, is what is occurring in what he calls 'post-democracy'. Community, for him, is polemically constructed, and cannot be grounded or deduced from the idea of the 'common good', a thought which also animates his critique of political philosophy, and its misunderstanding of the objectives pursued by both philosophy and politics.

In the first edition of *Angelaki*, we published an article by David Howarth criticising aspects of Doreen Massey's theorisation of space and politics. In this issue, we publish a contribution by Michael Reid, 'The Aims of Radicalism', which furthers discussion on the politics of space, time and community. In his short reply, Reid cautions against an overhasty weakening or even abandonment of ideas of community, particularity and tradition in the name of a universalising cosmopolitanism.

We wish to express our sincerest gratitude to the following people, without whom the publication of *Reconsidering the Political* would not have been possible: Pelagia Goulimari, Gerard Greenway, Ben Norland and John Peacock.

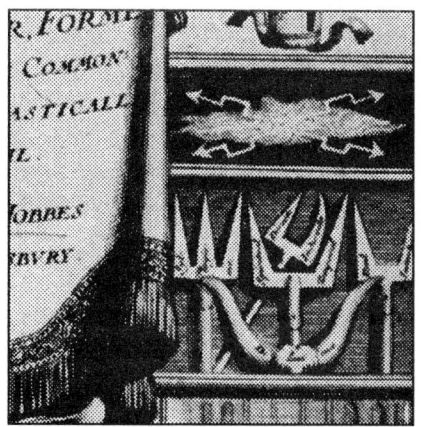

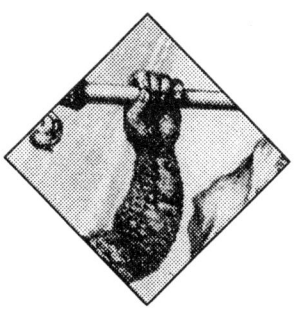

I the form of the political

Schmitt seeks to specify the political, to distinguish political phenomena from those that emerge in other spheres of exchange. The problem is that the continuous realignment of forces leaves the field of relations of the political in constant flux (Schmitt, 1963a: 4). This metastable state is its necessary, not accidental character. So the criterion must identify the political, convey its fluidity and ubiquity, and reflect upon its phenomena independently from the observable empirical content of politics. References to the state will not do, for the state does not exhaust the field and scope of the political. In fact, '[t]he concept of the state presupposes the concept of the political', he says, not the other way around (Schmitt, 1932: 19; see also de Giovanni, 1990: 35ff.). The formula *political=statal* did apply under absolute monarchies, when the state was the sole subject of politics, but the expansion of democracy and the politicisation of civil society has undermined it (Schmitt, 1932: 20, 22-5; Schmitt, 1971: 23-4).[1] Politics now spreads beyond the statal sphere; for Schmitt this spread reveals the field of the political:

> The classical profile of the state vanished when its monopoly on politics decreased and a diversity of new subjects engaged in political struggle with or without the state, with or without a 'statal' content. This marks the emergence of a new phase of reflection for political thought. The distinction between politics and the 'political' is introduced, and the issue of new bearers and subjects of political reality becomes the central theme of the complex problematic of the 'political'. This is both the starting point and the meaning of all the efforts to distinguish the multiple new subjects of the 'political' that become active in the political reality of pol-

benjamin arditi

TRACING THE POLITICAL

> itics, whether it is a statal reality or not ... the criterion of the 'political' that I have proposed is in fact an approximation to the recognition of this political reality. (Schmitt, 1971: 24-5)

He chooses to specify the political through a central antithesis or core opposition. A 'core opposition' is one that does not derive from and cannot be reduced to any other opposition. It can therefore be considered as an appropriate criterion to ground the specificity and relative independence of a given domain of phenomena (Schmitt, 1932: 26). The opposition between *friend* and *enemy* would be the distinctive trait of the political, just as those between good and evil, beautiful and ugly, and profitable and unprofitable are those of the moral, aesthetic and economic

tracing the political

sectors (Schmitt, 1932: 26). This, he says, is neither an exhaustive definition nor indicative of the substantial content of politics; it is only a definition in the sense of a criterion to which actions with a specifically political meaning can be traced. The criterion must be understood in its concrete existential sense rather than as a metaphor, a symbol, or a normative antithesis (Schmitt, 1932: 26, 27-8). The concept of the political and the public domain of its relations is characterised by the friend-enemy grouping, for he considers it gives rise to the most intense of oppositions. 'The weight of the political', he says, 'is determined by the intensity of alignments according to which the decisive associations and dissociations adjust themselves' (Schmitt, 1932: 59).[2] The specifically political tension of the opposition is born out of the real possibility of struggle. War is its *ultima ratio*, whether as war between sovereign states or as civil war within a state. It imposes on us the most political of all decisions, to distinguish who are our friends and who the enemies whom we must fight. It creates the most intense form of division or separation between groups, he says, '[f]or only in real combat is revealed the most extreme consequence of the political grouping of friend and enemy. From this most extreme possibility human life derives its specifically political tension' (Schmitt, 1932: 35). The political confrontation is the most intense of oppositions precisely because of the possibility of killing and dying.

His references to combat and killing do not suggest that the nature of politics lies in war. Schmitt does not identify politics with war itself. The political emerges if there is a *possibility* of real combat between opposing collectivities. War, he says, is not the end, or the goal, or the content of politics, but rather its *presupposition*, for a world finally

in peace, without enmity, 'would be a world without the distinction of friend and enemy and hence a world without politics' (Schmitt, 1932: 34-5). His argument here is typically Hobbesian. Hobbes conceives the state of nature as a condition of war of every man against every man. 'Warre, consisteth not in Battell only, or the act of fighting; but in a tract of time, wherein the Will to contend by Battell is sufficiently known... So the nature of War, consisteth not in actual fighting; but in the known disposition thereto, during all the time there is no assurance to the contrary' (Hobbes, 1968: 185-6). Notice that Hobbes doesn't reduce war to the moment of actual fighting. *Mutatis mutandis*, one can say that for Schmitt (a) a 'combat' need not be present to talk of the political, for a disposition to combat the public other suffices; and (b) while politics may involve killing, it is not of its essence.

None of the other oppositions – between good and evil, beautiful and ugly, or profitable and unprofitable – have the intensity that can lead to the decisive case of war.[3] Unless, of course, they manage to generate a friend-enemy alignment around them, in which case they cease to be 'purely social' and become political in the Schmittian sense of the word. For Schmitt it does not matter where the opposition arises, as long as it adopts the form of a friend-enemy antithesis. The political is characterised only by 'the activity of aggregating and defending our friends, and dispersing and fighting our enemies' (Bobbio, 1982: 1247-8).

Schmitt defines the 'friends' only indirectly, by reference to the enemy. So who is the political enemy and how can one distinguish it from other enemies? It cannot be the private adversary, the personal enemy whom one hates. The political enemy is simply:

[T]he other, the stranger ... [who] exists only when, at least potentially, one fighting

16

collectivity of people confronts a similar collectivity. The enemy is solely the public enemy, because everything that has a relationship to such a collectivity of men, particularly to a whole nation, becomes public by virtue of that relationship. The enemy is *hostis*, not *inimicus* in the broader sense. (Schmitt, 1932: 28)

From here it transpires that the political enemy (the *hostis*) is simply that which we are not; it is the other, that which is *different*. This allows Schmitt to set out the necessary distance, division or separation associated with the hostility that leads to friend-enemy oppositions without introducing value criteria to qualify the adversary. In the political field the enemy one fights is not the adversary or counterpart of a private conflict. If it was, the enemy would be *inimicus* rather than *hostis*. One fights a public other, an adversary whose status cannot be equated to that of the mortal foe (Schmitt, 1938: 102). That is why it is not necessary to hate the enemy personally (Schmitt, 1932: 28); the enemy need not be considered as pure negativity in order to become one. As Schmitt put it, 'the morally evil, aesthetically ugly or economically damaging need not necessarily be the enemy; the morally good, aesthetically beautiful, and economically profitable need not necessarily become the friend in the specifically political sense of the word' (Schmitt, 1932: 27). But the *hostis* is not simply that which is different, but also *similar*. As we saw, Schmitt says that the adversary (or 'them') that opposes the friendly grouping (or 'us') is 'a similar collectivity'. Both groups perceive themselves as positivities that struggle with one another in defence of a way of being, a project or a set of objectives.

The recognition of this double nature of the political enemy, a group or set of groups which are different yet similar to a certain 'us', indicates that its nature is not exhausted in being a pure and absolute negation of the friendly 'us'. In the political field, a group becomes an enemy only if it constitutes an obstacle or a resistance to our objectives, and is therefore considered a target against whom our strategy is mobilised. Politics seeks to control the opponent's force and fighting capacity, not to eliminate him.[4] The parties that intervene in a political struggle are complex entities whose identity does not depend on a confrontation with a single and unchanging adversary. Neither the conflicts nor the opposing groups need to exhaust the totality of antagonisms or involve all the subjects that roam the social field. The latter only occurs under total war and the absolutization of enmity this entails.

Three considerations follow from this. First, the political designates a form of confrontation (the public friend-enemy opposition), and is unconcerned about the concrete content of the confrontation. Secondly, as Leo Strauss acknowledged, the political can neither become a concrete particular sector nor a central sphere: it lacks its own central preoccupation, and it is capable of potentially encompassing every concern (Strauss, 1933: 99-100). The autonomy of the 'political' in relation to other spheres only means that the intervention of moral, aesthetic, economic or any other criteria is purely accidental or secondary *vis-à-vis* the domain of friend-enemy relations. If it is not a 'concrete sector', then the *autonomy of the political* should be understood to mean *specificity of the political*. Expressions such as 'sphere', 'realm' or 'domain' are only used in a figurative sense when applied to it. This allows Schmitt to retain his criterion of the political without giving up the mobile and ubiquitous nature of its relations. It also opens the possibility to think political confrontations without necessarily locating them in a formal public arena, or circumscribing them to a particular institutional setting. Finally, unlike Hobbes' individual contracting parties, Schmitt's adversaries are collectivities. For him the unit of analysis in a political relation is the group, not the individual. And if the friend-enemy opposition is constitutive of the political field, then at least two different groups – the friends, or 'us', and the enemies, or 'them' – must exist in order for the political to arise (Schmitt, 1963b: 125). Yet he also says that '[t]he political world is a pluriverse, not a universe' (Schmitt, 1932: 53). This suggests that the existence of a major friend-enemy opposition does not exclude others: the political *pluriverse* is inhabited by multiple friend-enemy oppositions, and therefore by a multiplicity of groups.

II the ubiquity of the political

A different view of the political begins to take shape. It departs from traditions that attempt to circumscribe it to a particular ensemble of institutions and normalised practices that both define its conditions and create a perimeter or enclosure for its action and effectivity. I am obviously referring to parliament, political parties, government and state institutions in general. For Schmitt the political can encompass the totality of relations of the polity – at least in principle – in the sense that everything is *politicisable*. The political might be seen as a form that is coextensive with the 'social'. As Frye put it, Schmitt chose to use the adjective *political* rather than the noun *politics* because he wished to create a concept of politics that was not circumscribed to the territorial limits imposed upon it by liberal thought (Frye, 1966: 821). That is, a concept freed from the topographical location assigned to politics since the consolidation of

the nation-state. It therefore becomes a means to recognise the emergence of the political in the least expected folds of the social fabric:

> The political can derive its energy from the most varied human endeavours, from the religious, economic, moral, and other antitheses. It does not describe its own substance, but only the intensity of an association or dissociation of human beings whose motives can be religious, national (in the ethnic or cultural sense), economic, or of another kind and can affect at different times different coalitions and separations. The real friend-enemy grouping is existentially so strong and decisive that the nonpolitical antithesis, at precisely the moment at which it becomes political, pushes aside and subordinates its hitherto purely religious, purely economic, purely cultural criteria and motives... In any event, that grouping is always political which orients itself toward this most extreme possibility. The grouping is therefore always the decisive human grouping, the political entity. If such entity exists at all, it is always the decisive entity, and it is sovereign in the sense that the decision about the critical situation, even if it is the exception, must always necessarily reside there. (Schmitt, 1932: 38)

It is unimportant whether or not these groups appear in the form of political parties, or if their conflicts unfold within parliament, or if their enmity is or is not contingent upon the objective of controlling sites in the state apparatus. The political does not necessarily require an intervention of that which society formally recognizes as part of the field of politics. It is a *form* of confrontation (as friend-enemy) that can originate in religious, economic, moral or other fields.

An example can clarify this. In the early

1990s there was a wave of neo-Nazi attacks against hostels housing refugees seeking political asylum – and therefore permanent residence – in Germany. Several were beaten, some hostels were burned down and a few died in the blazes. Police and other authorities were conspicuously slow to respond, and bystanders apparently encouraged the attackers. But others went to the streets to show they would not stand idle in the face of this resurgence of racism. Perhaps the images of Jew-bashing in the 1930s lingered in the collective memory of many Germans, and of immigrants who had learned that history often repeats itself.

Let us review some characteristics of these events. Neo-Nazi attacks and anti-racist responses had no strict 'institutional' dimension. They might have been prompted by organized groups, specially in the case of neo-Nazis, but they were generally organized by *ad hoc* committees set up during the events. Institutional mediations came later. The participants were not motivated only by 'political' reasons. Attackers were enticed more by the prospect of hooliganism than neo-Nazi ideology, and protesters seem to have gone to the streets primarily because of their moral or ethical indignation against racism. The organizational forms – specially of protesters – had a minimal level of formalisation; they had no significant duration either, for most *ad hoc* committees created during the events were disbanded soon after. These were quite different from more traditional and institutional forms such as workers' trade unions, which have offices, paid officials, hierarchical structures, recognized interlocutors (e.g., employers and government in collective bargaining) and regular protests. While the initiatives of both sides originated in 'private' civil society, and their confrontation was located in the physical site of the streets, they quickly acquired a 'public' dimension. But it was a most peculiar one. More often than not, it was a case of participants peeking into the formal public space, crossing the ('imaginary') frontier between the public and the private while remaining in a public space unconstrained by the institutional settings of politics. It was a *virtual* public space.

The events also had traits of the political as Schmitt understands it. There was a division of social space into groups of 'us' and 'them' (i.e., of 'friends' and 'enemies'). This division did not 'absorb' all others (e.g., class, gender or the wider split between rulers and ruled), but had a contaminating effect over many (e.g., on the division between government and opposition, or among the partners within the governing coalition). There was a willingness to identify and fight the adversary in such a way that the separation between the groups of friends and enemies adopted the intensity expected in a political confrontation. There was also some notion of a 'cause' or object of dispute. Neo-Nazi groups claimed to defend racial purity and German jobs threatened by immigrants, while anti-racist and immigrant groups defended the rule of law, the legitimacy of ethnic and cultural diversity, and the constitutional rights of immigrants. The enmity between these groups remained within the limits set by these conflicting 'causes', and not necessarily – or rather, not significantly – transferred to other aspects of their identity. Finally, the events did have effects in the institutional public arena, whether through the positioning of the media, public opinion, political parties or government and other statal bodies. In other words, the confrontation unfolded in the field of the political, but the groups also – and simultaneously – addressed claims to the state. In a way, politics in the institutional sense was never absent.

III politics and the political as interconnected registers

This example shows both the enactment of the political in civil society and the continual interplay between the political and institutional politics. This means that it is perfectly valid to talk of an overflow of politics beyond the state or the political system, but that it is also illegitimate to push it to the point of turning one's back on the statal sphere. The temptation is there, specially among those sympathetic to new social movements and their potential for political renewal – more generally, pluralist thinkers who address the processes of politicisation from the standpoint of civil society. Kirstie McClure seems to succumb to such temptation by posing a 'politics of direct address' – of rights claims addressed to each other rather than to the state (McClure, 1992: 122-123). She does say that it is not a question of escaping from the state or abdicating from conventional political participation. But her insistence on pluralist claims purely within 'the plurality of the social' tends to undermine that disclaimer. A politics of purely horizontal address within civil society overlooks the dangers of *balkanization* of social space.

The state – more precisely, the network of institutional mediations of the political regime – remains a powerful field and actor in our societies, in spite of the greater weight civil society has acquired. Not only because it intervenes in collective life through regulatory and distributive activities, but because of what Walzer calls 'the paradox' of the civil society argument. 'Citizenship', he says, 'is one of the many roles that members play, but the state itself is unlike all the other associations. It both frames civil society and occupies space within it. It fixes the boundary conditions and the basic rules of all asso-

ciational activity (including political activity)' (Walzer, 1992: 103). For him, civil society (the 'setting of settings') requires political agency for it generates radically unequal power relationships that only the state can challenge. For despite the claims of liberal theory, the state is not a mere framework for civil society: it is also the instrument of the struggle, used to give a particular shape to the common good. That is why citizenship does retain certain practical relevance among all our actual and possible memberships (Walzer, 1992: 104, 105).[5] Coming back to our example, this explains why neo-Nazi and anti-racist initiatives eventually addressed claims to the state. The former sought to institute an exclusive form of the public good, whereas the concern of the latter was to reverse the unequal standing of immigrants in power relations.

So the reference to the political does not entail a dissolution of the formal sphere of politics. It merely calls for a distinction between two registers that do not cease to intertwine with each other, to contaminate one another. The distinction between the adjective *political* and the noun *politics* is not purely grammatical, but conceptual. 'Politics' has its own public space or *locus*. It is the field of exchanges between political parties; of parliamentary and governmental affairs; of elections and representation; and, in general, of the type of activity, practices and procedures that take place in the institutional ensemble of the political system. Paraphrasing Duso, we could say that politics has the status of an *artifice* in the Hobbesian sense of the word (Duso, 1990: 147). Hobbes says that Leviathan – the sovereign, the state, authority, the body politic, peace – is not natural, but constructed as a result of a covenant or contract. Leviathan is created to domesticate the natural condition of conflict (*status naturalis*). It does not

efface conflict, but regulates its modes of existence within the institutional space of the state (*status civilis*). The 'political', however, is a type of relationship that can develop in any area of the social, regardless of whether or not it remains within the institutional enclosure of 'politics'. It includes but exceeds the field of 'politics'. It has no particular object, no unique actors, no necessary institutional support of its own. All that matters is the enactment of public engagements between friends and enemies: the political is being enacted whenever and wherever these are spotted. The 'political', then, is living movement, the magma of conflicting wills: conflict is the ontological condition of the political (dal Lago, 1990: 165-6). Like 'politics', it also has a public space, only that it is mobile and ubiquitous, not confined to – or defined by – institutional settings alone. We have already given it a name: virtual public space.

Yet there are still a few loose ends that need to be tied up. The nature of the friend-enemy opposition suggests that cleavages, collectivities that organize themselves to confront others, and relations of force and power are constitutive traits of the grammar of politics. While this is correct – the political seems to be unthinkable without a split between 'us' and 'them' – Schmitt's emphasis on conflict is problematic. Politics is not only a language of divisions and confrontations. Sartori claims that this only accounts for 'hot' or 'untamed' politics and, moreover, reverses the logic of his much-admired Hobbes: while Hobbes proposes the *status civilis* as a way out of the conflict-ridden state of nature (war of all against all), Schmitt reinstates the *status naturalis* as the condition in which politics manifests its gen-

uine essence (Sartori, 1989: 72-73).

I am not as worried as Sartori about the reversal. First because in a way it calls into question the 'givenness' of particular forms of the *status civilis*. The politicisation of gender relations shows that patriarchy is a form of construction of gender, that many consider it a rather undesirable one, and that reactivating the constitutive moment of conflict and division may enable the reconstruction of a different *status civilis* of gender relations. Secondly Sartori's reference to 'hot' or 'untamed' politics seems to suggest that the political connotes violent or unregulated conflicts. This is not necessarily so. We have already seen that Schmitt distinguishes the public nature of the political *hostis* from the personal *inimicus* and the mortal *foe*. Friend-enemy oppositions are never fully 'outside' conventions (*status civilis*), whether they unfold in the institutional setting of politics or in the magma of the political: we are still citizens, and as such, subjects of law and bearers of rights. Finally, conflict does not necessarily imply pure instability or permanent crisis. Niklas Luhmann says that conflicts are highly integrated systems due to the coercive behaviour they imply, whereas Julien Freund argues that the identification of an enemy suspends subjective uncertainty and stabilises expectations (Marramao, 1989: 75, 81). This might seem paradoxical, but a moment of reflection shows that it is rather common sense. Members of political communities (whether 'us' or 'them') rarely collaborate in harmony. This is not a problem, for political 'friends' need not like one another in order to remain friends in the political sense of the word. Yet they do need to forge some representation of their unity despite internal cleavages, something to enable members to say: 'Here is where I belong'. Their communion is more often than not 'imagined' in

tracing the political

Anderson's sense of the term, i.e., the image of communion lives in the mind of each one, even though most of them might not meet or know their fellow members (Anderson, 1983: 6). An actual or potential conflict with a 'them' can function as a means of cohesion. One only needs to recall the (perverse) certainty about identity that prevailed during the Cold War, when East and West had a clear notion of who was the enemy. The allies on both sides did not need to 'like' each other; and they often did not, but political friendship was sufficient for them to remain together. That is why the antagonism with a 'them' is not simply the disruptive 'outside' of our identity. It functions both as a threat and as a supplement of – hence also as part of – our identity; it is an 'internal periphery' that constitutes any 'us'.

The problem is that Schmitt enhances the moment of reversal without posing the reconstruction. To be more precise, he *does* pose it, but in an oblique and unconvincing fashion. Schmitt links the dissolution of the high politics of the *jus publicum Europaeum* with the decline of the state as a sovereign decision-making instance, separate from society and above it. This supposedly led to the resurgence of the political subordinated to the ontological reality of war. This is disputable. His nostalgia for a bygone era confers no theoretical or political validity to a zero-sum game between order and conflict. Schmitt seems to think that the proper statal order (*status civilis*) must resemble Hobbes' Leviathan, that is, the prototype of the absolutist state, and that otherwise we are back in a civil war-like environment (*status naturalis*). Yet conflict and its 'other' (order) are not mutually exclusive. Whoever talks of political conflicts must also include within the same speech ways to overcome and/or suspend them. Otherwise conflict becomes the end of the political, which is either nonsensical or dangerous, for then one would be forced to conclude that the *raison d'être* of friend-enemy oppositions is the perpetuation of a friend-enemy opposition.

This notwithstanding, the friend-enemy criterion can be retained by adding two provisos. The first one refers to the difficulty of enclosing the friend-enemy opposition in itself. Schmitt insists on the *binary* form of the political as the aggregation of friends and the dispersion of enemies, when in fact it has, of necessity, a *triadic* structure. The collectivities of friends and enemies are two of its components; the third is the disputed 'something' that is at stake in the contest and can be obtained through that very contest. This third element can be many things: sites and objects of power coveted by both sides, the support of those who are still uncommitted *vis-à-vis* the friend-enemy opposition under consideration, the recognition of claims and claimants, the introduction of an issue in the public agenda, the defence of a principle, or simply the pursuit of symbolic goods (solidarity, participation, and so on). We have seen this in the brief discussion of the 'causes' at stake in anti-racist initiatives in Germany.[6]

Secondly, the field of politics is a pluriverse of friend-enemy oppositions in constant flux, but this does not preclude the crystallisation of power in new institutional forms. Political engagements open up the question of existing configurations of power relations, but also aim to institute new configurations of the *status civilis*. Some can be pursued in the domain of cultural practice, e.g., the realignment of gender relations in non-patriarchal settings, or the transformation of a xenophobic hate of immigrants. Here is where I could see the effectiveness of McClure's 'politics of direct address'. It would resemble Donolo's idea of homeopathic strategies, i.e., the possibility of 'curing' society through horizontal politics unfolding within the social *without* going through the mediation of the political system (Donolo, 1982: 103-120). But other engagements often seek to modify formally instituted norms too, e.g., those that promote racial inequality, or deny citizen status to sons and daughters of settled immigrants. When this is the case, the political must necessarily manifest itself also in the institutional domain of politics to secure socially sanctioned and enforceable configurations. This corresponds to Donolo's idea of allopathic strategies, i.e., the treatment of the social through the formally 'external' instance of politics and its legislation, public policies or regulatory functions (Donolo, 1982: 103-120).

Once again we see that politics and the political are not mutually exclusive registers. The institutional order of politics intertwines with the magma of the political. This seems to be the way Laclau interprets Husserl's dialectic between sedimentation and reactivation. Reactivation occurs when the 'givenness' of order is contested. 'To show the original sense of something', he says, 'is to question its obviousness, to refer it back to the absolute act of its institution … Thus, the ground on which this absolute act of institution takes place is what we call *politics*, and the desedimentation of the social consists of revealing its political essence' (Laclau, 1990: 213).[7] Notice the analogy between sedimentation and politics on one hand, and between reactivation or desedimentation on the other. In both cases the disruptive conflicts of the political are neither the failure nor the 'other' of politics. Rather, as in the case of identity, they are its ineradicable internal periphery. Politics institutes an order to overcome the threatening conflicts of the political. Yet 'order' (any order) is only a regulative idea whose

absolute moment (*pure* order) can never be fulfilled. The permanence of the political prevents the institution of a full being – in this example, of pure order, one that has finally effaced all traces of its ontological substratum of becoming.

This failure of pure order is not a bad thing. It introduces a healthy dose of humbleness into the politics of institutions, the state, and the party system: politics cannot encompass everything it wishes to govern. It also curbs the often far-fetched critiques and expectations of those who dwell in the deterritorialized space of the political. We know that reactivation reveals the political essence of an order. But what happens when an effort is successful, e.g., patriarchy is shown as a particular and not a 'natural' form of organization of gender relations? The restoration of a pure *status naturalis* (no rules for gender relations) and the institution of a new and definitive *status civilis* (purely egalitarian gender relations) are impossible options. What remains is a partial order that cannot put an end to the interplay between politics and the political. The ensemble remains in a metastable state.

IV repetition and involvement

As in Marx's formula of the expanded reproduction of capital, M-C-M', the interplay leads to a cycle: the institution of politics-as-order, followed by the political life subversion that seeks to institute new (different) figures of political order, and so on. However, in the case of politics, the M' of the new figures is not *prima facie* bigger or better than the original M; it is simply different. Does this cycle entail a notion of time akin to Nietzsche's 'eternal return of the same', only applied to politics? In a way it does. Not in the sense of a *circularity* of its time, for the various enactments do not take the ensemble back to square one. It is more like *spiralling* time, which opens the question of its direction. Does the spiral wrap its way inward? No, for then it could be mistaken with a self-reflective exercise, or with a quest for its own essence. The cycle is unconcerned about the (non-existent) true essence of politics. Does it reach outward? Perhaps, but then one would be hard-pressed to say where it would go without abandoning the specificity of political time, which has no universal normative orientation. Is it downward (towards its origins), then? Not really. We have seen that Schmitt's longing for the high politics of the *jus publicum Europaeum* betrays a questionable assumption, i.e., the loss of (or fall from) political Arcadia. If the aim of politics is a restoration of a lost paradise, then one would have to conclude that politics is inherently conservative. And upward (forward) it is definitely not, unless one is willing to introduce a notion of *telos*, of a predefined destiny, whereby the cycles would be successive moments in a process of political self-development (a transparent, emancipated society at last).

Instead, the time of politics is the return of the 'same' as *repetition*, in the Deleuzean sense of the term: a mask of a mask that has lost its original. Political temporality as pure repetition is a staging of never-ending cycles of power and opposition, of domination and resistance. It adopts the paradoxical formula of an *invariable change*. One might struggle for freedom, justice and power to make the world a better place to live in. But in a world without meaning and *telos*, nothing is definitive and history absolves nobody. May 1968 was a rejection of disciplinary and hierarchical models; its protagonists and many observers perceived it as a passage from rigidity to flexibility, from constraint to freedom. But often new holders of power can be corrupted; after a while the spirit of change becomes conformist; and new injustices always seem to mushroom in the most unexpected places. Change is an invariable repetition for there is no end to the cycle of transformers and despots, commitment and betrayal, good faith and manipulation, and mistakes generally. The Bolsheviks overthrew the Tsar, but soon found themselves with Stalin and the *nomenklatura*.

The scene of repetition seems to suggest a cynical, or at least a disenchanted view of politics. Disenchanted it certainly is. But disenchantment, as Vattimo put it, 'can be understood neither as the grasp of a true structure of reality, nor ... as a "transposition" into the world of undisguised relations, that is, of pure relations of force' (Vattimo, 1992: 99). Rather, it means that everything is posited and that the play of forces 'operates only if it is "presented" in the form of a "conflict of interpretations", that is, in the production of meaning or symbolisation' (Vattimo, 1992: 98-99). In the field of symbolisation, nothing guarantees that a successful interpretation will be the best, or better than the rest, or even good, which means that a priori nothing guarantees the goodness of an instituted order. God, he says, has been exiled as a guarantor of objectivity. From the point of view of disenchantment and the temporality of politics as repetition, there is no difference between Ghandi and Pol Pot.

Does this mean that (political) emancipation is defunct? Can one still address it in some way? The answer is yes, you probably can, but not in the context of a purely theoretical account. This can show the interplay between politics and the political, or the spiralling time of repetition. But it cannot assess the value of each turn. The positive or negative value of a particular turn can only be assessed from the perspective of those involved, of those moved into action to change or maintain a state of affairs. Not because action has an ontological primacy over discourse, or because it provides an Archimedes point to judge the correctness of a choice and guarantee the goodness of the outcome. Rather, it is because involvement facilitates a basic existential leap. Total mastery over a situation is impossible, so a degree of uncertainty about the consequences of a decision is unavoidable. But a decision does not require full mastery to be made. It only needs the acceptance of risk. Whoever is engaged in a situation has already taken a decision, and therefore accepted a risk. Involvement introduces the passion and the will needed to suspend (rather than abolish) the indeterminacy of a relativised world in which every political perspective or possibility is equally valid, at least in principle. 'Only the actual participants can correctly recognize, understand, and judge the concrete situation' (Schmitt, 1932: 27). It reveals the concrete existential sense of Schmitt's criterion of the political: it is the moment of taking sides, of distinguishing who are the allies and who the adversaries.

This echoes Vattimo's rendering of the overman's perspective, described by Nietzsche in *The Gay Science* as a willingness 'to continue dreaming knowing that you are dreaming' (Vattimo, 1992: 9-10, 40). To dream is to believe that being – whether it is essence, order or truth – is the foundation of the real, that there is an ultimate explanation for everything, or that it is possible to find an objective referent to judge the goodness of an order or a project. It amounts to the belief that the movement of becoming has been fixed by the stability of being. The awareness of dreaming, though, is a recognition that being (a model of society, a type of subject) is a limitation, not a cancellation of

becoming. Existential involvement is the 'as if' of being in the political field: it is to dream of being, knowing that it is a dream. It is the turning point that enables one to assess M' or Ghandi not simply as something different from the M of Pol Pot, but also preferable, and better, while remaining forever in the terrain of pure repetition. This means: we believe that Ghandi is preferable without forgetting that Pol Pot can succeed him.

notes

1 Max Weber believed it still applied. For him, '"politics"... means striving to share power or striving to influence the distribution of power, either among states or among groups within a state' (Weber, 1961: 78). Unlike Schmitt, I do not think that their arguments are ultimately incompatible. They simply addressed different subjects: Schmitt worked on the 'political', whereas Weber was concerned about 'politics'. I'll come back to this in the final part of the article.

2 However, as Ulmen observed, in *Theory of the Partisan* Schmitt says that 'the core of the political is not enmity but rather the distinction between friend and enemy, which presupposes both friend and enemy' (Schmitt, 1963b: 125). That is why he concludes that 'the key to the concept of the political is not enmity but the *distinction* itself' (Ulmen, 1987: 189).

3 I am aware of his ambiguous use of the 'intensity' criterion. As Sartori says (Sartori, 1989: 66), why is intensity an exclusive prerogative of the political? Why should racial, moral or other intensities yield to the political one? Why can't wars be waged for purely religious, economic or other motives? We should also consider the ambiguous *scope* of friend-enemy oppositions: can the criterion be extended to include a split between astrophysicists who support the 'big-bang theory', and those who claim that the universe is contracting? If so, wouldn't this

dilute the conceptual efficacy of the criterion? Schmitt does not address these questions conclusively, perhaps because they have no formal answer. The notion of 'anexactness' might help us, at least to qualify the fuzzy and shifting contours of intensity and scope. Deleuze and Guattari use it to describe 'vague' or 'nomadic' essences, i.e., those that are 'essentially and not accidentally inexact'. 'Roundness' is an example: it is neither an ideal and fixed essence like a circle, nor something round like a wheel or a vase. In the case of anexact figures 'all that counts is the constantly shifting borderline' (Deleuze and Guattari, 1988: 367). The 'open texture' of law mentioned by H.L.A. Hart poses something similar: '[u]ncertainty at the borderline is the price to be paid for the use of general classifying terms in any form of communications concerning matters of fact' (Hart, 1961: 125). The scope and intensity of friend-enemy oppositions would be anexact by nature, they would have an open texture. The same applies to everyday use of the term 'politics'. People often refer to 'politics' as shorthand to designate a *residual register* of that which cannot be settled through epistemology or debate alone. It is perceived as a *register of closure/completion* where issues are settled or decided through contestation (which does not exclude negotiation or compromise). But it is an anexact or open-textured closure, for contestation can reopen settled issues again and again, blurring their borderline. This might suffice as a preliminary answer. For the time being we can agree at least on the heuristic value of the friend-enemy criterion: it reminds us that conflict is a constitutive dimension of the political and

that political relations are relations of force and power. 'Force' refers to a capacity to impose something upon others, whereas power is used in Foucault's sense of a capacity to structure the possible field of action of others.

4 Although something along these lines appears in a passage of *The Concept of the Political* (36), it was actually added as a footnote to that same passage in the edition of 1963. It appears in the Spanish and Italian editions, but not in the English one.

5 To say that 'only' the state can challenge unequal power relations is an overstatement. It is also misleading, for the state is not a priori a unified or cohesive ensemble that intervenes at will to redress social injustices. State institutions are both objects and sites of struggle, and they usually need to negotiate a policy or a piece of legislation with social and political forces.

6. José Carlos Rodríguez believes that politics is more like a quadrangle than a triad: it does not occur in a vacuum, but in a context that provides the fourth element. Different types of context (e.g., democratic, totalitarian, or military) shape actual politics in different ways. This reinforces the criticism of Schmitt's emphasis on a binary logic. Others claim that in real politics the binary logic rules, and hence the primacy of power dissolves the triad into a binary bind. Remember Ulmen's claim that the nucleus of Schmitt's concept of the political was not so much in the enmity between collectivities, but *in the distinction* or, rather, *in the capacity to distinguish* enemy from friend. This is correct. But Schmitt's argument is somewhat ambiguous, for the emphasis

on the distinction was explicitly introduced in 1963 with the publication of *Theory of the Partisan*. Until then, the central theme was enmity that led to a friend-enemy criterion. Still, at first glance the behaviour of professional politicians seems to confirm both possibilities. The career of a politician, or the good or bad performance of a political group, depends largely on their capacity to distinguish and to act accordingly. Those who come together today might confront one another later, and then join forces again. We see it all the time. It does not matter if today's friend is ugly and mean, and the enemy good and kind; aesthetics and moral concerns play a minor role when positions of power are at stake. In real politics you survive if you manage to be on time in the right place with the right group. Notions of 'cause' are often conflated with the immediate interests of the participating groups. But even then, a third element – the logic of power – is present in this scenario, which supports the idea of a triadic structure of politics.

7 Laclau also says (1990: 214, 219, 244) that conflict, as the moment of negativity, is the constitutive 'outside' inherent to every instituted system. I would modify this claim and take the inverted commas that frame his reference to the 'outside' to mean a supplement that partly configures the system. Conflict might be the 'outside' of a system, but it is also 'internal' insofar as its supplementarity makes it one of its constitutive dimensions. In a word, conflict, as an 'outside' or supplement, is the *internal periphery* of the system. We already saw how it works in the case of identities.

references

Anderson, Benedict, *Imagined Communities* (London: Verso, 1983).

Bobbio, Norberto, 'Política' in *Diccionario de política*, vol. 2, eds Norberto Bobbio, Nicola Matteucci and Gianfranco Pasquino (México: Siglo XXI, 1982).

dal Lago, Alessandro, 'El sentido de las palabras' in *Pensar la política*, ed. Martha Rivero (México:

Instituto de Intestigaciones Sociales, UNAM, 1990).

de Giovanni, Bagio, '¿Qué significa hoy pensar la política?' in *Pensar la política*, ed. Martha Rivero (México: Instituto de Intestigaciones Sociales, UNAM, 1990).

Deleuze, Gilles, and Félix Guattari, *A Thousand Plateaus* [1980] (London: The Athlone Press, 1988).

Donolo, Carlo, 'Sociale', *Laboratorio politico*, vol. II (January-February 1982).

Duso, Giuseppe, 'Pensar la política' in *Pensar la política*, ed. Martha Rivero (México: Instituto de Intestigaciones Sociales, UNAM, 1990).

Frye, Charles E., 'Carl Schmitt's Concept of the Political', *The Journal of Politics* XXVIII, 4 (1966).

Hart, H.L.A., *The Concept of Law* (Oxford: Oxford University Press, 1984).

Hobbes, Thomas, *Leviathan* [1651], ed. C.B. Macpherson (Middlesex: Penguin Books, 1968).

Laclau, Ernesto, 'Theory, Democracy and Socialism' in *New Reflections on the Revolution of Our Time* (London: Verso, 1990).

Marramao, Giacomo, 'Palabra-clave (metapolítica). Más allá de los esquemas binarios acción-sistema y comunicación-estrategia' in *Pensar la política*, ed. Martha Rivero (México: Instituto de Intestigaciones Sociales, UNAM, 1990).

McClure, Kirstie, 'On the Subject of Rights: Pluralism, Plurality and Political Identity' in *Dimensions of Radical Democracy. Pluralism, Citizenship, Community*, ed. Chantal Mouffe (London: Verso, 1992).

Sartori, Giovanni, 'The Essence of the Political in Carl Schmitt', *Journal of Theoretical Politics*, vol. I, 1 (January 1989).

Schmitt, Carl, *The Concept of the Political* [1932], tr. George Schwab (New Jersey: Rutgers University Press, 1976).

Schmitt, Carl, 'Corolario No. 2: Sobre la relación

existente entre los conceptos de guerra y de ene-migo' [1938] in *El concepto de lo 'político'* (México: Folios Ediciones, 1984).

Schmitt, Carl, 'Premisa' [1963a] in *El concepto de lo 'politico'* (México: Folios Ediciones, 1984).

Schmitt, Carl *Teoría del partisano* [1963b] (Madrid: Instituto de Éstudios Políticos, 1966).

Schmitt, Carl, 'Premessa All'edizione Italiana' in *Le Categorie del 'politico'*, eds Gianfranco Miglio and Pierangelo Schiera (Bologna: Societa Editrice Il Mulino, 1971).

Strauss, Leo, 'Comments on Carl Schmitt's Der Begriff Des Politischen' [1933], included as an appendix in *The Concept of the Political*, tr. George Schwab (New Jersey: Rutgers University Press, 1976).

Ulmen, Gary L., 'Return of the Foe', *Telos*, 72 (Summer 1987).

Vattimo, Gianni, *The Transparent Society*, tr. David Webb (Cambridge: Polity Press, 1992).

Walzer, Michael, 'The Civil Society Argument' in *Dimensions of Radical Democracy. Pluralism, Citizenship, Community*, ed. Chantal Mouffe (London: Verso, 1992).

Weber, Max, 'Politics as a Vocation' [1919] in *From Max Weber: Essays in Sociology*, eds H. Gerth and C.W. Mills (London: Routledge and Kegan Paul, 1961).

Both politically and philosophically our age has, during the last thirty years or so, experienced some radical dislocatory effects. Philosophically or theoretically, the foundationalist tendencies in the different traditions have been exposed to an increasing dis- and re-articulation from such different 'post-positions' as post-structuralism; post-analytic philosophy; post-Heideggerian hermeneutics; and post-Marxism – movements among which one of the best examples is perhaps Derrida's deconstruction. Politically, during the last few years, the Communist regimes in Eastern Europe and the Soviet Union have collapsed; students have mobilized in China; Apartheid in South Africa has been seriously questioned; many countries in Africa and Latin America have begun to move towards multi-party systems; and in the Western world, in 'advanced' industrial countries, there has been the emergence of a plurality of political actors, the so-called 'new social movements'. Among other things these dislocatory events have questioned the traditional – metaphysical – focus on politics as a more or less autonomous subsystem in a social formation, redirecting the spotlight of political theorizing to the very constitution of the social, whether relations, identities or formations.

Since the end of the fifties Derrida's deconstruction has questioned the Western metaphysical tradition from *within*. The problem with which he has been working can be formulated as that of how it is possible to think otherwise than the tradition penetrating our way of thinking, our culture. However, deconstruction has been criticized for having no political relevance. Throughout the eighties the relation between deconstruction and politics has been the topic for many discussions of which the latest manifestation can be seen in the so-called 'Oxford-Cambridge debate'.

michael
cholewa-madsen

ENACTING
THE POLITICAL

Among the many more or less critical 'commentaries' on deconstruction there are, as far as I am concerned, two approaches to politics and the political which situate themselves at the limit of deconstruction. One is the 'French debate' initiated in and around the *Center for Philosophical Research on the Political*[1]; another is 'discourse analysis' as recently developed in the programme of 'Ideology and Discourse Analysis' and around the *Center for Theoretical Studies in The Social Sciences and The Humanities* at Essex University.[2] The French debate promotes the question of the *retrait du politique* in deconstruction, and the project of the Center exploits both senses carried by the word *retrait* in French: first a withdrawal from *la politique* or politics, referring to empirical events; and second a retracing of *le politique* or the political, referring to the 'essence of the political': a re-treat and a re-tracing. As Fraser (1984) has shown the debates were centred around the tension between a 'politicization of deconstruction' and a 'deconstruction of the political'. Ernesto Laclau and Chantal Mouffe's discourse analysis can also be seen as an approach to politics and the political at the margins of deconstruction. As Laclau argues in the preface to *New Reflections*, it is necessary to attempt to think politics rather than constantly having detailed discussions of concrete political problems (1990: xvi). Laclau and Mouffe have – via a reactivation of recent anti-essentialist theoretical developments – questioned the radical political tradition of the West. Their main focus has been on the Marxist tradition, and, via a deconstruction of this tradition, an anti-essentialistic theory of hegemony has been developed which has enlarged the field of theory and politics in an illuminating way.

In situating this article in the above framework I hope to develop an 'approach of modesty', in that it is an attempt to recognize and account for the insurmountable limitations of from where to act. By focusing on the political at the borderline of deconstruction I propose the following thesis: it is possible and – if we want to engage ourselves in an anti-totalitarian political project – necessary to position ourselves at the 'limit'; not only acknowledging, but taking to heart the political consequences of the 'impossibility' of any fixed position. This I call 'enacting the political'.

everything is political

As the so-called 'Oxford-Cambridge debate' has recently testified, Derridian deconstruction can hardly be said to be an uncontested approach in contemporary philosophizing. While at Oxford there has been an appreciation of the significance of deconstruction in or at the limit of the philosophical tradition,

some philosophers at Cambridge were rather sceptical in acknowledging its contribution. This was especially clear in, for example, the cataloguing of the 'dismaying implications' of Derrida's 'absurd doctrines':

> [I]n literature they dissolve the character of authors and periods; in history they deny that old documents have meanings independent of the reading we choose to impose; in law they imply that neither precedents nor statutes have meanings; in politics they deprive the mind of its defences against dangerously irrational ideologies and regimes; and finally by denying the distinction between fact and fiction, observation and imagination, evidence and prejudice, they make complete nonsense of science, technology and medicine. (*The Independent*, 1992: 19)

'Gosh!', as *The Independent* comments, 'is nothing safe from this menace?' (1992: 19). The ninety-two Cambridge signatories joined the chorus accusing deconstruction of avoiding discussions of ethical and political responsibility. A 'hard' version of this critique can be found in Frank, who argues, via a displacement of Adorno's comments on Heidegger, that Derrida's 'Heideggerianism' is 'fascist right down to its innermost components'. Frank argues that:

> The new-French theories are taken up by many of our students like a gospel ... I think the phenomenon is frightening, because it seems to me that young Germans are sucking back in, under the pretence of an opening to what is French and international, their own irrationalist tradition, which had been broken off after the Third Reich. (*Frankfurter Rundshau*, 1988)

Another version of this critique, which does not go so far as to label deconstruction 'fascist', is from those:

[W]ho think that he is a clever intellectual
fraud, a 'prophet' of nihilism, a whimsical
destroyer of any 'canons' of rationality, a
self-indulgent scribbler who delights in irre-
sponsible word play, punning, parody, and
even self-parody. (Bernstein, 1991: 172)

There is also the absolute reverse
approach, characteristic of literary circles in
America, for which Derrida has become 'an
intellectual guru whose texts are treated as if
they were "sacred"' (Bernstein, 1991: 172).

While I can in no way associate myself
with the above-stated preposterous, senseless
or idolising criticism, there is a 'softer',
more reasonable and responsible, and therefore more subtle and productive critique of
the (early) Derridian *retrait du politique*, his
withdrawal from politics or the political.
This withdrawal is sometimes rendered as
amounting to either an amoral anarchism or
a de-politicized quietism (Critchley, 1992:
195-196), i.e. that deconstruction has no
political or ethical pertinence. But the *retrait
du politique* of deconstruction – which is the
theme of the French debate – does not signify a failure to touch upon the political.
Rather deconstruction is to a large extent
dominated by 'that which has always linked
the essence of the philosophical to the
essence of the political' (Derrida, 1982: 111).
As Fynsk argues, on the one hand Derrida
abstains from any direct engagement with
political questions and resists demands for
an explicit, immediate politicization of his
work – as suggested at Cérisy by Spivak and
Rogozinski, in 'revolutionary' and 'reform-
istic' versions respectively (Fraser, 1984:
128) – but on the other, he affirms that his
practice is political, and that philosophical
practice in general is a political practice
(Derrida, 1982: 111). In the French disputa-
tions there is an attempt to clarify this
apparent contradiction via the statement
that *everything is political*, which, as

Lacoue-Labarthe and Nancy argue, necessi-
tates a re-treat from the empirical *la politique* and invites a re-tracing of the essential
le politique.

The nodal point on which the strategy of
Lacoue-Labarthe and Nancy hinges is the
meaning of the assertion that 'everything is
political'. That 'everything is political'
builds on the hypothesis of the *co-appartenance* (the essential belonging-of-one-anoth-
er) *of the philosophical and the political*.
Philosophy, in this context, is understood as
what Heidegger and Derrida articulate as
'Western metaphysics of presence', and the
political is conceived as the fulfilment of the
philosophical, being that which is consum-
mated in the discourse of 'the great
"enlightening", progressive, secular-escha-
tological discourse of Revolution as humanity's self-appropriation and self-actualization'
(Fraser, 1984: 139). This 'double consummation'[3] results in the 'immanentist' or
closed 'totalitarian character' of the political.[4] Lacoue-Labarthe and Nancy's approach
can thus be seen as a quasi-reactivation of
the Heideggerian claim that metaphysics is
completed or fulfilled in modern technology,
as a reoccupying reiteration resulting in the
declaration that we live in the age of the
'total domination of the political' (Fraser,
1984: 138).[5] The thesis that 'everything is
political' illustrates, they argue, that there is
no longer any distinction between the political and the non-political as the specificity of
the political has disappeared. As a corollary,
a scientific empirical investigation of the
political has to be avoided because such
investigations themselves issue from and are
determined by a pre-established closed
philosophical field. Discourses which articulate the political as an autonomous positive
domain or as subordinated to some other
autonomous domain have philosophical presuppositions, and as Lacoue-Labarthe and

Nancy argue, these discourses necessarily bear the marks of the *co-appartenance* of the philosophical and the political in the Western tradition. This totalizing and totalitarian 'closedness' of both philosophy and the political does, consequently, necessitate a break with *la politique*, with politics.

By emphasizing the closed character of philosophy, the one-to-one correspondence between the philosophical and the political, and consequently the closed totalitarian character of politics, simultaneously with their project of thinking the political in a 'wholly transformed' way (Fraser, 1984: 146), of thinking a 'wholly other politics' (Critchley, 1992: 201), Lacoue-Labarthe and Nancy inscribe themselves in an ambiguity. On the one hand, they argue for the consummation of the philosophical and the political, and on the other they acknowledge some internal dislocations in the philosophical tradition. Examples of the latter would be Nietzsche's 'European nihilism', Heidegger's 'overcoming of metaphysics' and Derrida's 'deconstruction' (Fraser, 1984: 139). These propositions do not fit together, for if such internal dislocations are a possibility then the unity or totality of the 'Western metaphysics of presence' cannot be all-encompassing.

In spite of their retreat from *la politique*, the thesis that 'everything is political' is also seen as an indication that the 'actually existing social formation' has to be conceived as a totality dominated by the political. But if 'society does not exist' as a self-identical and self-referential entity, if 'society is impossible' as a closed totality (Laclau and Mouffe, 1985: 122), then a contingent, historical, and (to a greater or lesser degree) sedimented social formation has to be seen as having an open, differentially structured, relational constitution. If this is the case – to which I shall return – then it makes no sense to articulate an entity as a totality.

Furthermore this 'homogenization-thesis', namely that 'everything is political' can be seen as counteracted by de Tocqueville's notion of the 'democratic revolution', which suggests that the West has since the French Revolution experienced 'an increasing fragmentation of society, a proliferation of new antagonisms, and a consequent increase in political possibilities' (Critchley, 1992: 212) via 'a logic of displacement supported by an egalitarian imaginary' (Laclau and Mouffe, 1985: 168). However, I think, it is obligatory to perceive the 'revolution' not only as democratic, but as 'radically democratic', in the sense that there is simultaneously a 'democratic logic of equivalence' and a 'liberal logic of difference', thereby 'installing' a certain 'tension and openness' in the social (Laclau and Mouffe, 1985: 190). In an analogous way, Critchley's thesis of the 'proliferation of new antagonisms', has to be seen in the light of the forms of these new antagonisms. That is in the light of the clearly delimited antagonisms which are characteristic of the horizon of the 'democratic revolution' (Laclau and Mouffe, 1985: 131). Political frontiers are no longer clear-cut. And if political subjects are seen not as unified, homogeneous entities, but as nonfixed, articulatory, overdetermined ensembles of 'subject positions' (Mouffe, 1992b: 372), then political frontiers can even be seen as piercing each and every 'individual' (Mouffe, 1990: 64-5). In this way Lacoue-Labarthe and Nancy's thesis that 'everything is political' can be radically questioned.

A key corollary of the proposition that 'everything is political', is Lacoue-Labarthe and Nancy's forewarning against 'political engagement'. Their political strategy can be seen as a Heideggerian 'politics of awaiting', that is 'a politics based upon the realization that human action cannot transform the world and that we must therefore wait for the transformation to come from within Being itself' (Critchley, 1992: 215). With Fraser, this '(non)position' can be seen as one of lapsing into political quietism and despairing resignation, because of a 'fear of dirty hands' (1984: 149-150). This is why Lacoue-Labarthe and Nancy tend to fall back into the assumed Derridian non-position, the very 'position' the Center attempts to transcend. This paradox has again to be seen in the light of their ambiguous but still over-totalizing view of the philosophical tradition and their emphasis on the *co-appartenance* between the philosophical and the political. Historically there are of course examples of such a political approach, e.g. Plato's dream of a 'philosopher-king'. However, there are other possibilities. Democracy can be interpreted as both a project emphasising its 'futural character' and as a political form that is 'founded' on the absence of any metaphysical foundation (Critchley, 1992: 212). I shall return to this possibility later.

These critical comments are not made in order to oppose Lacoue-Labarthe and Nancy's warning against a 'gesture of foundation' or *instauratio* of the political by the philosophical. But it may be that they are too much bound to the Heideggerian opposition to the 'activity of the will'. Of course it is correct to warn against the desire that a people can create itself anew as a *Gesamtkunstwerk*, as a vast collective entity represented by a Führer who incarnates the whole society (Lacoue-Labarthe, 1989: 64). But this does not necessarily have to result in a denial of a 'new formation of man himself' (1989: 66). Even in acknowledging and enacting the very impossibility of an absolute foundation, we still have to 'create' a new. As Laclau argues:

> [T]his will be a hero of a new type who has still not been entirely created by our culture, but one whose creation is absolutely neces-

sary if our time is going to live up to its most radical and exhilarating possibilities. (1991: 98)

Rather than avoiding 'dirty hands' we should perhaps attempt to identify ourselves, if not with such a new hero, then at least with the position from which such a hero will be possible. In short, we must not deny the desirable character of a 'radical democratic citizenship' (Mouffe, 1992: 235-238); or, in order to reactivate the radical tradition, a 'post-modern prince' who in all its 'finitude' can 'enact the political'.

Despite my scepticism regarding the thesis on *co-appartenance*, the positing of an actually existing more or less 'soft totalitarianism', and particulary their political strategy of 'awaiting' – in short the consequences they draw from their thesis that 'everything is political' – the project of Lacoue-Labarthe and Nancy is not without pertinence. There is another more important 'reason' for the necessity of a retreat from *la politique*, namely the inadequacy of some traditional approaches to politics and the political reducing thinking on the political to questions of a pre-constituted, positive, and (more or less) autonomous realm in the social formation. This is not just an 'innocent theoretical failure', but an approach which has had its own political effects. The horizon of politics in the post-war period can be seen as having been subordinated under what can be called the 'socio-economic imaginary'. As Fynsk argues, politics has therefore been reduced to a concern with questions of administrative decision-making, interest-mediation and an obsession with the putatively non- or pre-political problems of 'national housekeeping' (Fraser, 1984: 135-36). The problem with this conception of politics is that in the delimitation of the domain known as 'the political', the very notion of 'limit' derives from a desire for an 'objective' definition. This is the case whether we are dealing with the political theory, political science or political sociology which has developed through our century. As Lefort has shown, the different 'descriptivist', 'functionalist', 'Marxist' or 'relationist' perspectives share the operation of breaking down social data in order to find something intelligible, from which 'to deduce *society*' (1988: 216-20). In this way they can be seen as engendering an essentialist approach. Even though many of these approaches have emphasized the relational character of the social, they do not account for the very space of inscription on which the social depends. An analytic distinction between the political and the non-political is conditioned by an idea of the dimensionality of the social always already involving its constitution – a constitution which is itself political (Laclau, 1990: 35). As Žižek has argued, it is as if this positivist sociologism in its desperate

> attempt to convince us that politics is only a sub-system ... echoes an imminent danger of 'explosion' whereby politics would again 'be all'... There is an unmistakable *normative* undertone to this persuasion, bestowing on it an air of conjuration, it *must remain* a mere sub-system. (1991: 194)

These critical comments make possible a rearticulated notion of the phrase 'everything is political'. If it is the case that the political refers to the very constitution of the social then everything can be said to be political in the sense that nothing exists which does not have a political 'origin'. It is in this sense that the project of Lacoue-Labarthe and Nancy has – in its rearticulated form – to be seen not as a retreat to an 'apoliticism', but rather as a 'non-traditional', 'non-socio-techno-economic' political gesture or enactment.

Provided that the above rearticulations are taken into account they support an engagement in the project of 'retracing the political' in the sense of 'reflecting' on the very constitution of the social.

However, that which Lacoue-Labarthe and Nancy name and want to retrace, the 'essence of the political', the transcendence or alterity of the political *vis-à-vis* the social, also has to be questioned, since what they want to think is a 'wholly transformed alterity' of the political (Fraser, 1984: 148). The question is whether such a total transcendental movement is possible.

the essence of the political

The 'necessity' to attempt a move 'beyond' *la politique*, and hence to retrace *le politique* raises the question of how this outside should be conceptualized.

The interrogation of the *essence of the political* displays an inherent ambiguity. Fraser shows that Lacoue-Labarthe and Nancy oscillate between taking a position at the level of *la politique* and drawing back to meta-philosophical reflections in the retracing of *le politique* (1984: 148). However, there is also an ambiguity between a metaphysical and a non-metaphysical conception of *le politique*. On the one hand, they argue that the retracing of the political is not a simple restoring of the 'beyond' of a transcendental signifier of God, Man or History, and that it is necessary to rethink the political without 'nostalgia for a lost plenitude of presence' (Critchley, 1992: 217). On the other, in their assimilation of the Arendtian approach, they tend to conceive the political as a completely autonomous sphere without any relation to *la politique*.[6]

Hannah Arendt conceives of the political as 'a public space for normative deliberation about common ends'. Building on the

Aristotelian conception of politics as *polis*, the political life of Antiquity is located in a sphere of freedom, a sphere made possible because the constraints of physical necessity are handled in another sphere. This is why political action presupposes leisure and slaves, who are not (defined as) citizens but make it possible for others to cultivate citizenship. As Arendt argues, the concept of ruling and being ruled, of government and power was perceived as something prepolitical and belonging in the private rather than the public sphere (1958: 29). In this way the *polis* is seen as a special and freely chosen form of human organization sharply distinct from other power structures and societies, a self-governing community of equal citizens, such that all are involved in a shared public life (Arendt, 1958: 14). The Aristotelian doctrine, that man is a political animal, a *zoon politikon*, can be seen as indicating that (only) in the *polis* is it possible to be aware of the 'innumerable perspectives on a shared public enterprise' and of 'the experience of participating in reconciling these perspectives for common action' (Pitkin, 1972: 217). This approach therefore articulates the political as an additional concentric circle of society in which a political life of freedom, participation and responsibility is possible and desirable; a possibility which has as its condition a sharp distinction from the sphere of necessity, economics and coercive power. Lacoue-Labarthe and Nancy assume in their reiteration of the Arendtian approach as well as in their thesis of the *total* withdrawal of the political (Critchley, 1992: 212) that the 'essence of the political', or the

'beyond', has an absolute autonomy. Such an absolute or total independence or autonomy, however, is meaningless because, as Laclau has argued, 'if an entity was *totally* autonomous, it would mean that it was totally self-determined', and in that case 'the concept of autonomy would be absolutely redundant (what, exactly, would it be autonomous from?)' (1990: 37). Lacoue-Labarthe and Nancy point to a more adequate non-metaphysical approach to the 'project of the beyond' when they ask which non-dialectical negativity withdraws in the very constitution of the social (Fraser, 1984: 142), i.e. what is 'forgotten' in the very processes of institution or sedimentation of the social. In short, what is the specific character of *le politique*, the 'beyond', the outside of *la politique* or the social?

One starting point for addressing the question of an 'absolute outside', of the possibility of positioning oneself totally outside the social, could be the debate between Derrida and Foucault departing from the latter's writing on madness in the early sixties. This debate can illustrate the impossibility of taking a 'wholly otherwise' position, as Lacoue-Labarthe and Nancy seem to attempt. Moreover, this debate illustrates that deconstructive approaches should not be seen as a simple 'reversal' of the metaphysical tradition, and therefore are not equivalent to a total denial of any rationality, as was indicated in the initial criticism of Derrida.

In that debate, Derrida argues against the possibility of an absolute 'outside', and against there being any (access to a) real referent, i.e. madness as an invariable. Rather, the strategy must be to indicate the 'decisive' moment, the articulation which simultaneously connects and separates reason and madness (1990: 61). In this way, it is not a total exclusion, but rather an exclusion in the form of a dissension within thought, that is interior to meaning or logos in general (1990: 38-39). If Derrida's argument is accepted, then the 'retracing of the political' can no longer be simply a question of placing oneself in a position of an absolute outside. Thus *le politique*, the 'essence of the political', cannot be seen as something totally separated and autonomous from *la politique*:

> Now, if the 'outside' can no longer be conceived as something absolute, then how is it possible to think a non-absolute outside? Here the deconstructive installment of a permanent and constitutive undecidability in the very structures themselves can be drawn upon. This *undecidability* can be seen as a 'logic of in-between', as an operation that *both* sows confusion *between* opposites *and* stands *between* the opposites 'at once'. What counts here is the *between*, the in-betweenness. (Derrida, 1982: 212)

Undecidability denotes the terrain of simultaneity of the conditions of possibility and conditions of impossibility. In this way conditions of (im)possibility can be seen as what Gasché refers to as the 'space of inscription' (1986: 156-163). This 'empty space' 'coinciding' with the inscribed must be presupposed in relation to any inscription. From the point of view of the inscribed, whether in the form of our tradition or the social – from that into which we are thrown and from which there is no escape – the space of inscription – even though it only comes into 'existence' in the process of inscription – can be seen as the 'absolute outside'. Lacoue-Labarthe and Nancy's project of retracing the 'essence of the political' is thus to be seen as an attempt at reaching such an 'absolute outside', to which there is no access.

The inscribed, the social, which Lacoue-Labarthe and Nancy articulate as a closed entity characterized by the immanentism of 'everything is political' is also an impossibility. And even though the inscribed and the space of inscription 'coincide', that is, are given in relation to each other, any process of inscription will always establish a gap between the inscribed and the space of inscription because no inscription can manage to represent fully the very emptiness of the space of inscription. The inscribed has in this way to be seen as something partial and therefore precarious.

The initial conclusions to be drawn from the above are, firstly, the inadequacy of focusing on an 'absolute inside'. Secondly, this has to be supplemented by an articulation of the problematic nature of focusing on an 'absolute outside', i.e. the problematic nature of what could be called the 'postmodern metaphysics of absence'.[7] The problem with these two equally absolutist positions is that they attempt the impossible, to reach the ultimate instance of an essence either in the form of 'presence' or 'absence'. There is always something other which subverts the purity of such absolutist positions. These positions can only be reached via an ethical-theoretical decision or 'hegemonic intervention' which tries to eradicate the undecidable character of everything that exists.[8] It is in this terrain of undecidability that the political has to be 'located'.

enacting the political

Laclau and Mouffe's notion of 'the impossibility of society' (Laclau, 1983) is important, in that it is the condition of possibility for political events. If society is seen as something which fully manages to constitute itself as an objective totality, then the political in the sense of an event would cease to be, since any development will thus be a determinated 'internal' transformation. But the social never manages to constitute itself fully as 'society', in that everything in a social configuration is penetrated by its limits (Laclau and Mouffe, 1985: 127). The social has thus to be seen as an open field of inscribed differential identities in which relations and identities are contingent, historically specific, and a sedimented result of power and struggle (Laclau, 1990: 31-36).

The way in which the social is inscribed and obtains its partially fixed existence is a fundamental *political praxis*, and this is why the political can be seen as having an 'ontological' status (Laclau, 1990: 61). However, political inscription is always a reinscription, because we are always already thrown into one social order rather than another. The social is therefore (re)constituted through the political, and a 'normal' state of the social is 'secured' subsequently via processes of *sedimentation* (Laclau, 1990: 34) or institutionalization. The social thus ceases to be political when there is a decisive moment of interruption or suspension of the political event, in the sense that the social takes on the character of an 'uncontested set of meaningful practices' (Bertramsen, Thomsen and Torfing, 1991: 30). However, this sedimentation can never be complete because there will always be a *trace* of the political origin in the social (Laclau, 1990: 60). This trace installs an ontological vulnerability in the social, which in turns makes possible a new politicization or *reactivation* of the social. The necessary relation of the inscribed to the space of inscription is acknowledged, and in this way it is recognized that no inscription can be seen as a metaphysical foundational act or as *instauratio* which manages to ground the

social fully (Laclau, 1990: 28-31). Hence also Laclau and Mouffe's emphasis on the inescapably 'impossible' character of everything which 'exists'.

Such an anti-essentialist conception of the political clearly demarcates itself from more traditional 'spatial' conceptions of politics and the political. A distinction between politics and the political can thus be made, so that politics becomes the separate social subsystem 'interacting' with other subsystems, and the political becomes the very moment of openness when the structuring principle of society is questioned or reactivated by antagonizing subjective forces. In this sense, the political can be seen as doubly inscribed: it is one among other moments in the social formation, and it is the very 'terrain' or 'non-space' (i.e. temporality) from which an attempt is made to decide the future of the social.

The 'terrain' of the political is that of undecidability, an undecidability which affects everything right down to the social structures (Laclau, 1990: 31).

This inescapable undecidability can be seen as indicating the permanent 'impossibility' of the social, i.e. in the words of Žižek an 'antagonism as real' (1987). But as Laclau also argues, 'in practical life we are constantly faced with decisions to take which are algorithmically undecidable but which, nevertheless, have to be taken' (1987: 172). The argument concerning the non-algorithmic character of decision is that given that the identity of the social is never perfectly achieved and sutured, the social cannot be determined. Decisions do not follow automatically from the 'actually existing situation'.[9] To take a decision thus implies *creating* something which, however, at the same time, implies cancelling out of existence other possibilities which will not be realized (Laclau, 1987: 171). This means, and this is

enacting the political

the crucial point, that in the case of 'collective decisions ... it is highly *probable* that those other possibilities ... may be chosen by other groups' (Laclau, 1987: 171, emphasis added), whereby 'the relation between them will be one of antagonism' (Laclau, 1990: 31). If these arguments – concerning the inescapability of undecidability; the necessity of enacting decisions or, put another way, of enacting identifications; and the inevitability of such enactments involving 'exclusions' – are accepted, then it will be possible to view antagonism as a 'probable' corollary of enacting a decision, i.e. a way of giving the inescapable 'impossibility' a specific articulation. This means that decisions taken under the horizon of undecidability or 'antagonism as real' will probably result in antagonistic relations, or in Žižek's words in 'the social *reality* of the antagonistic fight' (1987), because of the cancelling out of some identities or poles of identification. In this way 'antagonism as *real*' can be seen as necessary, i.e. unavoidable, and this kind of antagonism is what Laclau reconceptualizes as dislocation in *New Reflections* (1990: 39f.).[10] The status of antagonism as 'antagonistic fight of social reality' can thus be seen as a non-necessary but probable result of taking a decision in an undecidable structure. With this distinction between dislocation and antagonism the question arises as to whether all decisions or identifications – even though they all involve power and the exclusion of alternatives – necessarily take on the same form, or whether there are different forms of decision and therefore the possibility of different and more or less antagonizing social relations? This is a question which has radical political consequences as I hope to indicate in the following.

One starting-point in this respect could be a distinction between those political projects which acknowledge the radical impossibility

of their project and those which do not 'account' for this 'impossibility'. The first type of project articulates its 'impossibility' as something 'internal' to its own identity, whereas the second type attempts to direct attention from its impossibility by locating the problem in an 'externality'. That the latter type does not accept their constitutive 'impossibility' can only be due to the fact that they presuppose the 'impossible', i.e. a full self-referential identity. In other words, in such projects a 'strong' conception of 'We' is constructed. In this way the project must necessarily take on the character of striving for the realization of an impossible fullness or consummation. As has been shown, such a total consummation is impossible. When such projects denounce their 'internal' 'impossibility', the latter has to be articulated as something 'external', and this is typically in the form of the 'past' or the 'outside' or 'Them'. For a project with a 'strong' we, references to an outside – given the relational character of identities – demand the construction of a 'strong' them: for Stalin it was the 'Traitors', for Hitler the 'Jews', for the West 'Communism', etc. The 'outside' in these circumstances of 'strong' identification represents the impossibility of the 'inside'. The problem with this kind of approach is not only that it is 'impossible'[11], but also that it leaves only two strategies open. Either a 'Total Strategy of Segregation', an absolute separation for example between the 'old' and the 'new', or between the 'inside' and the 'outside', is postulated. Or in the case where the 'past' or 'outside' is not only seen as something totally 'otherwise', but as something which is seen as a threat to the 'new' or the 'inside', the only possibility is a 'Total Strategy of Extermination'. These two strategic possibilities consist in either the denial of any relation at all with the 'otherwise' (and therefore the uncontaminated character of both 'camps') or the supplement of this with a total Elimination of the other. In principle I do not see these strategies as fundamentally different.

If this is seen as inadequate, not only theoretically (essentialism) but also politico-strategically (totalitarianism), then the only strategy is to accept fully the constitutive 'impossibility' of the social. This would be followed by an attempt to 'account' in a political way for this 'impossibility', i.e. an attempt to see the 'impossibility' as something penetrating and subverting (y)our own project and identity. This means that the constitutive 'impossibility' has to be articulated as something positive, and not as something for which there should be an attempt to find a 'solution'. As has been shown, the 'impossibility' is only seen as something which has to be 'exterminated' if the starting-point is 'false', i.e. if an 'essential fullness' is presupposed.[12] Even references to so-called 'strategic essentialism' have to be avoided, because they – as is the case in all essentialism – make possible an eschatological dream of purity, which is in fact a totalitarian dream. As Laclau has argued, it leads to the view that the 'new' has to be, or is, an uncontaminated fullness, purity, presence; and consequently to a view of the 'past' as something essentially impure (1990b: 95). But which strategic possibilities are thus left in an anti-essentialist framework? Recalling the earlier hesitance towards a Heideggerian 'politics of awaiting', is this strategy thus replaced by a totally empty 'strategy of impossibility'?

At this point it should be clear that a deconstructive approach has an 'ethical pertinence': a possibility exists of enacting an 'ethics of the political'. One theoretico-political articulation of such a 'political ethics' can for example be found in the work of Norval

and Laclau. Norval argues in 'Postscript – Post-Apartheid?' (1990) that given the relational character of identity in a situation of post-apartheid a simple reversal is inadequate for what I have called an 'ethics of the political' in that such a position will remain in the terrain of apartheid so that the systems of domination and signification which have constructed apartheid will continue to have effects. Laclau generalizes this argument in 'Universalism, Particularism and the Question of Identity' and argues that:

> [I]nstead of inverting a particular relation of oppression/closure in what it has of concrete particularity, [it should be inverted] in what it has of universality: the *form* of oppression and closure as such. The reference to the other is maintained here also, but as the inversion takes place at the level of the universal reference and not of the concrete content of an oppressive system, the identities of *both* oppressor and oppressed are radically changed. (1992: 11-2)

Now, the strategic possibilities which are left in an anti-essentialist framework do not amount to a totally empty 'strategy of impossibility', but to a possibility of 'enacting the political'. This means first of all that constitutive 'impossibility' has not only to be fully acknowledged, but the political-ethical-strategical consequences have to be enacted. There are at least two strategies for such an enactment. Firstly, given the 'impossibility' of the social, a (Socratic) 'strategy of suspicion' – a constant questioning of any 'actually existing situation', which by definition will always be a particularistic configuration. There is therefore an obligation to engage in the political, i.e. in constant struggles, contestations and negotiations. Secondly, and in so far that it is necessary not only to question and contest a given order but to enact another political project, a 'strategy of radical democracy'.

This is because 'radical democracy' in its deconstructive and discourse analytical sense, is a project which has at its 'heart' constitutive 'impossibility'.

I cannot imagine a better way to 'end' and thereby 'begin' this 'enacting of the political' than that of 'suspending' the perhaps excessive 'critical comments' enacted throughout this paper, and so of sending out an invitation to 'my' tradition via a reiteration of its articulation of some of the 'in-between' characteristics of radical democracy:

Radical democracy is something *tensional* (Laclau and Mouffe, 1985); it is something to be *attempted*; something which has a *futural* (Derrida, 1991b) or *différantial* (Critchley, 1992) character – it is always democracy *to come*; it is a *vanishing point* (Žižek, 1991), i.e. something to which we must constantly *refer*, but which can *never be reached* (Mouffe, 1992b); its value is *indeterminate* (Laclau, 1989), *incomplete* (Laclau, 1992b); and its subject is a proliferation of *finitude*, a subject whose limitations are the sources of its strengths (Laclau, 1992); and it does not have any particular objectives (Laclau, 1992), in short *an 'impossible' task which makes radical democratic relations possible.*

notes

1 The 'French debate' was initially played out in the conference entitled (with reference to Derrida, 1982) *The Ends of Man: Spinoffs of the works of Jacques Derrida*, held at Cérisy in France in the summer of 1980. The discussions mainly took place in and around the *Center for Philosophical Research on the Political* at the École Normale Supérieure, Paris, organized by Philippe Lacoue-Labarthe and Jean-Luc Nancy, who delivered the *Ouverture* on December 8, 1980. The Center lasted until November 16, 1984, when an indefinite suspension of its activities was announced in a memorandum.

2 Ernesto Laclau and Chantal Mouffe's discourse analysis is developed especially in *Hegemony and Socialist Strategy: Towards a Radical Democratic Politics* (1985), in 'Post-Marxism without Apologies' (1987), and later in Laclau's *New Reflections on the Revolution of Our Time* (1990) and Mouffe's *Dimensions of Radical Democracy: Pluralism, Citizenship, Community* (1992).

3 This 'double consummation' is, in fact, a 'single' one because if it is the case that there is a strict one-to-one correspondence between the philosophical and the political, then the completing transformation is an internal 'self-development', in the sense that 'it is a wholly positive process that *explains itself* in terms of the identity of the constituent elements' (Laclau, 1990: 17-18).

4 Lacoue-Labarthe and Nancy expand Claude Lefort's conception of totalitarianism into a 'soft' version, i.e. in the form of 'immanentism' which also refers to so-called Western liberal democracy (Fraser, 1984:144f.), and in this way the traditional distinction between democracy and totalitarianism is problematized.

5 Quasi-reactivation is used to indicate that Lacoue-Labarthe and Nancy, in the words of Dominique Janicaud, tend towards being 'more Heideggerian than Heidegger' (Critchley, 1992: 212).

6 Critchley has a similar critique, when he argues that *la politique* will always leave some traces in *le politique* (1992: 215), but does not theorize this relation, in that he does not elaborate *how* there 'remains a trace' of *la politique* in *le politique*.

7 The phrase 'post-modern metaphysics of absence' is used to indicate that it is not enough – as some 'wild' nihilistic postmodernisms have attempted – to argue that 'in the *final instance* no objectivity can be referred back to an absolute ground' (Laclau, 1990: 27), in that 'just to say everything is contingent ... is an assertion that would only make sense for an inhabitant of Mars', and 'no important conclusions can be drawn from this, since the social agents never act in that final instance' (1990: 35).

8 The Derridian notion of ethical-theoretical deci-

sion can be seen as analogous to Laclau and Mouffe's notion of hegemonic intervention (Laclau, 1991b: 5).

9 Here it is important to emphasize that this is not to say that any enactment is irrational but rather that it can never be 'legitimized' by reference to an absolute foundation. The decision can thus still be reasonable (Laclau, 1990: 31).

10 As Laclau argues, this reconceptualization is enacted because the idea of radical antagonism still involves the possibility of a radical representability, and this is why it has to be complemented with the notion of dislocation which is previous to any kind of antagonistic representation (1992: 16, note 2).

11 By referring to the 'impossible' character of such totalitarian projects I do not mean that it is impossible to attempt such a project, but rather that the agents of such a (in Heideggerian terms, 'inauthentic') political project would have to wear 'blinkers' in order to imagine that they can escape the impossibility of everything which exists.

12 Of course, if the situation is conceived as a situation of apoliticism, then an activation of the 'apolitical people' has to be enacted, but I do not think that this necessarily involves reference to, for example, an 'absolute evil'.

references

Arendt, Hannah The Human Condition (Chicago: University of Chicago Press, 1958).

Bernstein, Richard J. The New Constellation: The Ethical-Political Horizon of Modernity/Postmodernity (Cambridge: Polity Press, 1991).

Bertramsen, Rene, Jens Peter Frølund Thomsen and Jacob Torfing State, Economy and Society (Unwin Hyman, 1991).

Critchley, Simon The Ethics of Deconstruction: Derrida and Levinas (Oxford: Blackwell Publishers, 1992).

Derrida, Jacques 'The Ends of Man' in Margins of Philosophy, tr. Alan Bass (Chicago: University of Chicago Press, 1982 [1972]) p109-37.

Derrida, Jacques 'Cogito and the History of Madness' in Writing and Difference, tr. Alan Bass (London: Routledge, 1990 [1967]) p31-63.

Derrida, Jacques '"Eating Well", or the Calculation of the Subject: An Interview with Jacques Derrida' in Who Comes After The Subject, eds Eduardo Cadava, Peter Connor and Jean-Luc Nancy (New York: Routledge, 1991b) p96-119.

Frank, Manfred 'Kleiner (Türbinger) Programmentwurf. Philosophie heute und jetzt – Ein paar Überlegungen', Frankfurter Rundschau (5 March 1988).

Fraser, Nancy 'The French Derridians: Politicizing Deconstruction or Deconstructing the Political?', New German Critique, 33 (Fall 1984) p127-54.

Gasché, Rodolphe The Tain of the Mirror: Derrida and the Philosophy of Reflection (Cambridge, Mass.: Harvard University Press, 1986).

'Is Jacques a Cambridge Chap?', The Independent (15 May 1992) p19.

Laclau, Ernesto 'The Impossibility of Society', Canadian Journal of Political and Social Theory, vol. 7, 1 & 2 (1983).

Laclau, Ernesto 'Letter to Aletta' in New Reflections on the Revolution of Our Time (London: Verso, 1990) p159-74.

Laclau, Ernesto 'The Signifiers of Democracy', paper delivered at the conference on 'The Legacy of C.B. Macpherson', University of Toronto, October 1989.

Laclau, Ernesto New Reflections on the Revolution of Our Time, tr. Jon Barnes (London: Verso, 1990).

Laclau, Ernesto 'Totalitarianism and Moral Indignation', Diacritics (Fall 1990b) p88-95.

Laclau, Ernesto 'Community and its Paradoxes:

enacting the political

Richard Rorty's "Liberal Utopia'" in *Community at Loose Ends*, eds Miami Theory Collective (Oxford: University of Minnesota Press, 1991) p83-98.

Laclau, Ernesto 'Universalism, Particularism and the Question of Identity', paper delivered at University of Essex, 1992.

Laclau, Ernesto 'Beyond Emancipation' in *Emancipations, Modern and Postmodern*, ed. J. Nederveen Pieterse (London: Sage, 1992b).

Laclau, Ernesto 'Power and Representation' in *Politics, Theory and Contemporary Culture*, ed. Mark Poster (New York: Columbia University Press, 1993).

Laclau, Ernesto and Chantal Mouffe *Hegemony & Socialist Strategy: Towards a Radical Democratic Politics*, trs Winston Moore and Paul Cammack (London: Verso, 1985).

Laclau, Ernesto and Chantal Mouffe 'Post-Marxism without Apologies', *New Left Review*, 166 (1987) p79-106.

Lacoue-Labarthe, Philippe and Jean-Luc Nancy (eds) *Le retrait du politique* (Paris: Galilée, 1983).

Lacoue-Labarthe, Philippe and Jean-Luc Nancy eds *Les fins de l'homme: à partir du travail de Jacques Derrida* (Paris: Galilée, 1981).

Lacoue-Labarthe, Philippe *Heidegger, Art and Politics: The Fiction of the Political*, tr. Chris Turner (Oxford: Basil Blackwell, 1989).

Mouffe, Chantal 'Radical Democracy or Liberal Democracy', *Socialist Review*, 2 (1990) p57- 66.

Mouffe, Chantal 'Democratic Citizenship and the Political Community' in *Dimensions of Radical Democracy: Pluralism, Citizenship, Community*, ed. Chantal Mouffe (London: Verso, 1992) p225-39.

Mouffe, Chantal 'Feminism and Radical Politics' in *Feminists Theorize the Political*, eds Judith Butler and Joan W. Scott (New York: Routledge, 1992b) p369-84.

Norval, Aletta J. 'Postscript – Post-Apartheid?' in

Ernesto Laclau *New Reflections on the Revolution of Our Time* (London: Verso, 1990) p155-7.

Pitkin, Hanna Fenichel *Wittgenstein and Justice: On the Significance of Ludwig Wittgenstein for Social and Political Thought* (Berkeley, Los Angeles: University of California Press, 1972).

Žižek, Slavoj 'Beyond Discourse-Analysis' in Ernesto Laclau *New Reflections on the Revolution of Our Time* (London: Verso, 1990) p249-60.

Žižek, Slavoj *For They Know not What They Do: Enjoyment as a Political Factor* (London: Verso, 1991).

E rnesto Laclau represents one of the most influential theoretical voices in contemporary debates about the future of radical politics. In his various writings, including those co-written with Chantal Mouffe, he explores the political and social consequences of post-foundational and post-structuralist thought. In this interview we seek to situate his work in the broader theoretical and philosophical traditions from which it emanates, and then seek to clarify the implications of this for our contemporary political situation.

NEGOTIATING THE PARADOXES OF CONTEMPORARY POLITICS
an interview with ernesto laclau

In New Reflections on the Revolution of Our Time there seems to be a clear movement towards reworking aspects of the tradition of political theory and philosophy. This movement complements your longer standing interest in psychoanalysis and deconstruction, to name but two of the wellsprings of your thought. A series of questions arise out of this articulation of philosophical and socio-political concerns. Is there not a dissolving of the differences between philosophical traditions, and a reduction of philosophical concerns to social and political analysis by your treating of 'anti-essentialist' philosophy in a very general way as a reflection of the dislocation of the subject in post-modernity? Is not Wittgenstein's wish to dissolve philosophy into life, for example, left undifferentiated from Derrida's work on philosophical texts which remains within a tradition of philosophical reflection? Would not a more specified account of these sources of discourse theory allow a more precise theoretical outcome? Moreover, some of the deconstructive and psychoanalytic categories you employ are notoriously evasive of, or even resistant to, active projects of radical social transformation. There are also, as Žižek argues, profound tensions between these intellectual strands. Is there still significant work to be done in this area? Finally, how do you see the relation between the more philosophico-theoretical aspects of your work (derived as they are from standpoints which have strongly problematised systematic ethical commitments), and their articulation to a political project which has a clear normative content?

Ernesto Laclau: Regarding your first point everything depends, of course, on the viewpoint that one adopts. It is not so much that intellectual currents are not differentiated one from the other, but that these differentiations take place within a certain horizon defined by problems that all currents of thought, whatever their orientation, have to deal with. For instance, in a post-Communist era, in which there is an explosion of new identities – ethical, sexual, racial, etc. – you can have very different political responses, which range from an extreme multiculturalism to an affirmation of the universal values of reason around which the 'Republic' – à la Régis Debray – is based; but in all cases these are all (although very different) responses to challenges which would have been unthinkable twenty years ago. The comparability between these responses is given by the fact that all of them react to a new situation, which constitutes the political and intellectual medium in which all of them move. Fascism and Communism in the inter-war period were certainly very different, but both of them shared an unmistakable *Zeitgeist*.

All this, of course, is not to deny the intellectual differentiations that you are establishing. But even here we should be clear about the status of this differentiating gesture. It would be wrong, for instance, to assume that once the differentiation has been made, it is just a matter of *choosing* between them. The *penchant* for a final choice, that aspiration to ultimate and systematic coherence, is only a leftover of a half-repressed Cartesianism. The fact is that our own experience is fragmented, that it has been organized by many differentiated intellectual and political discourses, and that the most that we can do is to subvert or 'reactivate' some of them by the others to produce new hegemonic articulations between their themes, but without any pretension to produce systematic effects at the level of a mythical ground. We are thus condemned to be perpetual *bricoleurs*, to go on forever confronting Plato and Kant, Lacan and Derrida, Wittgenstein and Hegel in order to produce new effects of meaning. Thus, it is possible to open new avenues for historical action, but without the pretension of either reaching any ultimate meaning which would put the whole series together,

or – what is its symmetrical equivalent – to make an absolute choice between intellectual currents which would allow us to discard three quarters of the intellectual patrimony of our time. Any intellectual life worth living is based on indefinitely postponing the moment of an absolute approval or an absolute rejection.

It is partly for this reason that I do not think it is right to accuse deconstructive or psychoanalytic categories of being evasive or resistant *vis-à-vis* projects of radical social transformation. In the first place, the historical effects of categories which were elaborated without having in mind effects of social transformation, can lead to the latter in unexpected ways. This is possible insofar as the categories do not govern from the beginning the totality of the effects which can be derived from them. A category such as 'overdetermination' was thought by Freud without the slightest intention of producing effects of social transformation but, as you know, it opened the way to a theorization of the unfixity of meaning which, if radicalized in *certain directions* (others are, certainly, equally possible) can lead to a theory of hegemonic articulations and of indeterminacy as the milieu for a democratic politics. In the second place, categories which were *explicitly* designed to promote radical social transformation led exactly to its opposite – think, for instance, of the destiny of Leninism. The point to be made is that the use which is historically made of a certain category is not predetermined by the range of effects it was thought to contain at the moment of its initial elaboration.

This is also my response to your last question concerning political projects, and ethical and philosophico-theoretical commitments. Let me tell you, to start, that I do not see why you say that the philosophical-theoretical traditions I am close to are 'standpoints which have strongly problematised systematic ethical commitments'. I cannot find a single line in the works of, for

instance, Lacan, Derrida or Wittgenstein that would grant such a conclusion. What seems to be behind your question is the assumption that, while social theory is possible outside a foundationalist approach, an ethical theory has to be necessarily foundationalist. But I do not see the slightest ground for this assertion. The only thing that an antifoundationalist approach would deny is that normative propositions can be established outside all systems of belief, but it would certainly not deny that once people believe in certain things a normative argumentation becomes possible. The problem is more complex when people do not belong to established and homogeneous communities, when social fragmentation and a multiple belonging can lead to differentiated and even contradictory subject positions. What would it be, in these circumstances, to be an ethical *bricoleur*? I think I have something to say in this connection, although I cannot develop it here. But it is clear, anyway, that

these are ethical questions whose relevance is stressed by the fact that there is not a ready-made answer to them, and that the denial of their existence is not even the beginning of an answer.

Would it be accurate, in your opinion, to invert Marx and claim that the specificity of the present period lies in the solidification of the state and the concomitant 'withering of civil society' as Hardt and Negri claim in their most recent publication?

E.L.: Oh no, I think that it is a totally misleading characterization of present-day societies. It is undoubtedly true that civil society is less capable than in the past to ensure its self-reproduction, but it is wrong that there is at hand an instance such as 'the State', capable of ensuring social reproduction. If something is occurring today it is exactly the opposite: a loss of unity of the various State functions as a result of the globalizing contexts within which contemporary States are inscribed. And this globalization does not mean that there is a transference of decisions to higher instances but, on the contrary, that it is increasingly difficult to constitute any stable centre. The idea of an inversion of Marx's claim concerning the relation between State and civil society has the serious inconvenience of maintaining the notion of a separation between the two. Now, if anything characterizes the situation of contemporary societies it is, I think, the blurring of the division between State and civil society. Currents circulate between both spheres which make illusory the idea of a confrontation or even a delimitation between the two as fully fledged autonomous entities. Just think about the way of conceiving the radicalization of a democratic process. We cannot accept the

view of those who affirm that the radicalization of democracy consists in the deepening
of the line of demarcation between State and
civil society, and in the defence of the latter
against the former, because in many
instances the advance of democracy requires
progressive legislation, for example, that
goes against many deep-seated interests in
civil society; but we cannot accept either the
Jacobin idea of the public sphere as the
locus of an absolute and omnipotent popular will. Democratic politics requires many
and complex strategic moves which cut
across the two spheres and dissolve the
clear-cut differentiation between the two.

Your work, notably Hegemony and Socialist
Strategy *co-written with Chantal Mouffe,
has been influential in justifying and supporting what may be called 'the politics of
difference', that is, the emphasis on an
increasing plurality of potentially liberat-
ory political subjects, and the downplaying
of global and universalising political projects. However, central to the social ontology of the discourse approach you have been
articulating is the necessity of drawing
boundaries and constructing political frontiers. This political imperative is made
more pertinent in a world context marked by
the emergence of radical, particularistic discourses such as Islamicist movements, new
'ethno-nationalisms', and certain variants
of 'political correctness', all of which have
directly challenged existing liberal democratic forms of life. This poses a number of
questions: where, and on what basis, do
political boundaries have to be drawn?
What, by contrast, does the politics of difference mean for the values and institutions
of liberal democracies? How is a relationship towards 'otherness' and 'concrete others' from within liberal democracies to be
cultivated?*

E.L.: Your questions address important issues
in contemporary politics. I would say that I
see the latter as dominated by a set of paradoxes – that is, by postulates which, if pro-
longed to their last consequences, are incompatible with each other. Now, there are two
forms of dealing with a paradox: one is to
try to find a solution which actually *solves*
the paradox by avoiding its antinomic consequences; the other is to accept that the
terms of the paradox are unavoidable, so
that the paradox is ineradicable, and to
explore the strategic movements that it is
possible to develop within those antinomies.
I think that the first response is a blind alley
and that only the second provides the basis
for a political thought adequate to our present situation. Let us consider your three
questions from this perspective.

Where should political boundaries be
drawn? Let me tell you that the answer to
this question is ancillary to another which is
more basic: what is the need for political
boundaries in the first place? As I have tried
to show in different works, political boundaries are neither the result of a contingent
imperfection of society, nor even of an
empirical impossibility of overcoming the
latter but, instead, of the impossibility of
constituting any social identity except
through acts of exclusion. But this, far from
being the solution to anything, is rather the
starting point of a set of difficulties. For if
social division is the condition of any communitarian identity, community is possible
only as far as it is impossible. We are submitted to two contradictory movements: on
the one hand we have to constitute society
as an objective social order; on the other,
this objectivity contains, as its internal
requirement, that which makes social objectivity impossible – i.e. a social division.
Now, I would argue that the terms of this
undecidability are not only ineradicable but

also politically productive, because the inevitably incomplete character of society opens the terrain for the permanent need for political initiatives which attempt to constitute that impossible entity. The range of strategic language games which it is possible to play within the social is thus considerably expanded. So, I respond to your question by saying that it cannot be answered at the level at which it is posed – i.e. a general theory of politics – because, given the undecidability just pointed out, there are no aprioristic grounds which would transform it into a meaningful one – it is, using an example from Quine, like asking what points are starting points. Only reference to a concrete situation can provide the grounds for a meaningful answer.

And you actually provide such a reference with your second and third question concerning 'difference', 'otherness' and liberal democratic institutions. Here you can easily see the paradox of possibility/impossibility in full operation. Taken from the particularistic point of view of the supporters of the 'politics of difference', the paradox traverses their identity through and through: if they want to preserve their identity unchanged, they have to abstain from participating in the institutions of the liberal State; but if they want to advance their causes and the extension of their rights, they can only do it precisely through that participation. Even more: the more particularistic the identity of the group, the more universalistic will have to be the discourse of rights on which that particularism is based. Identity can only be asserted through the very process in which it is lost. Hybridization is the destiny of all social identities in present-day societies. But the same paradox dominates liberal institutions: if they are consequently pluralistic, they will have to accept the coexistence of many values and princi-

ples of other communities which are incompatible with those which accompanied the installation of the liberal State. At the limit, the very principle of pluralism could be put into question. Again, inevitable hybridization. In practice, this means that a politics of difference which is compatible with the coexistence of a plurality of groups within a community cannot logically solve any of the paradoxes just mentioned, but this does not mean that it cannot negotiate them politically. And this – it is at least my hope – means that new abilities and forms of identification of the groups involved in the negotiation can be developed, thus enriching and expanding the strategic language games at the disposal of the community as a whole to politically manage its own impossibility.

In a recent interview you have argued the following: '[w]e no longer regard ourselves as the successive incarnations of the absolute spirit – Science, Class, Party – but as the poor men and women who think and act in a present which is always transient and limited; but that same limitation is the condition of our strength: we can be ourselves and regard ourselves as the constructors of the world only insofar as the Gods have died. There is no longer a Logos, external to us, whose message we have to decipher inside the interstices of an opaque world' (New Reflections, 189). Many of your political interventions and positions replicate this double movement: the recognition of the dissolution of foundations on the one hand, and an overall optimism about the political consequences of this increasing human awareness of limits and contingency on the other. Our question concerns the grounds of this optimism. When other critical traditions such as the Frankfurt School, the later Heidegger and even some so-called post-modernists (such as Baudrillard), dwell on the constant 'enclosure' and 'ensnarement' of human action in the all-encompassing logics of capitalism or technology, why do you insist on emancipatory possibilities in late modernity? Is this optimism a conjunctural appeal, or is it grounded in the immanent tendencies and logics of our present situation? Does your commitment to human beings 'as the constructors of the world' run the risk of a traditional humanism or a 'subjectivism' which is inconsistent with your questioning of philosophical foundations?

E.L.: In the first place, let me tell you that I am not particularly optimistic about the possible outcomes of the present world situation. If I could have given the impression of being so, it is because I have strongly reacted against the grounds which some contemporary currents, such as the Frankfurt School, have presented for their pessimism. All I have said is that the present situation is one of indeterminacy in what concerns its possible outcomes, that the future is largely open and undecided, and that there are no 'objective grounds' for either an aprioristic pessimism or optimism. Anyway, I deeply distrust such sweeping stands as a *global* optimism or pessimism. In my view, the pessimism of *some* of the tendencies to which you refer (the case of Heidegger is much more complicated) is the direct result of the fact that the notion of a universal class, incarnating the future of Humanity, is on the wane. That decline of universalism is only too evident but, in an era of disorganized capitalism, the decline in the ability of the ruling groups to establish an unchallenged domination is also evident. The point is that as all systems of domination are contingent, they can never be total, and will always be unable to reach some spaces of freedom, from which a war of position can be initiated. Can you imagine what would

have happened if, in South Africa, the militants of the ANC had adopted in the mid-sixties an Adornian view of the future of capitalism? Or if De Gaulle, in 1940, would have accepted the view that, as a result of 'objective tendencies', modern societies irresistibly advance towards a totalitarian nightmare? Both the prophets of gloom and the prophets of a sunny future are well inscribed in that modern terrain of the 'universal' which is best expressed by the philosophies of History. What I am saying is that since all groundings are ultimately contingent, limitation is a feature shared by *all* social actors, for none of them is the game definitely over. If I have taken special issue with the prophets of pessimism, it is because over the last decade the Left has been only too prone to indulge in a monotonous *mea culpa* and masochism, and much less prepared to explore the new possibilities of social and political action opened by the contemporary scene. But I am equally critical of any optimism based in assumed immanent and necessary logics developing in our present situation. In that sense, if I have said that human beings are 'the constructors of their world', what I mean is that the world is not guaranteed to them by any immanent necessary logic and that, as a result, all historical construction will ultimately be groundless, contingent and transient. This is, I think, enough to delimit my position from any subjectivism or humanism, which precisely requires some foundation deeper and previous to any contingent human action.

In your work the category of dislocation has taken on a more and more central role. This is so especially with regard to your claim that 'dislocation is the source of freedom'. A number of questions regarding the relation between dislocation and freedom, and the nature of freedom itself, arise here. It is with the nature of the movement from dis-

48

location to 'freedom' that we are mainly concerned. How are we to understand the nature of this freedom? You distance yourself very clearly from accounts which emphasise the 'freedom of a subject with a positive identity' (NR, 60), arguing that freedom here is that of a 'structural fault'. Thus, freedom has no positive contents but is 'mere possibility'. However, seen from the vantage point of dislocation, there is no freedom here. The failure of the structure fully to constitute the subject, forces the subject to be subject, to take a decision, to act, to identify anew. We have to respond, we are not free. It seems, therefore, that the relation of dislocation/freedom could be thought more productively, by emphasising both the dimension of possibility and its impossibility. That is to say, rather than simply being free to act, to choose in a Sartrean sense, the moment of freedom and possibility is simultaneously the moment of my greatest constraint, of unfreedom. Taking this latter dimension into account could – to come back to our contemporary situation – help to make sense of the experience of dislocation as not being ipso facto something positive and worthy of celebration. In other words, would you agree that stressing the terror and force at the heart of freedom, has to form part of our very account of the possibilities arising out of severe dislocation?

E.L.: I could not agree more with your conclusion. As you cogently point out, the experience of dislocation is not ipso facto 'something positive and worthy of celebration'. But this also means that, if freedom and dislocation are related in the way I have suggested – that you seem to accept – the very experience of freedom is ambiguous. For that reason, although as I said, I subscribe to your conclusion, I cannot follow you in one of the intermediate stages of your argument, when you assert that, because the failure of the structure 'forces the subject to be a subject', when we are forced to respond we are unfree. If this was so, we would certainly be in the best of all possible worlds: the villain of the piece would be 'dislocation', while 'freedom', as complete lack of constraint, would be preserved as an uncontaminated positive value. But, as you yourself recognize, this impeccable solution is impossible: freedom and dislocation cannot be separated that way. On the one hand, a freedom that dislocation does not coerce to choose, would not be my freedom, but the freedom of the structure which has constructed me as a subject. On the other hand, a freedom which is my freedom, which avoids both the pitfalls of the Spinozian freedom, reduced to be consciousness of necessity, and the Sartrean freedom of being a chooser who has no longer any grounds to choose, can only be the freedom of a structural failure – i.e. dislocation. But in that case the ambiguity of dislocation (what you call 'the terror and force at the heart of freedom') contaminates freedom itself. Freedom is both liberating and enslaving, exhilarating and traumatic, enabling and destructive. In a fragmented and heterogeneous society, the spaces of freedom certainly increase, but this is not a phenomenon which is uniformly positive, because it also installs in those spaces the ambiguity of freedom. As a result, the possibility emerges of more radical attempts at renouncing freedom than those that we have known in the past. If freedom and dislocation go together, it is in the terrain of a generalized freedom that experiences such as those of contemporary totalitarianism become possible. If this is so, it means that the quest for an absolute freedom for the subject is tantamount to a quest for an unrestricted dislocation and the total disin-

49

tegration of the social fabric. It also means that a democratic society which has become a viable social order will not be a *totally* free society, but one which has negotiated in a specific way the duality freedom/unfreedom.

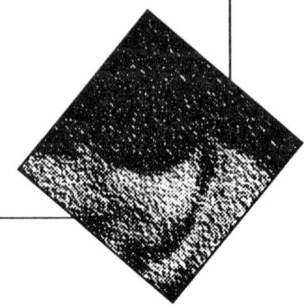

interviewers: david howarth and aletta j. norval

contributors to questions: david howarth, aletta j. norval, timothy s. murphy, barry stocker

U ntil recently, the history of Marxism followed a dialectical pattern of development, carried along on the antithetical horns of the method that was also its constitutive dilemma: investigation of the mechanisms of domination on the one hand, and constitution of a revolutionary subject position on the other. This pattern found its model in Marx himself, in the formal and substantial antithesis of *Capital*, the objective treatise on domination, to the earlier *Grundrisse*, the subjective account of insurrectionary organization. This dialectic may be found as well in Lenin's thought, where it has had the most far-reaching practical consequences, but also in Lukács' *History and Class Consciousness* and in the writings of Rosa Luxemburg and Antonio Gramsci. In the work of the Frankfurt School and its descendants, however, one of the terms of this dialectic falls away: the constitution of the revolutionary subject all but disappears, leaving only the critique of mechanisms of domination. Revolutionary subjectivity is no longer possible in light of contemporary techniques of domination like the culture industry. This is the source both of Theodor Adorno's pathos and of his 'negative dialectic', which, like Herbert Marcuse's one-dimensionality, bear witness to the expansion of capitalist contradiction beyond the ability of the dialectic to resolve it. The influence of this monological version of Marxism has been tremendous, especially on those who seem to have taken it a step further, as Jean-François Lyotard and Jean Baudrillard have done. Even Marxists who do not explicitly renounce theories of constitution often give no place to them; one would be hard-pressed to find revolutionary subjectivity inscribed in the writings of Fredric Jameson, for example. Recent attempts, like those of Ernesto Laclau and Chantal Mouffe, to found a radical democra-

timothy s. murphy

HERCULEAN TASKS, DIONYSIAN LABOR

michael hardt and antonio negri on the contemporary state-form

cy by recuperating the Gramscian notion of hegemony show a great deal of promise, but they are premised on critiques of Marxist 'essentialism' rather than on analyses of the functioning of the contemporary state, and they retain the idea of 'civil society' as if that concept had not been rendered problematic by Frankfurt School and postmodernist criticism.

This is the situation into which Antonio Negri and Michael Hardt intervene. The problem that they work to extend is this: is it possible to return to the theory of revolutionary subjectivity without reducing it, through the dialectic, to the theory of domination, in the manner of the Frankfurt School? In other words, is a relation of domination and revolution that would preserve their difference possible? The task which forms the focal point of Negri's career has been the determination of the conditions of possibility of such a relation, and in the face of what he calls the real subsumption of society under capitalism, that task has been truly herculean. Negri taught state doctrine at the University of Padova (Italy) from 1959 until 1979, during which time he also helped to organize several successive incarnations of extra-parliamentary leftism, among both students and factory workers; the most famous of these groups were Potere Operaio (Workers' Power), which dissolved in 1973, and Autonomia (Autonomy), which succeeded it. Negri taught at the Ecole Normale Supérieure in Paris at the invitation of Louis Althusser between 1977 and 1979, in addition to his professorial and organizational duties in Italy. His popular fame, however, rests primarily on his incarceration, without trial, as the mastermind behind the Red Brigades' assassination of former Italian Prime Minister Aldo Moro. He was arrested on April 7, 1979, and charged with 'subversive association' for his work as a militant organizer and Marxist philosopher, under an Italian law that still stands. He was imprisoned for four years without trial.[1] He has always maintained his innocence, and indeed his writings are explicitly critical of what he calls the 'regicide' strategy of the Red Brigades. While in prison, Negri was elected to Italian Parliament as a representative of the Radical Party; parliamentary deputies are granted immunity from prosecution, so he was freed to take his seat in 1983. Debate soon turned against him, however, and he fled to Paris to avoid returning to prison. He has been sentenced to thirty years imprisonment in his absence. Negri has taught political science at the Université de Paris VIII (Vincennes à St. Denis) since the late nineteen-eighties, and has given several seminars at the Collège International de Philosophie. Michael Hardt, who was educated at the University of Washington and the Université de Paris VIII and who now teaches at Duke University, was Negri's student for several years, and has collaborated with him on the Parisian journal *Futur antérieur* as well as on *Labor of Dionysus*.

Negri and Hardt's intervention takes as its point of departure Marx's distinction between the formal subsumption of society within capital and real subsumption. Formal subsumption, in which already existing relations and practices of production are enclosed within capitalist systems of exchange but are not transformed by them, dates from the Industrial Revolution; Romanticism in philosophy and literature, which exalts affect and the sovereign individual against the instrumental rationality and general equivalence (of commodities and laborers) upon which capitalism is based, are reactions to this form of subsumption. Real subsumption, on the other hand, takes place when capitalist relations of production invade all of the spaces of society, transforming the socius into an immense factory for the extraction of surplus value. Capital remakes all social relations in its own image, like a virus remakes the cells of its host into contagious images of itself. This, according to Negri and Hardt, is the situation we have lived through since 1968: the transition from formal to real subsumption. Coeval with this transition has been the completion of the internal development of capitalist relations of production: the de-differentiation of labor. Through mechanization and computerization, the skill level required of labor has been systematically reduced, rendering all workers, no matter what their training, interchangeable. The same mechanization, Marx notes, allows capital to 'reduce labor time to a minimum, while it posits labor time, on the other side, as sole measure and source of wealth' (1973: 706). Negri and Hardt call this tendency the 'crisis of the law of value'. The absolute reduction of human labor time necessary to drive production is visible in the rise in unemployment and the concomitant political interest in protectionism everywhere in the industrialized world. It is also visible in the extreme polarization of incomes that characterizes the demographic make-up of the U.S. and Europe, to say nothing of the rest of the world: the managerial class, whose income depends on the control of resources, saw its percentage share of wealth balloon during the nineteen-eighties, while the share of the working classes, whose income depends on generic time worked, declined just as precipitously.

To this point, Negri and Hardt merely provide an alternative terrain for the analysis of domination in the contemporary period, which alone would make their work important. But they do not stop there; in fact they do not even start there. I have presented their critique of domination first in the belief that it resonates with other contemporary critiques and thus provides an accessible point of entry into Negri's earlier works on the constitution of revolutionary subjectivity. These works present an argument for the logical and ontological priority of labor over capital as follows: capitalist domination in this century has developed in reaction to the mass movements of labor, from the Bolshevik revolution in Russia through the Great Depression up to May '68 and beyond. Keynesian economic planning and the New Deal, for example, arose as attempts to forestall a Western communist uprising that would match Russia's, like the dispersal of factory production in the nineteen-seventies and eighties arose in response to demands of labor unions and workers' groups. Negri views capital as a profoundly conservative force, in the sense that it does not expend profit on innovation unless its profit-generating systems are directly threatened, nor does it posit new values beyond the dialectic of profit. Labor, on the other hand, is innovative in its constant evasion of capitalist control and in its ability to revalorize the exchange values handed to it by capital. This innovative power of labor has been harnessed by capital through the dialectics of value and governmentality for use as the motor of production, but this does not mean that labor and capital are inextricably linked. The crisis of the law of value has revealed the dialectic to be a ploy of capital, and it has also revealed the logical and ontological disjunction that separates it from labor. The dialectic only functions in one direction: capital necessarily requires labor, at least as the power to purchase and consume, but labor does not necessarily require capital. Unlike the conservative power of capital which, like the dialectic, preserves as it destroys in order to extract profit, the Dionysian power of labor is a pure aggression that destroys completely in order to construct totally new forms of value. In the contemporary period, this power of labor is multiply incarnated: in AIDS activism, in eco-feminism, in the immaterial labor of the burgeoning tertiary or service sector.

The essay that follows is a section of Negri and Hardt's new book *Labor of Dionysus: Critique of the State-Form* (Minneapolis: University of Minnesota Press, 1994). The book is an analysis of the gradual construction of the contemporary State, in response to mass political movements, in the course of the twentieth century. The first section of the book moves from a consideration of post-World War I Keynesian economic policies and the crisis of 1929 through a detailed analysis of the post-World War II Italian Constitution, which declares in its first article that Italy is a 'democratic republic founded on labor', and the philosophy of law inherent in it. The second section criticizes inadequate communist models of the State and goes on to analyze the ways in which public spending has been used as a tool to manage recalcitrant labor through the 'social wage' of welfare or dole payments. The final and most provocative section argues that it is civil society, rather than the State, that has 'withered away' in our time; postmodern law, like John Rawls' *Theory of Justice*, attempts to legitimate the abstraction and atomization of mass politics along with the concomitant privatization of the public sphere (i.e., the reconstruction of the State in the image of private enterprise). It is from this penultimate chapter that the following excerpt is taken. The book concludes with an assessment of the 'potentialities of a constituent power' *separate* from the power of capitalist domination. This account dramatizes the collapse of the dialectical mediation upon which capitalist domination was premised, and the potential triumph of the autonomy of what Negri and Hardt, following Spinoza, call 'the multitude'. The labor of this multitude, no longer subordinated to the capitalist control of time as surplus value, is the labor of Dionysus, a labor that is savage in its ability to exceed and evade the categories of capitalist value production and delirious in its creative force. Dionysian labor is the only viable response to the herculean tasks that face the Left today, precisely because such labor is bound not by the moral duty of the individual hero-subject but by its own collective desire; the only 'heroism' possible will be such a delirious, collective 'heroism', like that of the micro-collectivity that has produced this book.

* * *

We have given this excerpt from *Labor of Dionysus* the same title as the chapter from which it is taken, even though the chapter contains much more than any excerpt could

adequately show. I have written an introduction summarizing the preceding part of the chapter so that the excerpt can stand alone here. We would like to thank Antonio Negri, Michael Hardt and the University of Minnesota Press for their kindness in allowing *Angelaki* to publish this text.

postmodern law and the withering of civil society
summary of preceding part

Chapter Six of *Labor of Dionysus* is a critical account of the philosophy of law and justice underpinning the contemporary capitalist State. It begins with a reading, against the grain, of John Rawls' monumental *Theory of Justice* (Cambridge, MA: Belknap/Harvard, 1971), which attempts to break with both transcendental and utilitarian models of juridical foundation. Rawls 'invites us to accept or reject his vision of the just basic structure of society on the basis of the philosophical coherence and moral necessity of the founding contractual moment and the procedure it puts in motion'[2], rather than on the basis of transhistorical ideal norms or existing concrete social relations. His model distributes justice on the basis of its procedural structure, not precepts of 'reason' or analyses of society. Negri and Hardt's reading identifies this model's almost-effaced moments of confrontation with the State's others: the historical events of the French and American Revolutions, which Rawls reduces to formal contractual procedures even as he uses them to demonstrate the continuity of ideal justice and actual juridical practice; and the creative social activity of labor that produced those revolutions. Rawls and his followers must control these forces of rupture, either by excluding them from the juridical system or by incorporating and domesticating their antagonisms within a more substantial State. Negri and Hardt label the first tendency the 'postmodern' interpretation of Rawls, and the second the 'communitarian' interpretation. The first is postmodern because, as we will see in the excerpt, it renounces the field of production to concentrate on the sphere of circulation; Jean Baudrillard, though not an interpreter of Rawls, clearly exemplifies this tendency in his analyses of the 'implosion of the social in the media'.3 Negri and Hardt expose the stasis and abstraction of Rawls' procedures of legitimation, and then choose to analyze Richard Rorty's extension of Rawls' principle of tolerance to the point where it becomes a principle of exclusion and neutralization of conflict.

notes

1 On this detention, see Amnesty International's annual reports for the years 1980-1983. See also 'Do You Remember Revolution?', 'The Revolt at Trani Prison' and 'Negri Before His Judges' in Negri (1988: 229-243, 253-258, 261-268).

2 Hardt and Negri (typescript 309).

3 Poster (1988: 207-19).

references

Marx, Karl Grundrisse (Harmondsworth: Penguin, 1973).

Negri, Antonio Revolution Retrieved: Selected Writings (London: Red Notes, 1988).

Hardt, Michael and Antonio Negri Labor of Dionysus: Critique of the State-Form (Minneapolis: University of Minnesota Press, 1994).

Poster, Mark (ed.) Jean Baudrillard: Selected Writings (Stanford: Stanford University Press, 1988).

other works in english by antonio negri and michael hardt

antonio negri:

'Capitalist Domination and Working-Class Sabotage' in Working-Class Autonomy and the Crisis (London: Red Notes/CSE, 1979) p93-137.

Marx Beyond Marx: Lessons on the Grundrisse (New York: Autonomedia; London: Pluto Press, 1984, 1991).

Revolution Retrieved: Selected Writings (London: Red Notes, 1988).

The Savage Anomaly: The Power of Spinoza's Metaphysics and Politics (Minneapolis: University of Minnesota Press, 1990).

with félix guattari:

Communists Like Us (New York: Semiotext(e), 1990).

The Politics of Subversion (Cambridge: Polity Press, 1989).

Constituent Power (Minneapolis: University of Minnesota Press, forthcoming).

michael hardt:

Gilles Deleuze: An Apprenticeship in Philosophy (Minneapolis: University of Minnesota Press, 1993).

An interpretation of Rawls adequate to a postmodern conception of law, an interpretation focused on the antifoundationalist aspects of the system, should be situated as a development in the tradition of juridical formalism – a development, however, that constitutes a qualitative leap.[1] The formalist tradition has always been haunted by the questions of foundation and the positive sources of the production of norms. On one hand, transcendental currents in the Kantian tradition have sought to resolve this problem through the foundation of right in the dictates of reason. The rational articulation of this foundation constructs an ordered and universal juridical system. These strictly formalist theories, however, have proved vulnerable to charges that they are arbitrary, abstract, and impractical. On the other hand, another current in juridical formalism has argued that law can function as an adequate analytic of civil society, as a faithful representation of social forms. Here the formal system is grounded on a material foundation and articulated along its lines. This current, however, must struggle to create a certain detachment from the incoherent and inconstant elements of society, to give representation the relative autonomy that a formal system needs to propose the order of a juridical arrangement. Many of the most sophisticated elaborations of juridical formalism, of course, combine these two strategies – Hans Kelsen, for example, brackets the material foundation in the *Grundnorm* and then articulates it through a rational, scientific deduction – but this combination or mediation does not resolve the problem of the foundation.

An 'antifoundationalist' theory of right represents, in effect, the adequate realization of these tendencies latent in the formalist juridical tradition. We will argue in

michael hardt
antonio negri

POSTMODERN LAW AND THE WITHERING OF CIVIL SOCIETY

the following section of this chapter that Rawls manages to navigate between the twin dangers of traditional foundationalist solutions: he avoids both the empirical foundation in the material constitution of society and the transcendental foundation in the precepts of reason. By rejecting these foundations and seeking support instead in a reasonable and circular network of procedures, Rawls constructs a formal system that is both autonomous and practical. Here the juridical form becomes a motor, an abstract schema of normative production and circulation. The concept of procedure is a perfect candidate to fill this role: a procedure is a form in motion, a dynamic schema. The procedural republic, then, provides us with a means of understanding how the basic structure of postmodern society – the simulacra of social reality detached from production and labor – can generate and maintain itself.

the genius of the system: reflection and equilibrium

While the postmodern interpretation of Rawls flattens the tension in the text we identified earlier, it does in fact find resonances in *A Theory of Justice* and particularly in some of his more recent articles. Specifically, in Rawls, the autonomy of the formal juridical system is supported by a line of development that extends from our sense of justice and our considered convictions to the idea of reflective equilibrium and finally to the notion of systemic stability. Circularity and reflection give the formal schema a depth and stability that serve to displace the problems of the foundation of the system and the sources of normative production. The genius of the system is its discovery of stability without foundations and procedure without movement, which effectively displace social antagonisms and conflict from the institutional arrangement. Circulation comes to replace production as the center of juridical theory, creating an overlapping system of supports and thus guaranteeing the security of a well-ordered democratic regime.

The circularity of the juridical system is announced, or perhaps prefigured in Rawls' method of argumentation. The 'moral geometry' (121) that he presents in *A Theory of Justice* differs radically from traditional conceptions of geometric development. Seventeenth-century arguments in *more geometrico*, for example, base their validity on the unilinear line of deductive demonstrations from definitions and axioms to propositions and conclusions. Rawls' geometry on the other hand rests on a circular form of exposition in which the argument's point of departure and its conclusion presuppose one another. We get a hint of this circularity simply by looking at the progression of themes in Part One of the text. The argument unfolds in an unusually complex order. Rawls begins with a series of tentative propositions that gradually become less provisional through a process of adequation or adjustment until the point when these very same propositions, no longer tentative, constitute the conclusions of the argument. The network of hypotheses are 'proven' by their mutual support. In effect, all of the theory must be laid out before any of its elements can hold; the argument must be finished before it can properly begin. Paul Ricoeur points out, for example, that the two principles of justice are formulated (section 11) and interpreted (section 12) before we have investigated the situation in which they would be chosen. Nearly one hundred pages later we are presented with the full description of the situation of the choice of the two principles (sections 20-25) and the reasoning that justifies that choice (sections 26-30). 'How can one formulate and interpret the principles, precisely insofar as they are principles, before having articulated the argument that is supposed to establish that those are truly the principles, that is to say the first propositions?' ('Le cercle de la démonstration', 81-82). Obviously, Rawls has a particular notion of what constitutes a principle.

Since Rawls' presentation refuses linearity, it in fact makes little sense to conceive of certain elements as prior or posterior to others. 'We are not dealing with a linear argument, but with a development that consists rather in the progressive elucidation of that which is already anticipated' ('Le cercle de la démonstration', 83). Since this is not a rationalist geometry in any conventional sense, perhaps we should call it a *reasonable* argument. Rawls appeals to the Kantian distinction between the Rational and the Reasonable to emphasize that his argumentation is not metaphysical but political, in other words, that the theory does not refer to a transcendental order of reason but to a practical realm of convictions ('Justice as Fairness', 237, note 20 and 'Kantian Constructivism', 528-32). While rational development is described by a straight, unidirectional movement, reasonable argument is conducted through a back-and-forth motion, within the conditions of feasibility. In fact, the reasonable argument is characterized not so much by motion but by a balancing procedure that arrives at a point of stasis, in other words, by the gradual elimination of motion.

The particularity of Rawls' methodology should indicate to us that he not only has a special understanding of geometrical development in a theoretical arrangement, but also of contractual development in a social arrangement. Like many formulations in the contractarian tradition, Rawls' contractual procedure is purely hypothetical, but it is novel in the way he conceives the authorship of the contract and the relationship of the parties entering into it. At the scene of the contract, in the original position, there is not a plurality of persons, not even hypothetical or representative persons. The background for the contractual argument is not an image of social difference and conflict, such as for example the state of nature in many early modern contractual arguments. In fact, several commentators have pointed out, with a certain perplexity, that Rawls' contractual procedure does not deal with difference at all: it is 'non-interactive' and does not involve any bargaining, negotiation, nor even any choice – in effect, it does not involve a contract in any conventional sense. (See Kukathas and Pettit, 34 and Sandel, *Liberalism and the Limits of Justice*, 130-32.) In a first instance, then, Rawls' contractualism refers not to any actual or hypothetical agreement but to a *condition* of the-

oretical discussion. 'It is at this point that the concept of a contract has a definite role: it suggests the condition of publicity and sets limits on what can be agreed to' (*A Theory of Justice*, 175). It thus seems that 'what matters is not so much the actual contract that would be made as the contractual situation' (Kukathus and Pettit, 68). At the same time, the public nature of the contractual situation defines the agent in that situation. Even though Rawls himself notes that the term 'contract' implies a plurality (16), there is only one subject in the original position and this subject is public, not in the sense that it represents a social average, but in that it is generic. The subject in the contractual situation can be best conceived as a displaced social subject: the limitations on knowledge imagined with the veil of ignorance create a subject that belongs to a specific society but is ignorant of its place in that society. Insofar as it is displaced, the subject can be understood as a sort of Rousseauian general subject, as distinguished from either an individual subject, a subject of the many, or the subject of all. Insofar as Rousseau's conception of the general will is invoked by the subject in the original position, however, we should note that it is invoked not as a center of democratic will, or popular subjectivity, but rather as a center of logical imputation. It would be completely inappropriate, Rawls insists, to link the generality of the original position to the actual positions of social subjects, in the way that Rousseau at times seems to link the general will to the forces of democratic participation:

> [T]he original position is not to be thought of as a general assembly which includes at one moment everyone who will live at some time; or, much less, as an assembly of everyone who could live at some time. It is not a gathering of all actual or possible persons.

To conceive of the original position in either of these ways is to stretch fantasy too far. (139)

Seen in this light, Rawls' original position is perhaps very close to a European tradition of constitutional thought (following in part a particular interpretation of Rousseau) that also emphasized the logical (not subjective) quality of the general will as foundation of the system. The first element of Rawls' contractualism, then, is its positioning of a single displaced subject in a contractual situation. Once we have established this condition, we can recognize that there is, in fact, a procedure of negotiation and agreement involved in Rawls' argument, not between persons but within the single subject found in the contractual situation. The process is oriented toward finding a fit between our sense of justice on one hand and the available theoretical principles of justice on the other. The convergence of these two lines will allow the subject in the original position the necessary support for proposing fair terms of social cooperation and thus for designating a well-ordered and just basic structure of society. We should look more closely, however, at the movement or progression involved in this contractual procedure. First of all, Rawls describes our sense of justice as our common moral capacity. Like our sense of grammaticalness in Chomskian linguistics, our sense of justice fills the role of intuition in Rawls' system: it is our innate ability to grasp an underlying structure of justice in the social field of moral signs (47). Our sense of justice provides the raw material for a moral theory, but it is not necessarily reasonable. Rawls presents a refined version of our sense of justice as our considered judgments, 'those judgments in which our moral capacities are most likely to be displayed without distortion' (47). These judgments represent our firmest convictions and reflect

our innate capacities for justice under the best conditions. They form a sort of natural substrate, the 'facts' (51) that give a solid social foundation to the system. On the other side of the balance, we have the organizing alternatives of the possible theoretical descriptions of our conception of justice. From one side, then, these alternative principles are weighed against our judgments and selected on the basis of their agreement. From the other side, our judgments are modified to conform with the selected principles. Eventually, this back-and-forth movement achieves a balance. 'This state of affairs I refer to as reflective equilibrium. It is an equilibrium because at last our principles and judgments coincide; and it is reflective since we know to what principles our judgments conform and the premises of their derivation' (20). Reflective equilibrium is a sort of contract in which reasonable convictions and rational principles have settled their differences and come to terms. To say that a certain conception of justice would be chosen in the original position means simply that certain principles would agree with our considered judgments in reflective equilibrium (138).

This particularly abstract notion of contract does not address the differences among persons, but nonetheless seems to indicate a movement toward social stability through the rationalization of our convictions in a reasonable agreement. This is what gives the appearance of contractual progression in Rawls' system. When we look more closely, however, this contractual procedure, like Rawls' argumentative procedure, is comprised of a perfectly circular movement. The circularity, in fact, is what guarantees the stability. At first sight, it appears that we are dealing with a process that engages the differences within an empirical substrate (our sense of justice), negotiates them through the contract of reflective equilibrium, and thus arrives at the consensual construction of an institutional structure. As we noted earlier, the term 'contract' connotes a plurality of parties or agents, and in this specific case it seems that the term 'sense of justice' is what characterizes the open field of plurality and differences that come to be organized in the contract. One might assume that the back-and-forth motion leading to reflective equilibrium would involve some adjudication or negotiation among different senses of justice. We find, however, that there is no real plurality of beliefs, but rather there is effectively only one sense of justice in the system, just as there was only one subject in the original position. To understand the function of the sense of justice in Rawls' system we should not consider it as related to the beliefs or desires of real individuals, or even hypothetical or representative social subjects. On the contrary, the sense of justice is grounded strictly in the institutions of a democratic regime: 'given that a person's capacity for fellow feeling has been realized by his forming attachments … and given that a society's institutions are just and are publicly known by all to be just, then *this person acquires the corresponding sense of justice* as he recognizes that he and those for whom he cares are beneficiaries of these arrangements' (491, emphasis added). In a well-ordered society, the institutions effectively inculcate a sense of justice in the individuals (515). The sense of justice, then, is not a reference to a social plurality outside the system, to external 'facts' or inputs, but rather a unique derivation of the convictions already embedded in the institutional structure. The theory can thus take an analytical short-cut, ignoring the sense of justice in the person and focusing instead on the 'corresponding sense of justice' embedded in the institutions.

At this point the circularity of the argument is perfect, completely insulated from the destabilizing influences of social difference and conflict. The sense of justice leads through the contractual procedure to the choice of the just social order, and the just social order, in turn, inculcates the sense of justice. As Ricoeur noted with respect to the method, we are not dealing with any sort of movement, but with 'the progressive elucidation of that which is already anticipated'. The democratic regime, or the well-ordered society, is not only the endpoint but also the point of departure for the contractual process. The circular movement of self-reference gives the system a perfect equilibrium and thus the idea of a social contract is reduced to tautology. The system manages to achieve autonomy by avoiding or excluding any external inputs. The appearance of negotiation, dialectic, and mediation in the contractual procedure is only an appearance. No difference, in fact, disturbs the equilibrium of the system. Reflective equilibrium, then, perhaps best describes the stability achieved when the system is reflected back on to itself. The regime is democratic precisely insofar as the system freely elects itself to power.

weak subjects and the politics of avoidance

The postmodern interpretation of Rawls' theory of justice gives us a simulation of social reality, a depopulated horizon, emptied of all social contents. The machine that would go of itself marches through the social simulacra. Two elements have emerged as central to the 'de-centered' postmodern juridical machine — two elements that are essential (paradoxically, since the concept of essence seems to be excluded here) for a system without foundations. First, even though the system often alludes to pluralities, it only accepts an abstract unitary subject within its bounds. A postmodern unity is not created by mediating or even coercing a multiplicity to order, but rather by abstracting from a field of differences to free the system and thus pose a generic unity. There is not a plurality of persons in the contractual situation, nor even a single person, but merely an abstact, impersonal agent. The system itself is the single agent that chooses the contract. Second, time is negated or short-circuited in the system by an infinite circular motion. In effect, time is stripped of production, leaving it a hollow mechanism of movement. Postmodern time gives the illusion of movement, a buzz of activity that gets nowhere. In both elements we can recognize the elimination of living labor from the juridical arrangement: the social differences of its creative energies and the temporality of its productive dynamic are absent from the system of right. The genius of the system sweeps aside all ontological referents and achieves an efficient abstraction from social being, imposing in its stead a pure *Sollen.* Our reading of these postmodern elements in contemporary juridical theory has thus confirmed Marx's intuitions about the role of machines in capital's phase of real subsumption and taken them to an apocalyptic extreme. Mechanical activity has completely eclipsed human labor-power so that society appears to be a self-regulating automaton, beyond our control, fulfilling one of the perpetual dreams of capital. It seems, then, that the system has been abstracted from human judgment: a theory of android justice.

This postmodern reading of Rawls seems to be leading us away from political theory toward the realm of science fiction. Let us try to bring the discussion back to real questions of power and understand how Rawls' work can descend from its theoretical heights and gain a purchase on real social terrain. In fact, Rawls' more recent work has focused on bringing to light precisely the sense in which his work is political. (See for example 'Justice as Fairness', 'The Idea of an Overlapping Consensus', and 'The Domain of the Political and Overlapping Consensus'.) He argues in fact that the juridical system is political not in the sense that it engages social differences or mediates social conflicts, but on the contrary precisely in the sense that it manages to abstract from the field of social relations. What comes to the forefront in this focus on 'politics' are questions of the efficiency of the system of rule. 'The shifts in emphasis' in the most recent articles, according to Kukathas and Pettit, 'come out most clearly in Rawls' increasing reliance on the *feasibility* arguments which dominated Part Three of his book, and in the corresponding downplaying of considerations of *desirability*' (142). Feasibility arguments direct the theory to concentrate on discovering a practical system that can maintain an enduring social order. The political goal in these arguments is to formulate an 'overlapping consensus', that is a consensus that exists despite the differences due to the various conflicting religious, philosophical, and moral doctrines existing in contemporary society ('The Idea of an Overlapping Consensus', 1). We soon learn, however, that the method of an overlapping consensus is not achieved by an engagement and reconciliation of social differences, but rather by an abstraction of the juridical system from the social field. Rawls calls this strategy 'the method of avoidance' (12). Through this method, he hopes to formulate a procedure whereby a democratic regime can avoid (not resolve) social conflicts and thus maintain the stable unity of its order. The regime is liberal in its openness to a plurality of ends and in its refusal of coercion as a method to achieve order; but this is an empty openness, an indefinite and barren expanse, since the system has effectively been detached from its limiting social parameters. Order, harmony, and equilibrium are achieved by excluding the points of social conflict from the workings of the system.

Richard Rorty seems to grasp the essence of this procedure and take it one step further when he extends Rawls' conceptions of tolerance and avoidance to mean a complete indifference to the determinations of social being. For Rorty, the goal of tolerance in postmodern liberal politics requires a weak conception of social subjectivity and the principle method of avoidance is the mechanism that achieves this end. Following Rawls, Rorty too tries to gain an argumentative authority by assuming the American revolutionary experience and the American Constitution as a point of reference. At this point, though, the revolution is adopted not as a source of power and creativity but only as a limitation, as a means of insulating the system from social contents. In Rorty's view the historical development of modern political theory involves the progressive isolation of politics from society. A first major step is represented by Jefferson, the modern revolutionary, inspired by the Enlightenment, who insisted that public affairs not be influenced by religious beliefs but guided solely by rational philosophical considerations. Rorty identifies Rawls the postmodern as representative of a second major step: social theory and rule should bracket off or discard not only religious questions but also philosophical questions ('The Primacy of Democracy to Philosophy', 261-62). If we look closely here we can recognize that Rorty is making a subtle but very important shift in Rawls' position. Rorty's essay is based on Rawls' proposal that 'we apply the principle of toleration to philosophy itself' and thereby achieve 'an "overlapping consensus", that is ... a consensus that *includes* all the opposing philosophical and religious doctrines likely to persist ...' ('Justice as Fairness', 223 and 225-26, emphasis added). Rawls understands the 'principle of toleration' to mean that the system includes conflicting views within its structure. Rorty, however, recognizes that a postmodern juridical system has no means for mediation or reconciliation. The language of inclusion, therefore, subtly shifts to that of exclusion. After all, the method of avoidance, which realizes the principle of toleration, is not a mechanism of inclusion but one of exclusion. In Rorty's hands, then, the realization of Rawls' tolerant system becomes dependent on its indifference to and avoidance of social conflicts.[2] Postmodern liberal tolerance is thus based not on the inclusion but actually the exclusion of social differences.

Rorty takes care to historicize this progression in liberal thought. While in the eighteenth century religion was the field of social conflict that produced the most dangerous threat to stability, today all fields of social conflict need to be avoided in order to create and maintain a stable system of rule. This 'will be a society that encourages the "end of ideology"', according to Rorty, 'that takes reflective equilibrium as the only method needed in discussing social policy. When such a society deliberates, when it collects the principles and intuitions to be brought into equilibrium, it will tend *to discard* those drawn from philosophical accounts of the self or rationality' (264, emphasis added). Expressions of social difference are simply ignored or discarded as matters of indifference to the public sphere; politics thus becomes the mechanical and pragmatic system of balancing abstract social inputs to establish the equilibrium necessary for order and legitimation. Just as a previous generation of democratic political scientists proposed that we escape from the premodern religious authority of the idea of God, today Rorty proposes we escape from the modern philosophical authority of the idea of a subject (264). Questions of labor, production, gender difference, racial difference, sexual preference, desire, value, and so forth, are all discarded because they are personal affairs and thus matters of indifference for politics. Democracy keeps its hands clean. This follows in Rorty's view from the general position that liberal political theory is deontological in the sense that it is not founded in any transcendental conception of the social good or any necessary and teleological structure of the human subject and human action. In fact he takes this negation to be an affirmation of its opposite: if liberal ethics and politics do not necessarily follow from a transcendental, ideal order, they must be posed as absolutely contingent, refusing any reference to the depth and weight of real social determinations. After excluding and neglecting the subjective field of social conflict as merely the affair of the private sphere, then, what remains is an antiseptic, mechanical, self-sufficient political system of equilibrium. As we have already seen, Rawls' conception of reflective equilibrium can be adequate to this task, because, from a perspective abstracted from the plurality of actually existing per-

sons (that is, the original position), reflective equilibrium balances the sense of justice embedded in the existing social system with the principles possible in that same system. The autonomy of the self-balancing system of right makes possible the avoidance or exclusion of social difference basic to Rorty's conception of democracy.

In Rorty's interpretation of Rawls, in effect, we can recognize the tendency of abstraction in the tradition of juridical formalism pushed to its extreme, so that now it resembles the systematism of Niklas Luhmann. Society, according to Luhmann, should be read as a self-referential or autopoietic system that poses an 'internal totality' and thus maintains a closure or autonomy from its environment:

> Autopoietic systems ... are not only self-organizing systems, they may not only produce and eventually change their own *structures*; their self-reference applies to the production of other *components* as well ... Even *elements*, that is, last components (in-dividuals) which are, at least for the system itself, undecomposable, are produced by the system itself. Thus, every thing that is used as a unit by the system is produced as a unit by the system itself. (*Essays on Self-Reference*, 3, but see also 1-20, 145ff and 228ff.)

Society is a system of communication that is not only self-regulating and self-organized but also self-produced. All that remains is solving the problems of complexity of the infinite specularity in this circular, autonomous world. Systematism is in effect the logical extension of the tendency in Rawls' work to pose the priority of feasability over desirability in moral theory; or rather, it makes this priority absolute by making feasibility the only possible issue in the context of the system. This focus on systematic maintenance can only view the social constituents as weak subjects. 'Within the world created by the operations of this system every concrete item appears as *contingent*, as something that could be different' (147). In this view of the liberal public realm, the system occupies the place of necessity and casts all of its components as contingent. The system is an equilibrium machine, abstracted from the passional field of social conflict and thus empty of all social contents.

Liberal governance is no longer an art but a science, a technical calculus of force designed to achieve a systematic equilibrium in a society without politics. The 'deficit of politics' in postmodern liberal theory implies a reduction of the State structure to its bare bones, a mechanical skeleton of rule. Does it consequently no longer make sense to pose the issue of power relations in society as a political question? Is the thin State, as Rawls would have it ('The Priority of Right', 260ff.), actually neutral or neutralized, in other words, ouside of power? We have seen in the development of the postmodern liberal argument that State power is not exerted according to what Foucault calls a disciplinary paradigm, nor does it create a 'transparent society' that illuminates and masters the structures of social interaction. (See, for example, Gianni Vattimo, *The Transparent Society*.) State power here does not involve the exposure and subjugation of social subjects as part of an effort to engage, mediate, and organize conflictual forces within the limits of order. The thin State avoids such engagement: this is what characterizes its 'liberal' politics. In effect, this line of argument extends the thin conception of the State to a thin conception of politics. Politics, in other words, does not involve engaging and mediating social conflicts and difference but merely avoiding them.

Precisely this politics of avoidance, however, shows the thin State as Janus-faced.

The benign practice of avoiding problems to preserve social harmony easily shifts to a more malevolent policy. It may be ironic, then, that the liberal notion of tolerance coincides here perfectly (and paradoxically) with a decidedly illiberal mechanism of exclusion. In this sense, the thin State of postmodern liberalism appears in effect as a refinement and extension of the German tradition of the science of the police. The police are necessary to afford the system abstraction and isolation: the 'thin blue line' delimits the boundaries of what will be accepted as inputs in the system of rule. Rorty says that the State will discard or set aside elements of difference and conflict, but when we pose the operation of discarding or setting aside on the real field of power it can only be understood as the preventive deployment of force, or rather the threat of ultimate force in the final instance. Rawls' conception of avoidance and Rorty's cherished insouciance take on a brutal exclusionary character when they are posed in such practical political terms. The crucial development presented by the postmodern *Polizeiwissenschaft*, however, is that now society is not infiltrated and engaged, but separated and controlled: not a disciplinary society, but a pacified society of control. (See Gilles Deleuze, 'Postscript on the Societies of Control'.) The police function creates and maintains a pacified society, or the image of a pacified society, by preventing the incidence of conflicts on the machine of equilibrium. The Disneyland of a fictional social equilibrium and harmony, the simulacrum of the happiest place on earth, is necessarily backed up by the LAPD. Rorty's 'primacy of democracy', in fact, is dependent on the continual threat that disorder impinge on the system and thus the continual need to keep the police function poised; the democratic system must be ever vigilant against 'thugs', be it a Soviet leader, Saddam

postmodern law

Hussein, Manuel Noriega, or African-American and Latino youths in Los Angeles. (See, for example, Richard Rorty, 'Of Theorists and Thugs'.) The method of avoidance, then, carries implicitly a postmodern *Polizeiwissenschaft* that effectively, and in practical terms, abstracts the system from the field of potential conflicts, thus allowing the system to order an efficient, administered society.[3]

Rawls' work, as we have noted many times, is animated by a truly democratic spirit and it should be clear that he would be very uncomfortable with this claim of the centrality of the police function to the liberal order. (See, for example, his objections to 'the oppressive use of state power' in 'Overlapping Consensus', 4 and 'The Domain of the Political', 235.) Rorty's interpretation certainly pulls the liberal system of right in this direction, but it is Gianni Vattimo who truly makes the leap and poses this connection in its strongest form. Just as Rawls does, Vattimo makes explicit the fundamental connection between the postmodern liberal notion of the State and Hobbes' Leviathan, but Vattimo confidently brings out its darker, illiberal face. 'The idea that the State is primarily the police', Vattimo writes, 'is hard to swallow for those who have imagined for so long a development of freedom also as a reduction of the repressive force of the State' ('Senza Polizia Non C'è Stato'). The real reduction involved in the thin or minimal State of liberalism, he points out, is not a naive, leftist reduction of repressive forces, but rather 'a reduction to the essential', and the essence of the State is the police: '[t]he State ... exists only and insofar as it is able to assure order'. Vattimo thus makes explicit and celebrates the often unstated but nonetheless essential hinge in the relationship between the postmodern theory of weak social subjects and a thin State. The police, even if it remains in the shadows and appears only in the final instance, is the linchpin that guarantees the order of the postmodern liberal State.

the strong state of liberalism: crisis and revolution in the 1980s

We see emerging in these postmodern theories a thin but functional State machine, abstracted from all material social contents and therefore all the more efficient in establishing simulacra of equilibrium and order. The weak social subject of liberalism is abstracted from the political power of social antagonism and thus simplifies the problem of liberal statecraft to merely a mechanical or instrumental matter of balancing abstract forces to order the government. The figure of the State as a social agent disappears in the system, in the equilibrium mechanism. The State is finally just one weak subject among others, a neutral guardian of order. One has to marvel at the theoretical perfection of this postmodern liberal vision of rule, at its imperturbable circularity, at its crystalline simplicity. When we now look to the plane of practical politics, there too we find the thin State, as a dream of the neoliberalism of the 1980s and the rhetorical centerpiece of the Reagan revolution. Let us break somewhat rudely, then, the line of our theoretical arguments, so that we can try to bring these liberal theories back to social reality and evaluate to what extent they are indeed functional to the practical needs and developments of the contemporary State.

First of all we should note a profound resonance between the interpretation of Rawls we have conducted thus far and the crisis of the Welfare State in the 1980s. We have emphasized the exclusion of the categories of production and labor in Rawls' theory of

right and the absence of any role for intersubjective bargaining or negotiation in his conception of the social contract. In a parallel fashion, the 1980s saw the end of corporatism and collective bargaining as methods of State legitimation and planning for social and economic stability. The traditional trinity of Welfare State political economy – Taylorism in production, Fordism in political planning, and Keynesianism in economic planning – was no longer able to guarantee political order and economic development.[4] The economic crisis was above all a crisis of capital's ability to master its conflictual relationship with labor through a social and political dialectic. Excessive demands of labor (whether recognized as high wages, insubordination in the processes of production, or refusal of the social mechanisms of command) pushed the dialectical process to a point of rupture, making mediation unfeasible. The strategies for crisis management, then, shifted from mediation to exclusion: both exclusion of the traditional processes of negotiation and the exclusion of labor itself from the site of production.

We can recognize the tendency toward exclusion of the mechanism of negotiation between capital and labor in part as the political project against corporatism, initiated in the United States in this phase perhaps by the Nixon administration and realized to a certain degree during the Reagan years. This project itself was composed principally of two efforts. First, there was an indirect campaign against corporatism, destabilizing the balance of the labor market and weakening the conditions of bargaining. As part of a campaign of retrenchment, social assistance programs were reduced and the rate of unemployment was allowed to rise. The expansion of the impoverished portion of society and the increased precarity of employment greatly weakened the collective bargaining power of workers with respect to employers. (See, for example, Piven and Cloward, *The New Class War*, 13 and *passim*.) The Reagan administration's efforts to repeal anti-trust laws and to deregulate and privatize industry contributed to the campaign to weaken the position of labor and upset the contractual balance that had existed in one form or another since the New Deal. Second, the State conducted a direct attack on corporatism, encouraging a complete refusal of collective bargaining with labor. Increasingly strikes have been met not with negotiations but a silent show of force and replacement workers, beginning perhaps most significantly with the strike of PATCO (Professional Air Traffic Controller's Organization) and continuing with the workers of Eastern Airlines, the New York Daily News, Greyhound buses, and Catapillar, among others. (See Bowles, Gordon and Weisskopf, *After the Wasteland*, 125-27 and, more recently, Aronowitz, *The Politics of Identity*, 1-9.) The power of organized labor and corporatist representation suffered a continual decline throughout the 1980s. The positive content of the new social contract heralded by the Reagan administration remained vague, but its negative content was very clear: the social contract will not be founded on collective bargaining or any mediated balance between capital and labor typical of the Fordist political equilibrium.

Complementary to these political mechanisms to weaken the position of labor as a bargaining partner there was also a tendency to reorganize the workplace through automation and computerization, and thereby actually exclude labor itself from the site of production. This involves both the mobility of capital and the tendency, in Marxist terminology, of the decreasing portion of variable capital and the increasing portion of fixed capital. In the course of this process, the previously existing balance between labor and capital is further tilted, or rather the question of balance itself becomes increasingly irrelevant when the worker is replaced in the production process by machinery. The transformation of the automobile industry provides an excellent example of how a once powerful workforce can be reduced, pacified, and defeated through automation. In Flint, Michigan as in Turin, Italy, the historical sites of the explosions of workers' subjectivities and power have become what Marco Revelli calls 'factory deserts'.[5] All of this goes hand in hand with a decline of unionism in general.

Just as the category of labor has been excluded from the constitution of the juridical order in postmodern liberal theory, bargaining and negotiation with labor has tended to be marginalized from the constitution of a political order in neoliberal practice. The exclusion of labor in the former, of course, can appear as passive (as if it were a lacuna or oversight of liberal theory) but in the latter an active, sometimes brutal exclusion is required. Despite these very real differences, however, this correspondence in the exclusion of labor from the constitution is perhaps a central element that explains why the contemporary political context has afforded Rawls' theory, and particularly a postmodern interpretation of it, a certain dominance among juridical theories and how in turn this version of liberal theory can be employed to further the neoliberal political project. In both liberal theory and neoliberal practice, we want to emphasize, the displacement or dispersal rather than the engagement and mediation of social antagonism functions through the image of a weak subject as the generic social actor.

The Welfare State was seriously eroded in the 1980s, then, in the sense that labor was progressively excluded from the constitution and the State's efforts toward full employment came to an end. If we take another perspective, however, and view the Welfare State in terms of State spending and State intervention in economic and social mechanisms it did not wither during this period but actually grew. The neoliberal project involved a substantial increase of the State both in terms of size and powers of intervention. The development of the neoliberal State did not lead toward a 'thin' form of rule in the sense of the progressive dissipation or disappearance of the State as a social actor. On the contrary, the State did not become a weak but rather an increasingly strong subject. 'Liberalization' was not a decentralization of power, not a reduction of the State – any reduction was perhaps closer to the heightened reassertion of the 'essential' State powers that Vattimo celebrates. Despite appeals to the rhetoric of classical liberal economics, State spending (even in most areas of social welfare provisions) and State intervention into market activity actually increased (LeGrand and Winter, 148). In this sense, the spending structures of the Welfare State showed signs of irreversibility and a remarkable resistance to the neoliberal attack (Piven and Cloward, *The New Class War*, 157-58). Neoliberalism could not respond to the economic crisis through a dispersal and decentralization of State power, but required on the contrary a concentration and reinforcement of authority on social and economic issues. While the heralded reductions were minimal, the expansion of State spending in new areas was dramatic, particularly in terms of military spending (Bowles, Gordon and Weisskopf, 130ff.). The neoliberal State thus did not act to reduce the structures of the Welfare State, but rather to redirect or restructure them. In this way, the neoliberalism of the 1980s con-

68

stituted a revolution from above maintaining the enormous economic powers and structures created by 50 years of Welfare State politics while diverting them to different ends.

This same process of maintaining and restructuring State powers also took place in the juridical realm, both through a direct appropriation of powers by the executive branch and through a complementary transformation of the judicial branch to bring it in line with the executive's initiatives. The 'Reagan revolution' in constitutional law was conducted through a series of appointments to the Supreme Court, the Department of Justice, and to the federal courts at all levels. Despite the claims of Reagan administration rhetoric, these changes of personnel did not free the judiciary from politics nor recreate a dream of pure interpretation of the Constitution, but only brought about a new paradigm of tendentious constitutional interpretation and 'judicial activism': liberal judicial activism has simply been replaced by conservative judicial activism. (See Ronald Dworkin, 'The Reagan Revolution and the Supreme Court'.) Although this new activism often operates under the cloak of federalism, refusing to consider cases on the federal level and pushing them back to the jurisdiction of the states, the executive has been no less effective in its pursuit of coherent ideological projects through the judiciary. The most serious effects of this shift were felt in the realm of women's reproductive rights, from the gag rule on doctors giving information on abortions to the right of abortion itself. In this way, just as the economic structures of the Welfare State and public spending were maintained and redirected, so too the extensive judicial powers have been preserved and oriented toward new goals, despite the rhetoric about a thin, nonideological State.

The re-enforcement of the State as a corpulent and strong subject, as the dominant social actor in both the economic and juridical realms, is a decidedly 'illiberal' face of the neoliberal State. This is perhaps most clear in the significant reductions of civil liberties in recent years. Throughout the series of wars launched in the past decade, not only the external wars on Panama and Iraq but also the internal wars on drugs and gangs, the Bill of Rights has been one of the most serious casualties. The foreign wars brought the temporary imposition of a semi-martial law, notably through curbs of the freedom of the press and the freedom of assembly, but the domestic wars have created a permanent state of semi-martial law. For example, the Fourth Amendment to the Constitution, prohibiting the State from conducting 'unreasonable' searches and seizures, has been dramatically curtailed while the powers of the police have been equally extended. Drug and gang-related 'profiles' are now commonly accepted as sufficient criteria for the police to stop and search citizens.[6] Adequate suspicion has been defined almost exclusively along racial and cultural lines. There is thus an enormously disproportionate number of racial minorities, particularly Blacks and Latinos, not only stopped and harassed by the police without reasonable cause, but also arrested, convicted and executed for crimes. (See Manning Marable, 'Black America', 12.) The attack on the Fourth Amendment, then, coincides to a certain extent with a (re)institutionalization of racism in America. In general, the recent decline of the Bill of Rights has served to re-enforce the traditional federalist project to stengthen the powers of the State against the danger of social disorder. A rising militarism on both foreign and domestic soil, then, and increasing recourse to a politics of social alarm, fear, and racism show the emergence of some fascistic elements of the State and the tendency toward the institution of a police state: the movement from *Rechtstaat* toward *Polizeistaat* has always been accomplished through fear, hatred, and racism.

A central problem facing the Reagan revolution, then, was how to give the powers of an autonomous and strong State a foothold in the material constitution of society, in order to create a real unity and consensus, in other words, in order to recuperate and tame the social base within its order. One contribution to this project was the movement to expand State intervention to include a moral plane. Much of the rhetoric of the Reagan and Bush administrations posed the contemporary crisis not principally as an economic crisis or even a crisis of law and order but as a crisis of values, of national direction, of the moral fabric. The intervention of the State, then, was increasingly conceived as an instrument for not only the economic welfare but also the moral welfare of the citizenry. Areas such as women's reproductive capacities, drug use, religious practices, family values, and sexual preference became more and more important as sites for direct State involvement. The country needed moral leadership and moral education. The strong subject of the neoliberal State, then, was in part consolidated on a moral plane through attempts to impose a national moral unity. We should point out that this is another 'illiberal' aspect of neoliberal practice that is particularly incompatible with liberal theory as we have presented it. The priority of right over good is the slogan that precludes the creation of such a moral unity in the context of Rawls' liberal argument, and it is precisely this freedom from a metaphysical foundation and from a moral teleology that allows writers such as Rorty to pose the confluence of the liberal and postmodern projects.

In summary, then, we can see that neolib-

eral political projects of the 1980s coincide with postmodern liberal theory in the attempt to exclude the category of labor from the constitution and thus displace the social contract of the Welfare State from its center on bargaining and negotiation. While this shift leads liberal theory to the proposition of a thin conception of the State and weak subject of politics, however, neoliberal practice moves in the opposite direction to reinforce and expand the State as a strong and autonomous subject that dominates the social field, in the realm of public spending as in that of judicial and police activity.

notes

1 Earlier we noted echoes between Rawls' work and the neo-Kantian tradition of moral theory, but here we find resonances with the neo-Kantian formalist tradition, which emphasizes formalist logics and a kind of schematism of reason. Eminent proponents of this tradition include Hermann Cohen and Paul Natorp.

2 If one were to consider A Theory of Justice alone, one would have to object that Rorty is stretching Rawls' argument to the point of distortion. In fact, we can find several passages in that text that are in patent contradiction with Rorty's thesis. For example:

> [L]iberty of conscience and freedom of thought should not be founded on philosophical or ethical skepticism, nor on indifference to religious and moral interests. The principles of justice define an appropriate path between dogmatism and intolerance on the one side, and a reductionism which regards religion and morality as mere preferences on the other. (243)

However, in Rawls' most recent articles ('Justice as Fairness', 'The Idea of an Overlapping Consensus', 'The Priority of Right and Ideas of the Good', and 'The Domain of the Political and Overlapping

Consensus'), his position is much less clear and does in certain respects support Rorty's reading. For a summary and analysis of this phase of Rawls' work see Kukathas and Pettit, p133-41 and particularly 148-50.

3 For a practical analysis of this 'method of avoidance' in relation to the urban development and the 1992 riots in Los Angeles, see Michael Hardt, 'Los Angeles Novos'. The architecture and territorial arrangement of Los Angeles provides a particularly clear example for investigating the practical relation between avoidance and exclusion. See Mike Davis, City of Quartz, in particular p223-63.

4 The studies of the recent collapse of the Welfare State trinity – Taylorism, Fordism, and Keynesianism – are too numerous to cite here. For one widely read example, see Michael Piore and Charles Sabel, The Second Industrial Divide.

5 For the history of the restructuring of the FIAT plant in Turin, see Marco Revelli, FIAT dopo FIAT. Benjamin Coriat has also done excellent work on the effects of industrial automation and the so-called Japanese model of production. See L'atelier et le robot and Penser à l'envers.

6 For a good discussion of the recent shrinking of civil liberties, particularly the Fourth Amendment, as a result of the war on drugs, see Stephen Saltzburg, 'Another Victim of Illegal Narcotics: The Fourth Amendment'. Mike Davis discusses the results of the Los Angeles Police Department's war on gangs for civil liberties in Chapter Five of The City of Quartz, 'The Hammer and the Rock', p265-322.

references

Aronowitz, Stanley The Politics of Identity: Class, Culture, Social Movements (New York: Routledge, 1992).

Bowles, Samuel, David Gordon and Thomas Weisskopf After the Waste Land: A Democratic Economics for the Year 2000 (New York: M.E. Sharpe, 1990).

Coriat, Benjamin L'atelier et le robot (Paris: Christian Bourgois, 1990).

Coriat, Benjamin Penser à l'envers: Travail et organisation dans l'enterprise japonaise (Paris: Christian Bourgois, 1991).

Davis, Mike City of Quartz: Excavating the Future in Los Angeles (London: Verso, 1990).

Deleuze, Gilles 'Postscript on the Societies of Control', October 59 (1992).

Dworkin, Ronald 'The Reagan Revolution and the Supreme Court', The New York Review of Books (July 18, 1991).

Hardt, Michael 'Los Angeles Novos', Futur antérieur 12/13 (1992).

Kukathas, Chandran and Phillip Pettit Rawls: A Theory of Justice and Its Critics (Stanford: Stanford University Press, 1990).

LeGrand, J. and D. Winter 'The Middle Classes and the Defence of the British Welfare State' in Not Only the Poor, eds R.E. Goodin and J. LeGrand (London: Allen & Unwin, 1987).

Luhmann, Niklas Essays on Self-Reflection (New York: Columbia University Press, 1990).

Marable, Manning Black America: Multicultural Democracy in the Age of Clarence Thomas and David Duke (Westfield, NJ: Open Magazine Pamphlet Series, 1992).

Piore, Michael and Charles Sabel The Second Industrial Divide (New York: Basic Books, 1984).

Piven, Frances Fox and Richard Cloward The New Class War (New York: Pantheon, 1982).

Rawls, John A Theory of Justice (Oxford: Oxford University Press, 1971).

Rawls, John 'The Domain of the Political and Overlapping Consensus', New York University Law Review 64.

Rawls, John 'The Idea of an Overlapping Consensus', Oxford Journal of Legal Studies 7.

postmodern law

Rawls, John 'Justice as Fairness: Political Not Metaphysical', *Philosophy and Public Affairs* 14.

Rawls, John 'Kantian Constructivism in Moral Theory', *The Journal of Philosophy* 88 (1980).

Rawls, John 'The Priority of Right and Ideas of the Good', *Philosophy and Public Affairs* 17.

Revelli, Marco *FIAT dopo FIAT.*

Ricoeur, Paul 'Le cercle de la démonstration', *Esprit* 2 (1988).

Rorty, Richard 'Theorists and Thugs: A Reply to Bernstein', *Political Theory* (November 1987).

Rorty, Richard 'The Primacy of Democracy to Philosophy' in *The Virginia Statute of Religious Freedom*, eds Merrill Peterson and Robert Vaughan (Cambridge: Cambridge University Press, 1987).

Sandel, Michael *Liberalism and the Limits of Justice* (Cambridge: Cambridge University Press, 1982).

Vattimo, Gianni 'Senza Polizia Non C'è uno Stato', *La Stampa* (September 22, 1991).

Vattimo, Gianni *The Transparent Society* (Baltimore: John Hopkins University Press, 1990).

Michael Hardt and Antonio Negri, *Labor of Dionysus: A Critique of the State-Form* (Minneapolis: University of Minnesota Press, 1994). Theory Out of Bounds series, volume 4. Pages: 350. ISBN: 0-8166-2086-5. Price: US$24.95/c. £17.99.

introduction

Against the historical experience of totalitarian societies in which an institutional separation between state and civil society has been refused, the debate on civil society has promoted discussions on important notions such as the good life, citizenship, community, the public and the private, and other related issues. Current studies on civil society investigate the relation between civil society and the state by showing how these spheres align respectively with *pluralism* and *order*. Some of the central claims which underpin the debate on civil society rely on the following assumptions:

• Democratic civil society is best promoted in social and political conditions where autonomy and maximisation of choice prevail. Pursuit of diversity is coupled here with the expression of difference in lifestyle, ideology, cultural codes, political organisation, economic activity etc. Against a singular notion of the common good which creates unity in conditions of political and cultural repression, pluralism offers the maximisation of partial fulfilments (Walzer, 1992).

• Civil society is a distinct social sphere which is institutionally separated from the regulative powers of the state (Keane, 1988). On this view a pluralist system of political and cultural powers entails an independent and secure civil society which can function as a safeguard against the totalitarian tendencies of a centralised state power (Mouffe, 1990).

• A pluralist civil society requires some form of mediation in the name of order so as to protect itself from collapsing into anarchy and the undifferentiated exercise of power. A strong view like Wood's claims that given the structural inequalities of capitalism, civil society tends to fall prey to the corporate interests of dominant and privileged groups,

yael shalem
david bensusan

CIVIL SOCIETY
the traumatic patient

which manifest themselves in fundamental class, gender and racial inequalities (1990). Hence the need for a centralised regulated state. Other positions attempt to reconstruct the possibility for civil society as a site of social and political organisation on the lines of partnership with the state (Keane, 1988; Walzer, 1992).

In South Africa the debate is carried forward within a similar set of distinctions. Here the domain of the civil is seen as 'the permanent and enduring pluralism ... capable of levying irreverent criticism on whatever pretensions the new state may assume' (Fitzgerald, 1990: 105). Common to this view is the argument that civil society is the home of social movements (Sayed and Carrim, 1992), of civil liberties (Enslin, 1990), and of political and economic rights (Glazer, 1990; Swilling, 1990). Yet in the light of the South African history of repression, in which capitalism and racism have produced a complex form

the traumatic patient

of exploitation, some local commentators have shown a strong objection to importing these notions to the local debates on democracy (Narsoo, 1991; Nzimande and Sikhosana, 1992).

What is common to the above claims yet not made explicit in the debate is a notion of agency which stresses the capacity to engage in diverse social activities and at the same time to attain some degree of self-regulation. In this debate the self is permitted to pursue personal freedom, to engage in new and proliferating lifestyles and yet to follow the rules of socialisation.

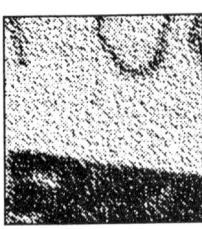

This results in an unproblematised tension which structures the debate along similar lines for the social and for the self. In respect of the social there is a tension between the requirements of a regulative social order and the wish for freedom. For the self a similar tension exists between the demand for the actuality of multiple expressions and the need to manage and hold them together.

The argument of this paper is that the conception of this tension arises from a dualist model of society and the self which polarises both into two discrete spheres, namely that which controls and regulates, and that which proliferates by generating diversity. This dualist approach limits the debate within the polarity of the demand for freedom and diversity on the one hand and the political requirement for the need to retain a measure of control on the other. As a result of this polarity the current arguments for pluralism and diversity are tied to a conception of order that unintentionally gives privilege to the organisational role of the state and thus leaves us with a politically weak account of the process of pluralism.

civil society located in the social

The central argument in the debate on civil society states that a pluralist civil society can secure democratic choice, social autonomy and cultural diversity and that this is conditional upon an institutional separation between the state and civil society. Such a view is strongly supported by Keane:

> The secret of liberty, whose maximization requires the maximization of complex equality among citizens, is the division of decisionmaking powers into a variety of institutions within and between civil society and the state. (1988: 13)

For Keane, this institutional separation means, *inter alia*, the decentralisation of decision making, localised forms of participation, innovative sites for public debates, voluntary associations, diverse forms of solidarity, non-singular means of distribution and conflict management, and multiple criteria of distributive justice. At the same time he entrusts the organisational and coercive functions of society primarily to the hands of the traditional sites of politics such as parliament, political parties and government apparatuses.

From this division of institutional interests between the state as the central organising machine and the propagation of diversity exterior to it, there is recognised to be an inherent tension characteristic of the nature of civil society:

> A democratic civil society which maximizes liberty and equality will never resemble a happy and contented family. It would always tend to be self-paralysing. Precisely because of its pluralism, and its lack of a guiding centre, a fully democratic civil society would be endangered permanently by poor co-ordination, disagreement, niggardliness and open conflict among its constituents ... Pluralism,

the multiplication of decisionmaking centres and spaces for individual and group autonomy, tends constantly to generate '*anarchy*'. (Keane, 1988: 22, our emphasis)

The tension insinuated above expresses for Keane the conflict between political desire for proliferation and the fear of anarchy due to the ambiguous nature of civil society. The response to this threat is the invocation in the 'last instance' of a central mediating faculty – the state. Through its administrative powers of financial organisation, and its legal and military forms of coercion it is taken as the main site for re-establishing the axis necessary for the maintenance of social order:

> But without the protective, redistributive and conflict-mediating function of the state, struggles to transform civil society will become ghettoized and stagnant, or will spawn their own, new forms of inequality and unfreedom. (Keane, 1988: 15)

Although Keane never brings to his analysis any explicit account of the self as social agent he nevertheless needs to assume a number of characteristics of the self for the elaboration of his social theory. This we gather from Keane's postulation of the tendency of civil society to lapse into anarchy in spite of the degree of freedom conferred upon social agents. In the domain of civil society Keane fosters a notion of the self which is compatible with the propagation of desires, the release of inhibitions and the maximisation of choices. (The concepts which incorporate this thinking include voluntary associations, participatory community, etc.) This self, a plural as against a monist conception of the self, appears to be torn between two different descriptions. The one face is the rational self which is capable of pursuing and choosing between multiple ends and to this extent optimises self-regula-

tion. The other face is the subservient self which is incapable of directing ends broader than its own needs. This conception perpetually holds out the prospect for self-destructive anarchical tendencies and consequently requires an external formal intervener to hold these tendencies in check.

Consequently, in the relation of civil society to the state, the state is located 'outside' as a high rational being which functions to liberate and release the body from the tyranny of power. On this view the self may be permitted to travel temporarily out of this augmenting home in so far as some form of resolution between the two descriptions can be maintained and secured by an external organising agent – the state. In other words there is a homologous relation between Keane's conception of the self as succumbing to a dual description and his account of an internally tense and unstable civil society.

Keane pushes the debate on civil society to the limits: irreconcilability between the pluralism at the social level and the conception of the unifiable self has required him to search for a centre in the social which will be able to *home* the differences and inconsistencies which emerge from trying to accommodate them under one theoretical position. The implicit requirement for Keane's pluralism is met by the establishment of a rationalisable order: a formal communication system through which society could be rendered orderly. Keane's strength is his attempt at maximising the possibility for pluralism. However he does this at the expense of an undeveloped notion of the self which unintentionally leaves him with a traditional dualist position.

A dualist position with an exclusive focus on the notion of diversity or pluralism at the expense of an unproblematised view of *order*, cannot take this debate forward as it is not successful in challenging the notion of the state as a centre of organisation and hence as the main site of power.

In identifying the problematic of 'order', we examine Walzer's notion of 'partial fulfilment' (1992), which he invokes against the presupposition of 'singularity' implicit in dominant accounts of society. As a response to the question 'What is the good life?', Walzer shows how this question has been contained in four mutually exclusive historical accounts: those of the consumer, the creator, the nationalist and the citizen. Each of these social identities is mutually exclusive of the others and requires a certain one dimensional source of social organisation.

Much like other contemporary theorists Walzer sees civil society as that conception in which plurality and multiple forms of social being are made possible in contrast with a society in which the state, the economy or the nation provide and protect in a mutually exclusive form the embodiment of singularity. What is being opposed here is a view which sees the only possible route for gratification in the enactment of one exclusive social role, which would necessarily preclude the possibility for the realisation of difference and diversity. Marx's singular self for example realises itself exhaustively through immersion in productivity (the highest form of creativity) to the neglect of the role of the citizen in public decision making.

Walzer's call for the proliferation of multiple styles of life is carried through to his reconceptualisation of the notion of the self – a self which can attain only partial rather than maximum satisfaction. On this view the self can no longer have an exclusive identity which would require a singular social setting to encompass it (or represent it). Walzer's project is concerned with taking the discrete singular selves represented in each of the above four types of social settings, and plu-

ralising them through the creation of a network of multi-associations.

Let us trace the details of the argument. Walzer's conception of pluralism emerges in line with the observation of the increasing diversification of the social. Like others, Walzer models his moral and political justification for a pluralist society on what he calls 'a more realistic view of communities and economies':

> On the ground of actuality (unless the state usurps the ground), citizenship shades off into a great diversity of (sometimes divisive) decision-making roles; and, similarly, production shades off into a multitude of (sometimes competitive) socially useful activities ... There is no ideal fulfilment and no essential human capacity. We require many settings so that we can live different kinds of good lives. (Walzer, 1992: 99)

The shift from productive to service economy, the pluralisation of forms of ownership, the decentralisation of political activity, and the proliferation of voluntary association and of multiple forms of social engagement of the self are evidence of a new particularity on the social level and of a sense of pragmatism – transition from total fulfilment to partial fulfilment – on the level of the self. Agents pursue different and contradictory ends, the market allows for the diversification of choices, and new forms of nationalism proliferate. Pluralism lies not so much in the partial maximisation of choices within these terrains but rather between them. To this end Walzer tries to bring the 'consumer self' in varying degrees of contact with the 'citizen self', which would mean putting political constraints on economic freedom and developing associational networks between them.

Walzer opposes the principle of singularity on both the fronts of civil society and state. A singular conception of the state would imply that state regulation aims to centrally unify any emergent forms of expressive difference by taking organic identities and abstracting them into public institutions. For example when the organisational incorporation of the self is performed by the state through central economic planning, the self is then reduced to the producer which incorporates/represses all the other selves. Alternatively this regulative process redescribes any organic identity into a higher form of social reconciliation, e.g. into nationalism which has a specific historical content.

On the other front, namely civil society, a central organic formation constructed in terms of class identity, blocks the occurrence of alternative identities by a process of reductionism which canalises state intervention into an instrumental body of class based regulation. Instead Walzer argues for a pluralist notion of state regulation – a regulating mechanism which is context bound and reflects a 'complex' rather than simple notion of equality. This complexity is reflected in the principle of regulation in which the initiative continually shifts from the state to civil society and vice versa and is also constructed differently under specific historical conditions.

Yet the idea of multiple construction gives rise to two important questions: why is this interrelated multiplicity more conducive to the realisation of the self than the pursuit of singularity? And how is it regulated? Walzer holds out two conditions for this:

(a) – That in different times and in diversified contexts, and through different attachments and relationships the self extends beyond the limits of a singular form of realisation and is constructed in multiple relationships through her engagement with the four (or other) identities:

Civil society itself is sustained by groups much smaller than the demos or the working class or the mass of consumers or the nation. All these are necessarily pluralized as they are incorporated. They become part of the world of family, friends, comrades and colleagues, where people are connected to one another and made responsible for one another. (Walzer, 1992: 107)

(b) – At the same time there must be some social setting that both frames the associations, gives them their freedom and at the same time occupies a space beyond them (i.e. beyond civil society). This space is filled by the role of citizenship:

[The state] fixes the boundary conditions and the basic rules of all associational activity ... It compels association members to think about the common good beyond their own conceptions of the good life ... A democratic state, which is continuous with the other associations, has at the same time a greater say about their quality and vitality. (Walzer, 1992: 103)

The two parts of the argument stand in a relationship of conflict with one another:

Condition (a) argues that no one conception of the self is more important than the other – what differentiates a fuller notion of the self is the forming of multiple relationships through maximisation of diversity. (It allows for various forms of nationalism.)

Condition (b) on the other hand argues that the fuller notion of the self is guaranteed primarily through citizenship as a higher form of incorporation. The extended self is that which limits the type and number of forms of partial expressions. (It precludes national chauvinism in the name of a common good.)

This tension is linked to an important question in the debate on civil society: how to respond to the conflicting demands between freedom and equality. Civil society, as the pursuit of freedom outside the constraints of the law of the state, stands for particular and diverse interests, wishes, and lifestyles, for decentralisation of the mechanisms for decision making etc. Yet the need for equality requires the development of some type of regulating mechanism that will, in a non-singular form, supervise the distribution of various systems of equalities and freedoms.

A rival conception to this is the Marxist one which propagates a reductionist view of freedom. By adopting the notion of the self as a creative producer Marxism invites a principle of total equality which coextends across the entire society. In this Marxism shows little sympathy toward a view of a pluralist society in which freedom of difference is also deemed desirable as a principle of regulation. Many current contributors to this debate, Heller amongst others, position themselves against this view by addressing what is referred to as the totalitarian implication of a reductionist, singular view of freedom.

In other words what the debate on civil society has brought to the fore is the understanding that the relationship between freedom and equality cannot be resolved by a single harmonising principle – be it 'man rich in needs', 'natural rights of man', 'rationality', 'God', or any other unitary process – and yet some form of regulation is still necessary.

Furthermore, this argument entails that the sought after regulative principles are required to represent the particular as well as the common in a person, institution, activity etc. and that any policy or law has to entertain sufficient complexity to be able to represent as well as somehow regulate this tension between freedom and equality, though not necessarily resolve it (Mouffe, 1990).

Walzer expresses the tension of a pluralist society (and hence of civil society) in his notion of 'paradox':

> [The state] both 'frames civil society and occupies space within it. (1992: 103)

This position situates civil society at the intersection of unresolvable conflict: between particular freedoms and inequalities (as a condition for the richness embodied in civil society) and a complex regulative mechanism at the general-state level (as a condition for its long term feasibility). A paradoxical relationship means that the state in one respect does not have a monopoly on questions concerning the common good nor any single principle for regulating this – in this respect it occupies a space alongside other spaces filled by civil society, and can only meet partial fulfilments. However in so far as it frames civil society and its partial discourses, the state occupies a space exterior to civil society – a meta-narrative which entitles it to a privileged organisation of power through its preferred relation to the common good. This, Walzer argues, is a positive paradox:

> For civil society, left to itself, generates radically unequal power relationships, which only state power can challenge ... [Hence] civil society requires political agency. And the state is an indispensable agent – even if the associational networks also, always, resist the organizing impulses of state bureaucrats. (Walzer, 1992: 104)

In these words Walzer indicates the need to move away from the singular self and to represent what is beyond particularity and partiality, in the name of the state. Walzer requires something that will hold the multiple and antagonistic encounters of the partial selves together, something which can further their outlook beyond their own conceptions of the good life. The self therefore as an agent of partial fulfilments is represented in the state as the agent – the citizen – empowered to unite multiple and conflicting fulfilments.

The problem inherent in Walzer's position is that in the final analysis 'complex equality' in conjunction with the view of the paradox cuts the reading of the paradox into a dualist conception and as we will show cannot justify its claims to pluralism. This reading stretches the notion of complex equality to the logic of 'the last instance' in which under particular historical circumstances the state frames its various regulating mechanisms through a single privileged form of intervention. For example in times of crisis the view which allocates the framing mechanism solely to the state would have to admit that only the state has the organisational capacity to intervene in a manner which can restrict its range of regulative principles. This view does not see the product of regulation as anathema to its aim. It emphasises rather the indispensability of the

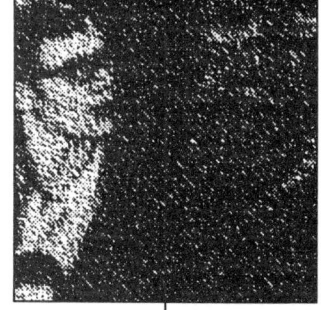

state for the process of unification in the face of resistance (see the above quotation from Walzer).

This conception of paradox leads the debate back into a dualism of space structured around various binary oppositions such as order and disorder, the general and the particular, the singular and the plural, etc., and the unintended consequences of privileging the former above the latter and hence the state above civil society. By retaining the notion of citizenship as that which is required – through formal rather than substantive procedures – in order to widen the scope of the particular in 'producer', 'con-sumer', 'member of a nation', it becomes another and a higher form of singularity encapsulated in the agency of the state. As a result the positive dynamic of the paradox is left unexplained and its consequences for pluralism remain obscured.

In a similar way to our criticism of Keane's account of civil society, we argue that Walzer's engagement with the paradox is blocked because it is captured by an undeveloped notion of the self: the partial self, that hinges upon the classical notion of the rational agent, that is the self that is faced with the actuality of multiple forms and antagonisms within and between the diversity of citizenship, economy, family, gender and nationalism, etc., but which needs to manage and hold them together. This is the incorporative/formal self – close to the 'republican self' (Mouffe, 1990) – as against the exclusive/substantive self as Walzer reads Marx's notion of the producer.

These limits of Walzer's analysis of the self call for a reconceptualisation of the self and by implication its relationship to the social. In response to this problematic, the following section will trace the conception of the ordered self, construct and explain its links with the dualist conception of social order, and show how this view of the self, despite its claim to pursue pluralism, results in a limited account of civil society.

In the light of the account thus far the debate on civil society renders the following available options:

Option I – Keane's unproblematised dualist conception of social order, which postulates a scenario in which the state could under certain circumstances share privileges with civil society, and under others refuse to. This position emphasises the necessity for institutional separation as a condition for the exercise of freedoms.

Option II – Civil society which modelled as an organic community represents a particular essence of the self in a maximum and exclusive form. It is less interested in giving multiple or partial expressions to the self than in rediscovering its lost nature. According to this view civil society is constituted in the name of a substantive good.

Option III – Walzer's notion of complex equality, which collapses the separation argued for in Option I and tends to consider the state on an equal footing with civil society in its ability to intervene in the name of different principles.

Option IV – Walzer's notion of paradox, which introduces the problematic of repression into the debate on civil society. The notion of the paradox admits that civil society and the state cannot be conceived as equal partners, but seeks moral significance in external regulation. According to this view freedom to pursue different forms of the good life is simultaneously combined with a selective process of framing and gives privilege to those particular forms of good life which identify with the common good of society.

Option V – A radical version of Walzer's notion of the paradox (developed in the last section of this paper), which asserts that the condition for freedom and equality in the form of partial fulfilment can paradoxically be met only through the process of repression. Ironically this unequal relationship, in which the state frames civil society but not vice versa, gives rise to the pluralism necessary for civil society.

dualist society and the socialised self

In the eyes of both Keane and Walzer the debate on civil society refers primarily to the forms of conflict created by competing claims of interested parties in propagating either different or the same social goods. We argue that this view relies upon an unproblematic account of social agency which assumes that the self is capable of coherent self-management throughout its process of construction. We contend that the conception of social order, which is prestructured by the view of the subject as internally ordered, reconstructs civil society through the agency of a rational mediator. Her task is to intervene whenever the internally ordered selves are frustrated by the pursuit of irreconcilable ends. The aim of this section is to show the implication for the debate on civil society of a conception of social order which hinges its analysis on a relationship between an internally coherent self (or what Taylor calls 'the disengaged self') and a conflicting social order (or the problematic observed by Keane and Walzer in the form of the permanent possibility of anarchy).

The development of an internally coherent view of the self can be traced historically to a modernist preoccupation with the question of order. By this we refer to the transference of the central principle of organisation in the cosmos to an internalised location, the self. This process set out to relocate the crucial axis on which order was structured by 'discovering' it initially in the figure of an external deity, transferring it to the regulating and symbolic power of nature (as natural law), then to the social as a central political faculty (Leviathan), and finally by accommodating it within the moral autonomous self (the rational agent).

Underlying every stage of this transference was a conception of an archimedean pivot, which entertained the belief in an axis on which the natural and social world could hinge. Initially this pivot helped organise man's fascination for and submission to the unknown by instating an epistemological anchorage, be it God, benevolence, harmony, or mother nature, as a counter to the terror of the 'out there'. Later the same axis helped fix the limits of society by juxtaposing central organisational structures, like the king, the queen, the Leviathan, as a counter to the threat of imbalance posed by war, accident and trauma.

This transference was carried to its logical conclusion when the axis of order came to rest in the self. The emergence of selfhood, a recent development in Western philosophy, meant the founding of identity upon one or other central pivot expressed in such ideas as a core, an inner sanctuary, a true self, even the rediscovery of the highest form of management, i.e. God as immanent. Kant's transcendental is a very clear example of the efforts of the Enlightenment to construct an identity for the self on qualities (like Kant's categories) which had previously been located somewhere 'out there'. Benn and Peters (1959) called this process the birth of the voice of the inner. This voice constituted the conditions of possibility for moral life or for a society in which conviction and will are intimately bound to our trustworthy inner nature. This nature became an origin to which everything could return at times of crisis and instability. It provided the security of an anchorage point from which the 'outside' in the form of society, nature and the cosmos, could reflect in an orderly fashion its own nature as if in a mirror.

There is a special relevance of the migration of order-as-axis from its location in God to its ultimate destiny in the self. For our analysis of civil society this relevance extends to whether the notion of an axis has been retained or finally dispensed with. We claim that the dominant tendency by current theorists is to challenge the axes which locate social order subordinate to the authority of God, nature and the state, but not to question the implications of an internally coherent self.

This notion of the self is traced in some detail by Taylor in *The Sources of Self* (1989). In this book Taylor traces the change from the Stoic order, in which the roots of the self were attributed to the providence of God, to the secular and mechanistic vision of the Enlightenment, which centred the self around instrumental control and procedural rationality (1989: 157). Epistemologically, the transition into the modern symbolises the movement away from the conception of meaning as immersed in nature – 'cosmos is no longer seen as the embodiment of meaningful order which can define the good for us' (Taylor, 1989: 149). In the new order, needs, the good, knowledge, etc., are a product of rational construction in that:

> [T]he notion of 'idea' migrates from its ontic sense to apply henceforce to intra-psychic contents, to things 'in the mind', [and hence] the order of ideas ceases to be something we *find* and becomes something we *build*. (Taylor, 1989: 144, original emphasis)

The modern self arrives at 'fullness of self-presence' through the achievement of rational clarity.

Of particular interest for us are the conceptions of 'the disengaged self' (Descartes) and 'the punctual self' (Locke) which underpinned the political and moral thinking of the Enlightenment – the historical root of the modern 'hegemony of reason' (Taylor, 1989: 148). The conception of the disengaged self (which is the product of the

Cartesian's process of 'radical reflexivity') is in essence a moral conception and is concerned primarily with the control of reason over passion. A rationalist like Descartes admires:

[G]reat souls ... whose reasoning powers are so strong and powerful, that although they also have passions, and often even more violent than is common, nevertheless their reason remains sovereign. (Letter to Elizabeth of 18 May 1645, quoted in Taylor, 1989: 150)

According to this view passions and desire are conceptualised on the side of experience, individual needs and custom, and are associated with error, confusion and lack of awareness. Reason on the other hand is correlated with certainty, instrumental direction and autonomy, and is associated with strength, firmness and resolution.

According to Taylor, Locke's separation of desire from reason continues this tradition. This separation splits the psyche into two separate poles: *desire* as equivalent to 'uneasiness' – 'pain of the body, of what sort soever, and disquiet of the mind' (quoted in Taylor, 1989: 169, our emphasis) – and *reason*. Uneasiness motivates us to search for the good. Yet not everything which is good for us could motivate us to choose it, only the good that can arouse discomfort and unease. To this extent the self-search for the good (or the will to the good) is driven originally by passion – by the desire to respond to the inner state of uneasiness – and not by reason, and therefore is not in itself a rational act:

Good and evil, present and absent, it is true, work upon the mind. But that which *immediately* determines the will, from time to time, to every voluntary action, is the *uneasiness of desire*. (Essay 2.21.33, quoted in Taylor, 1989: 169-170, original emphases)

This original state of uneasiness is replaced by reason, which acts as a weighting power characterised primarily by its ability to control and suspend desire. The process of determination comes full circle: the self holds back on its original relish and recreates it albeit in a rational form of a conscious and lawful reward. The relationship between the disengaged self and the expressive self (the cosmic self, the natural self, the concrete self, the passionate self) sets up an implicit *tension* between the two constituent elements in the self.

This split view of the self which defines its constitution primarily on the opposition between two positive contents is supported by a common and somewhat reductionist psychoanalytical reading of Freud's conception of the ego which we examine through the process of *internalisation*. The ego is seen to perform a management function similar to that of the disengaged self. The ego functions as a mediator and its main role is to try and bring the disparate agencies in the self into a compromised composition. In order to do this the ego is equipped with internal mechanisms of control which function under the constant supervision of external agents of socialisation. According to this analysis the self is divided into three components: the id as a repository of uncoordinated instinctual trends waiting for partial realisation in one form or another; the ego as the organising realistic part; and the super-ego, the father figure or ideal self, as the critical and moral function.

According to the internalisation view, both biological and socialisation processes direct the development of the self. The self is constituted as the synthesis of the conflicting relations between the demands of the external world, the erotic impulses of the id and the internal repressive demands of the super-ego, the libidinal structure of the

Oedipus complex. This is described by Freud as the transition from a weak sense of self to a strong ego which has successfully internalised the difference between itself and the other two powers (Freud, PFL 11: 374).

On Freud's account of internalisation the young and undeveloped ego is too weak to cope with the level of anxiety arising from extreme demands of the external world and the demands of the id. This tension within the ego is explained by Freud through the notion of the Oedipus structure, in which the child's desire for erotic love for the mother is threatened by the father. In this relationship a war is waged between the libidinal demand of the id for gratification and the father's refusal of this gratification. This refusal threatens not just the function of the ego but its very existence. As a compromise to the threat from the id, the ego internalises another agency, the father's super-ego: 'his infantile ego fortified itself for the carrying out of the repression by erecting this same obstacle within itself' (Freud, PFL 11: 374). The outcome of this is that the ego grows from an undeveloped state to maturity, yet at a price, namely that the ego antagonises itself: the ego itself becomes split in so far as it is torn between the demands of the super-ego and the instinctual needs of the id. In other words, in the process of internalisation of 'the other' a new identity is developed side by side with the old one:

> In so far as this super-ego is differentiated from the ego or *is opposed to it*, it constitutes a third power which the ego must take into account. (Freud, PFL 15: 377, our emphasis)

The internalised super-ego exhibits a number of well-defined characteristics such as intolerance and aggression, and an aesthetic and moral sense. In having a separate identity or full presence the super-ego acquires power to take control and to 'help' the ego to force the id to renounce its instinctual demands, i.e. to *master* it.

The view of differentiation in the ego consists of two processes which develop alongside one another. A certain psychical content which develops out of the experiences with reality as well as certain predominantly unconscious excitations are combined to form a manageable unity whilst incompatible instincts are split off and repressed. From this a division is created between those instincts that have social value and those that escape the socialisation route. The result is formation in which the socialisable desires of the self are located in an inclusive home whilst those that resist socialisation are cut off:

> In the course of things it happens again and again that individual instincts ... turn out to be incompatible in their aims or demands with the remaining ones, which are able to combine into the *inclusive unity* of the *ego*. The former are then split off from this unity by the process of repression, held back at lower levels of psychical development and cut off, to begin with, from the possibility of satisfaction. (Freud, PFL 11: 279, our emphasis)

Separateness and identity are inextricably bound and develop together. Through socialisation each agency matures into an identity of its own within a composition of opposites. The logic of the inclusive mode of unity, or what we call the mastering mode of the ego, generates 'spaces' within the ego in which certain of the 'needs' of the different agencies are transformed into a socialised consciousness whilst intransigent needs have to be repressed by invoking the private as the unconscious.

At the social level the split self is trans-

the traumatic patient

posed into the form of a dualist agency which enforces a spatial division of functions (control v. autonomy), of tendencies (organisation v. disorder), of needs (unity v. pluralism), and of morality (public duty v. private egocentric needs). We argue that a view which represents the social in the image of split tendencies between the disengaged self as common, rational, repressive and coercive on the one hand and the expressive self as particular, impulsive, narcissistic and aggressive on the other will ultimately seek redemption in a centralist and deterministic process of socialisation. In other words the notion of the split self will characterise the social relations between individuals primarily on the basis of the need to control the aggressive and unsocialised tendencies of the self.

In the following analysis we intend to show how the construction of the social vis-à-vis the debate on civil society draws on the opposition between the expressive and the disengaged self. One such view of this relation argues for the need to accommodate each description of the self in different social settings so as to avoid conflict between them:

> [The self is] split into private and public halves: his actions are totally subject to the law of the land, while his mind remains free, 'in secret free'. (Koselleck, 1988: 37)

This spatial metaphor, which expresses the bifurcation of the self from its desires and from its historical embeddedness, maintains a division of functions in which the respective components (the desires, the reasoning faculty) all know their place. Such a view is commonly referred to as the *social contract*.

According to this position the central problem facing modern society is that in the absence of any mediating mechanism each and everyone is self-authorised to freely pur-

sue multiple and expressive goals and desires. This implies that the concrete self of the pre-mediated will or even natural conscience is by the law of nature the sole authorizer of her own moral actions. As an alternative to this, the social contract is a formal agreement between individuals which tries to permit the prosecution of particular expressive interests by minimising the threat of conflict. Therefore the question of social order addresses the search for some or another form of *reconciliation* in favour of a higher conception of unity. This conception is evidenced in different ways by the Leviathan (Hobbes) or the constitutional government (Locke), and is found in various instrumental procedures of rationality. Civil society refers here to 'the perfect or less perfect result of that process of rationalisation of the instincts or passions or interests for which the rule of disorderly strength is transformed into one of controlled liberty' (Bobbio, 1979: 21).

In this process however, in which each of the respective selves is inserted into social relationships, formal institutional mediation effectively results in a compliance of the expressive self with a state of reason. One such conception of social order is represented in what Taylor identifies (1989: 330) as an instrumental-disengaged association of formally located individuals. According to Taylor, two important threads converge in the idea of an instrumental social organisation. The first of these is the belief in the benefit of a rationally organised life, which once freed from the constraints of prejudice reveals a picture of the universal and impartial good. The habits of custom, unexamined social mores and religious doctrines, amongst other forms of organic expressivism, all fall prey to new forms of planning and rationalisation. The other thread, and equally important, holds that the discrete and conflicting interests of each individual can be harmonised through mediating social principles and organisations. The practice of disengagement is hence seen as a vital emancipatory tool which through its range of disciplinary processes on the one hand and regulated autonomy on the other is able to guarantee the happiness of individuals within the social totality.

Although there are certainly different models of contracted civil society a common condition for all of them is that they each require a stronger or lesser degree of control in the name of formal mediating mechanisms. Contracted with pre-social forms of life, the state comes to be identified with forms of civilisation such as laws, customs and morals. This approach has a strong reformatory character to it which assumes that, through a methodical and disciplined form of intervention, the expressive self could be socialised:

> [In] the new philosophy, methods of administration and military organization, spirit of government, and methods of discipline ... is the growing ideal of a human agent who is able to remake himself by methodical and disciplined action. (Taylor, 1989: 159)

The emphasis on socialisation as a condition for order in the split self can be further seen from Freud's notion of the super-ego as an agent of punishment. The internalised conscience of the super-ego functions to punish the ego for displaying irrational and aggressive needs towards other egos:

> His aggressiveness is introjected, internalized; it is, in point of fact, sent back to where it came from – that is, it is directed towards his own ego. There it is taken over by a portion of the ego, which sets itself over against

the rest of the ego as super-ego, and which now, in the form of 'conscience', is ready to put into action against the ego the same harsh aggressiveness that the ego would have liked to satisfy upon other, extraneous individuals. (Freud, PFL 12: 315)

This is similar to the modernist political hope of gaining control over the expressive self through acts of disengagement. This view sees the expressive self as repository of positive contents, as an original and authentic voice comprised of certain concrete features such as lived experience, personal needs and private feelings. It also assumes that the expressive self has a certain location where it can give expression to its true nature and where it can be free to pursue its own needs. Yet this sense of free location is immediately hijacked by a rational pursuit of social order. Hence Freud's scepticism of one's ability to be satisfied with partial fulfilment, to self-direct and renounce one's aggressiveness:

> One would think that a re-ordering of human relations should be possible, which would remove the sources of dissatisfaction with civilization by renouncing coercion and the suppression of instincts, so that, undisturbed by internal discord, men might devote themselves to the acquisition of wealth and its enjoyment. That would be the golden age, but it is questionable if such a state of affairs can be realized. It seems rather that every civilization must be built up on coercion and renunciation of instincts ... One has, I think, to reckon with the fact that there are present in all men destructive, and therefore anti-social and anti-cultural trends ... This psychological fact has a decisive importance for our judgement of human civilization. (Freud, PFL 12: 185)

The degree of socialisation required by Freud is in line with the rationalist project of the social contract but it parts significantly from Walzer's project of partial fulfilment. Although it appears that both argue against the notion of a maximisable self – for Freud due to the conflicting nature of the-ego-as-a-synthesis, for Walzer due to social and political realities and a strong anti-totalitarian morality – their political views are very different. Freud parts way with Walzer on the issue of the partial satisfaction of the discrete selves. Where Walzer argues in favour of partial satisfaction as a limited form of resolution to the problem of human needs of self-realisation, Freud sees this possibility as a weak response to the imminent danger of the aggressive self.

We conclude then that if Freud's account of the self requires some or other form of agency to curtail the needs of the id, in social terms this can be translated into a need for a central authority figure such as the Father, the Teacher, the Leader, the State or what Freud calls 'the cultural super-ego' (PFL 12: 337). This central authority, in a way similar to the functioning of the super-ego, intervenes as a censoring mechanism and organiser of social cohesion against the unrestricted pursuit after social gratification. The same conception leads to a very sceptical view of pluralism, namely the belief that the id or the expressive self is the source of multiple but as yet unbounded selves, and the function of the super-ego is to give direction to this 'excessiveness' by manipulating it in favour of the ends of socialisation.

One of the conclusions to be drawn from this analysis informs us of the way in which the discourse of order has come to foster a centrally organised civil society, aligned in opposition to its tendencies of disorder. From the social contract account of civil society, we have noted how the distinction between a conception of the ordered self is set in contrast with civil society as the home of the irregular, the private, the conflicting and even anarchy. This dualist separation favours a site within society which has the ability to organise and to control but is also sceptical of civil society's ability to retain a sense of identity out of its disparate tendencies.

The implications of the above dualist conception of social order, which is ironically counterposed against a totalitarian unitary conception, is that it cannot adequately show how pluralism and the proliferation of difference could be developed. The expressive self which gets allocated to the private sphere is deprived of any effective political power. In the argument for the self which has both a regulating feature and an uncontrolled tendency the former ends up becoming the agent of domination. Such an agency commonly acts in the name of socialisation by extending the agent of domination within the self, i.e. the disengaged self, to the role of the state.

We conclude that the account of the split self which sees the self as emerging out of the tension and conflicts between the expressive and the disengaged aspects of the self leads to three options for social organisation:

Option VI – Civil society modelled as instrumental association, which gives primacy to the detached and punctual aspect of the self and which constrains the expressive self to a depoliticised realm of the private. Like Keane, this view assumes in an unproblematised way that the expressive self can be satisfied by being relegated to a portion of the social where it can give expression to its true nature and can be free to pursue its own needs.

Option VII – Civil society modelled in the image of the aggressive tendencies of the ego. In the name of civilisation this ego is compelled to forfeit its demands for satisfaction. This view gives no apologetic response to Walzer's admitted paradox but rather extenuates its consequences. Only forms of expressions which can be shown to further the common good are permitted to develop. Other have to be renounced.

Both of these options preclude the possibility of pluralism. Option VI strips off the expressive self from any real political power, whilst Option VII salvages human nature from its natural aggressive tendencies through a coercive socialisation process.

What remains for us is Option V, a radical version of Walzer's notion of the paradox, which asserts that the condition for freedom and equality in the form of partial fulfilment can paradoxically be met only through the process of repression. In so far as the state alone has the ability to frame civil society it has to assume the privileged role in this relation. Yet this unequal relationship produces the pluralism necessary for civil society.

The viability of this position depends on the reconstruction of two central notions, namely repression and abstraction, and on the ability to salvage them from being incorporated into the socialisation view. This can best be reconstructed through Walzer's paradoxical account of the relation of unity to pluralism. The point is not to see the whole question of the paradox of framing through moral eyes, as Keane and Walzer, various social contract positions, and a reading of Freud suggest, but rather to find the structural possibility for *pluralism* as it is inherent in the process of *framing*. To this end we have developed a 'traumatic' reading of Freud's triadic self.

civil society:
the traumatic patient

According to Walzer the state has to assume two incompatible functions simultaneously: the state occupies a place within civil society but it also frames it. On this reading the state is a participant alongside others but also stands in judgement over them and itself. Walzer arrives at his view of the paradox by effecting a spatial divide between two distinct social terrains which run on lines complementary to a model of the split dualist self. In the social for instance, the oppositional function of framing versus communal authenticity runs parallel to the oppositional function of the disengaged versus the expressive features of the self.

What is crucial about this duality is that it implies a view of socialisation which gives a particularly simplistic reading of repression and abstraction. For one thing it argues that conflict within the self must be managed through the intervention of an empowered disengaged self. Furthermore it also assumes that the expressive self has a pre-established identity. Through a process of instrumental abstraction certain features pertaining to this object are legitimised, whilst others are repressed. The former refer to shared political and social aspects such as claims to rights, natural faculties of reason, moral entitlements, conscience, technical efficiency, etc. The latter involve a range of features such as consumer voluntarism, chauvinist nationalism, moral egotism, gender and racial forms of social domination, etc.

What we wish to make clear in this is not that forms of regulation can be deemed undesirable and therefore wished to wither away. On the contrary we assert their indispensability for any social formation. Rather what is to be challenged is the assumption that the expressive self has an identity outside its relation to repression. By contrast we argue that the expressive self is constructed through a repressive agency, and that the process of abstraction and repression can only displace forms of expression from one location to another, multiply them but never control them. The paradoxical conclusion of this view is that repression and abstraction are the very conditions for the development of pluralism.

This can be pursued by an attempted reconstruction of Freud's notion of repression or what we refer to as a *traumatic reading of the self*. This reading involves a rethinking of Freud's discussion of the self mainly via the processes of transference and identification.

In parts of his work Freud insists that the idea that 'a man's ego is psychologically capable of anything that is required of it, that his ego has unlimited mastery over his id ... is a mistake' (PFL 12: 337). This suggests that the relation between the id, the super-ego and the ego can never achieve the differentiation which is required by the mastery view of the ego. Constituted in relation to the id, the super-ego thrives on the energy of the id and can therefore never completely detach itself from it:

> [E]very piece of aggression whose satisfaction the subject gives up is *taken over* by the super-ego and increases the latter's aggressiveness (against the ego). (Freud, PFL 12: 321, our emphasis)

According to the socialisation view, the process of transference is seen to be an after-development which follows on the back of internalisation. Once the pre-established identity of the father's super-ego has been set in place, aspects of aggression which precipitate off from the id are sorted out in a process of selection which in psychoanalytical terms is referred to as repression. In terms

of this, the abundant and prolific tendencies of the id undergo a reformative procedure in which its possible routes for satisfaction are slowly narrowed down and curtailed. Through the incremental establishment of order the super-ego gradually acquires a greater sense of aggressive control as its rules and regulations diversify in the process of sorting. Socialisation reaches an advanced state when a condition of homeostasis guarantees a regulated and orderly apparatus in which a healthy balance is reached.

This castrated view of the id (which is the other face of a mastery-ego) incorrectly assumes that conscience borrowed from the father's super-ego *causes* repression. Unlike the long tradition of morality which defends the rationality of the super-ego as a necessary agent for the mastery process of the ego, in particular for its war against the destructive and aggressive tendencies of the id, for Freud the super-ego is constructed only through the repression of the id: Freud's inversion is made on account of 'the paradoxical statement that conscience is the *result* of instinctual renunciation' (PFL 12: 321, our emphasis). This means that the constitution of the ego is conditioned on the id's ability to persist in its demands for instinctual satisfaction rather than on its successful submission. Rather than the id teleologically being transformed into the super-ego, the relationship between submission and aggression is structured in a vicious circle.

This anti-teleological view of the relationship between the super-ego and the id is explained in the following way: in the process of transference, undifferentiated latent

energy attaches itself to the libido and disguises it in an opposite form. Rather than the energy having to be relocated in a site exterior to the id, energy mutates the submitted element from the libido and articulates it into a new form. In this sense forbidden love can be seen as the other face of commitment and duty (Žižek, 1991: 160). This explains why every act of submission is also an act of betrayal. As Freud's analysis shows:

> [T]he docile and continent ego does not enjoy the trust of its mentor, and strives in vain, it would seem, to acquire it. (PFL 12: 318)

The importance of this process is that the articulated elements are not a matching representation of the element which they disguise, yet the latter can only find itself in the disguised form. The closest representation of this view is Marx's notion of exploitation which constitutes bourgeoisie freedom through the disguise of the freedom to sell one's labour. In this process of constitution what anchors the bourgeoisie system of freedom is the simultaneous presence of both freedom and enslavement (Žižek, 1989: 21-22).

While socialisation conceives of the transference relation as one in which a certain content is transported across social or psychic spaces, the traumatic view replaces content with an analysis of form. The concept which best illuminates the structural formation of the simultaneous presence of oppositions is *identification*.

According to Freud, identification occurs when the subject is no longer able to possess the object of his/her love. The child is forced into entertaining a compromise: in compensation for the given up object of love or the erotic tendencies which aim to *have* the other, the self gets constructed through a relation of *being like* the other (PFL 12: 135). Let us look at this relation:

> [The] relation [of the super-ego] to the ego is not exhausted by the precept: 'You *ought to be* like this (like your father)'. It also comprises the prohibition: 'You *may not be* like this (like your father)' – that is: you may not do all that he does; some things are his prerogative. (Freud, PFL 11: 374)

In the structure of identification the child wishing to be like the father is simultaneously alienated from the right to have the love-object (the mother). In terms of the formation of the self the decisive point of this relationship, i.e. the relationship to the super-ego, lies in the *form* that this relation takes: the process towards a self traverses through 'an other' ('you ought to be like this') which is constructed by its denial ('you may not be like this'). Hence the process of becoming is not an unfolding of something which was already there in an embryonic form but rather a confrontation with what one is not. In Freud's terms, the identification with 'the other' (the love for 'the other') is bound with the loss of the love-object (and hence the hostility for 'the other'). It therefore leads to a necessary but unsatisfying process. It is a necessary process because identification is the sole condition under which the id is prepared to give up its object (PFL 11: 368). It is eternally unsatisfactory because it is structured on a loss. Identification has what Freud calls a 'great economic disadvantage' for the self (PFL 12: 320). One form of this is the psychoanalytical experience of guilt: the more the ego succumbs to the demand of the super-ego (the more instinctual satisfaction is repressed) the stronger the ego's sense of guilt (Freud, PFL 11: 374):

> For the more virtuous a man is, the more severe and distrustful is [the] behaviour [of

the traumatic patient

the conscience], so that ultimately it is precisely those people who have carried saintliness furthest who reproach themselves with the worst sinfulness. (Freud, PFL 12: 318)

The double face of identification forces the subject into an endless chase in search of satisfaction. In the attempts to resolve the antagonism, the self finds that it has given birth to something which is incapable of being controlled, is continually elusive and is a real threat to the attainment of a complete identity. *Identification is the compulsion to try and resolve the wish for full expression, which however cannot be resolved.* Only by dissolving the wish and thereby finally annihilating it and oneself can maximum fulfilment ever be attained.

As a consequence the self has to find a way of coping with this impossibility, which it does by continually seeking new forms of identification. On the traumatic reading of the triadic self, pluralism of identity is an internal structural necessity. Yet this structure is not an unfolding process of an organic possession but rather a construction of reaction against a *contingent foe* – for Freud the father figure – in the impossible structure which combines love and hostility. Our relationship to the contingent foe is antagonistic: we come to identify ourselves in relation to that which is experienced as a threat to us. This cannot be conceived as an obstacle to be overcome, but following Freud's paradoxical view of the triadic self, as the sole condition of an identity, i.e. the structure of repression, which is embedded in a relationship to the foe.

In terms of the debate on civil society, this paper argues for the construction of the contingent foe through the form of democratic abstraction. This analysis will show that in the field of the social the paradoxical exercise of democracy produces 'organic selves' which are defined primarily by a double dynamic of a threat or repression. The first dynamic of the threat is in the democratic threat of abstraction. What characterises the process of democracy is what Žižek refers to as the 'violent act of abstraction' (1991: 163). This process, which is pursued through a pure and formal enactment, 'unifies' that which is common to each of the democratic subjects by a structure of negativity: the democratic subject is meant to be not racist, not sexist, not fundamentalist, not tribalist, not etc., not etc., not etc. As Žižek reminds us, the preamble of every democratic declaration begins with the statement: 'all people *without regard to* (race, sex, religion, wealth, social status)' (1991: 163). The attempt to construct a balance of features that can be shared amongst the particular selves (in the name of the citizen), or the attempt to frame the partial selves in a formal community, strips off the partial self from an organic state of identification. It uproots the partial self from its embeddedness in a communal lifestyle.

To this extent the relationship of the self to democracy is structured around the love for the abstraction of democracy which proclaims inclusivity on universal grounds. But this simultaneously alienates the subject from the right to organic expression. In the same way that the self is constructed in the process of identification on the loss of the organic relation to the mother, the subject is constructed in democracy *vis-à-vis* the common good, but also on the loss of an organic communal mode of life. In so far as the 'ideal' of a democratic unity is defined negatively (on the basis of an as-not relationship) it produces proliferating contestations in the search for a positive identification. The difficulty which this incurs for the self is that it refuses the self any positive identification in relation to the emptiness of the democratic project:

'[D]emocracy' is fundamentally 'anti-humanistic', it is not 'made to the measure of (concrete, actual) men', but to the measure of a formal heartless abstraction. (Žižek, 1991: 163)

In response to the heartless project of democracy, the self searches for a positivity which we know ironically from the structure of identification was never there. As the process of identification further reveals, the 'lost positivity' is experienced as a threat from an other. This other refers to that which in a particular historical form prevents the self from achieving a full identity. It is best exemplified in expressions such as 'the English always keep a foot in England', 'the Afrikaner is racist', 'it's not my home', 'the Jews are greedy', 'the Blacks are lazy', etc., etc. In this way the pure negativity of threat is displaced into a concrete and experienced repression constructed in relation to a particular other. The organic self as a positive notion is the antagonistic counter to the plural forms of repressing negativities which continually evade any embryonic identity, for instance, 'I am a patriot', 'I have a sense of commitment', 'I love sports', etc.

To use Taylor's language, not every act of disengagement diminishes the energy of the expressive self, but at the point of its experienced threat it displaces it to multiple forms of expression. In each of the above examples there is a certain achievement of satisfaction derived from the painful encounter with that which prevents us from finding our true expressive nature (Žižek, 1992). This tells us that the expressive self is located at the ambivalent point of intersection between pain and pleasure in so far as pleasure is constructed out of the former.

What this view tries to demonstrate is that the belief that a democratic civil society can be a home in which all different organic selves can rediscover themselves is a myth.

If one commences with a conception of the self that possesses certain attributes then one is tied to a view of democracy which is able to harbour each of the selves in an encompassing melting pot. Yet the notion of the home as a melting pot refuses to consider the double-edged face of repression and is limited by the constraints of socialisation theory. And this as we have shown is unable to give an adequate account of proliferation.

references

Benn, S.I. and R.S. Peters, Social Principles and the Democratic State (London: George Allen & Unwin, 1959).

Bobbio, N. 'Gramsci and the Conception of Civil Society' in Gramsci and Marxist Theory, ed. C. Mouffe (London: Routledge and Kegan Paul, 1979).

Carrim, N. and Y. Sayed, 'Civil Society, Social Movements and the NECC', Perspectives in Education, vol. 14 (1992) p19-33.

Enslin, P. 'The Limits of Community', Theoria, vol. 75 (1991) p27-36.

Feher, F. and A. Heller, Eastern Left, Western Left: Totalitarianism, Freedom and Democracy (Atlantic Highlands: Humanities Press, 1987).

Fitzgerald, P. 'Democracy and Civil Society in South Africa: A Response to Daryl Glaser', Review of African Political Economy, vol. 49 (1990) p94-110.

Freud, S. Beyond the Pleasure Principle in The Penguin Freud Library, vol. 11 (London: Penguin, 1991) p275-338.

Freud, S. The Ego and the Id in PFL, vol. 11, p350-401.

Freud, S. Group Psychology and the Analysis of the Ego in PFL, vol. 12, p95-178.

Freud, S. The Future of an Illusion in PFL, vol. 12, p183-241.

the traumatic patient

Freud, S. *Civilization and its Discontents* in PFL, vol. 12, p251-340.

Freud, S. *An Outline of Psychoanalysis* in PFL, vol. 15, p375-443.

Glaser, D. 'Putting Democracy Back into Democratic Socialism', *Work in Progress*, 65 (1990) p27-31.

Keane, J. *Democracy and Civil Society* (London: Verso, 1988).

Koselleck, R. *Critique and Crisis: Enlightenment and the Pathogenesis of Modern Society* (Cambridge: MIT Press, 1988).

Mouffe, C. 'Radical Democracy or Liberal Democracy', *Socialist Review*, vol. 2 (1990) p57-66.

Narsoo, M. 'Civil Society – A Contested Terrain', *Work in Progress*, 76 (1991) p24-27.

Nzimande, B. and M. Sikhosana, 'Civil Society and Democracy', *African Communist* (winter 1992) p37-51.

Swilling, M. 'Transition to Democracy: A Comparative Perspective', unpublished paper presented at a public meeting organised by IDASA, Pretoria, 22 May 1990.

Taylor, C. *Sources of the Self: The Making of Modern Identity* (Cambridge: Cambridge University Press, 1989).

Walzer, M. 'The Civil Society Argument' in *Dimensions of Radical Democracy: Pluralism, Citizenship, Community*, ed. C. Mouffe (London: Verso, 1992).

Wood, E.M. 'The Uses and Abuses of "Civil Society"', in *Socialist Register 1990: The Retreat of the Intellectuals*, eds R. Miliband and L. Panitch (London: Merlin Press, 1990).

Žižek, S. *The Sublime Object of Ideology* (London: Verso, 1989).

Žižek, S. *Looking Awry: An Introduction to Jacques Lacan through Popular Culture* (Cambridge: MIT Press, 1991).

Žižek, S. 'Eastern Europe's Republics of Gilead' in

Dimensions of Radical Democracy: Pluralism, Citizenship, Community, ed. C. Mouffe (London: Verso, 1992).

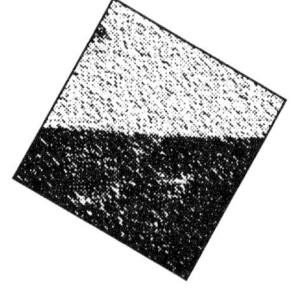

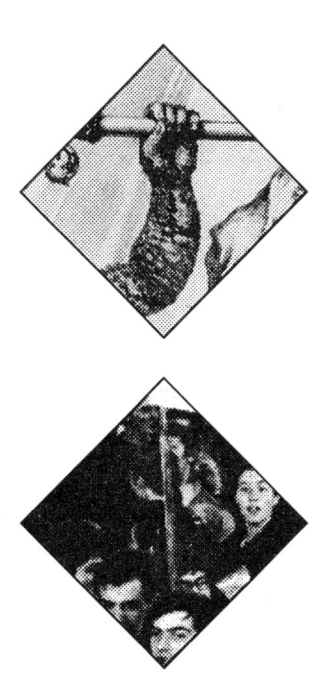

> How to describe a world that evades us, not because it is ungraspable but, on the contrary, because there is too much to grasp?
>
> *Maurice Blanchot[1]*

I want to take issue with (or perhaps, better put, I want to re-issue) three things: the problem of negation understood often as void or lack (and the abyssal logics therein implied); the privileging of temporality (and with it the so-called subordination of space); and, finally, the question of the [a-]moral interregnum and the possibility of a (contingently exiled) ethical ground. Shall we, maybe for the sake of brevity – though, maybe not – say that the intersection of these three axes creates a peculiar sort of land, a desert land, a land I shall name: curiosity.

As with every investigation, this 'curious' problem can best be situated with an echo from the past; in this case by beginning with Ricardo's now infamous suggestion of taking as a given the 'supposing that...' of science and of life.[2] Supposing that we are interested in, for example: change, not just for the sake of it, of course, but rather, because the democratic world toward which we strive and wish to partake, continually, happily, and in perpetuity, just does not seem to be quite 'here', at least, not yet. Supposing that, moreover, in thinking the possibility of such a radical political space called 'democracy', we start re-thinking the implicit assumptions inherent in what it is (and what it is not) to be human or for that matter, what this 'being human' could conceivably become. Immediately we are struck by the, not so subsidiary, problem of objectivity and, more to the point, of this seemingly slippery slope, off-handedly called 'the truth' – an objective/truth so very slippery especially when wanting to include (in that beingness of human) this fanciful thing called imagination.

sue golding

CURIOSITY*

Supposing that, finally, we are struck by the paradox that the very world in which we dwell does not at all resemble our picture of it – not because we have yet to discover or trace it properly – but because its boundaries elude the very landscape of our framework. If asked at point-blank range, 'show me the edge of the earth, the precise precipice, the absolute moment at which it goes otherwise into space', we could never point exactly to it and say 'look over here; here is where it is'. This does not, for a single minute, prevent us from having a picture of our world or, indeed, of our universe.

taking up the void

As we know from reading Hegel, particularly the Hegel of the *Encyclopedia* and, more to the point, of *The Phenomenology*, the immediate presence of a thing is always-already 'im-mediate'.[3] That is, it is always-already mediated by the division between the here and the not-here, ie, the this and its other. Or, to put it slightly differently, whatever one understands by the 'is' must always, of necessity, be set in relation to the that which is its 'not'. At once we have at our disposal the concept of the 'this' as something which must always be understood as a unity, a self-differentiating unity, whose totality exhausts the entirety of the real, in all its possible and impossible permutations. But at the same time, we are also confronted with the irritation that this positive/negative relationship – which, taken together includes all that might or could be thinkable – remains abstract, neatly grounded as it is (up to this point) only in the tautology of that which is its not. Enter the Hegelian dialectic.

Without repeating all the profound and subtle intricacies of this particular logic, suffice it to say that in deepening (or widening) the scope – that is, in contextualising any self-differentiating unity as a synthetic unity, made meaningful only on the basis of a teleological/dialectical synthesis, ie, on the basis of a becoming-ness from which it emerges and to which it points – we grasp the very relation around which identity, and therewith, meaning, is itself produced. It is on this basis that we come to understand that there can be no identity, and therewith no meaning, without a (relational) separation, a distinction, between the this and its negation, unified and plunged as it must, of necessity, be in the very movement of its immanent realization.

And yet, despite the insistence, logical or otherwise, on the immediacy of the split-shift, a whole set of worries emerges. It is a set of worries that can, partially, be summed up by the very different uses of one word: negation. For is it not the case, that often, in leaping from theory to practice (and back and forth again), we find in the very concept of identity, a whole series of oppositional relations which, taken as a unity are supposed to exhaust the entirety of the field; ie, differential unities claiming, say, woman as that which is distinct and opposed to man; or gay as that which is distinct and opposed to straight; or person of colour as that which is distinct and opposed to white; or Jew as that which is distinct and opposed to Christian – all of which, in the unity of their self-differentiality are supposed to circumscribe the whole of the field. Indeed, has not woman or gay or black or Jew or working class often been understood as Other or Lack or the Not-of-the-Something, always-already established as such?

Adorno was probably not the first, but he certainly was one of the more articulate of the worriers around this very problem. For him, negation could never be subsumed under the rubric of a positivity, be it dialectic, synthetic or otherwise. Indeed, negation was precisely the 'not-is' of the something, and therewith could not possibly be presented as if a homogeneous repository, let alone staged as the 'equivalence' of any category, be it woman or black or Jew or working class or the other or person of colour or void; ie, as the female 'castrated' container (as it were) of so-called otherness, always-already pitted against and utterly subsumed in terms of the 'phallic' real itself. 'Against this', says Adorno, 'the seriousness of unswerving negation lies in its refusal to lend itself to *sanctioning* things as they *are*' (Adorno, 1966a: 159) [my emphasis].

So, on the one hand, negation ought not to be understood as if standing outside, opposite, or apart from the is; nor, on the other hand, does negation cleverly disguise itself as affirmation, nor finally, does it seek to replace it, to become, that is to say, a positivity. Reflecting on the problem in his *Negative Dialectics*, Adorno clarifies it like this:

We can see through the identity principle, but we cannot think without identifying. Any definition is identification ... But ... *[n]on-identity is the secret telos of identification. It is the part that can be salvaged. The mistake in traditional thinking is that identity is taken for the goal.* (Adorno, 1966b: 149)[4]

[And yet the] nonidentical is not to be obtained directly, as something positive on its part, nor is it obtainable by a negation of the negative. *This negation is not an affirmation itself, as it is to Hegel.* The positive which, to his mind, is due to the result from the negation has more than its name in common with the positivity he fought in his youth. To equate the negation of negation with positivity is the quintessence of identification; it is the formal principle in its purest form. What thus wins out in the inmost core of dialectics is [actually] the anti-dialectical principle: that traditional logic, which *more arithmetico*, takes minus times minus for a plus. It was borrowed from that very mathematics to which Hegel reacts so idiosyncratically elsewhere. *[But] [i]f the whole is the spell, if it is the negative, [then] a negation of particularities – epitomized in that whole – remains negative.* (Adorno, 1966a: 158)

Not only, then, does this mean to say that objectivity cannot be 'static'; it always recruits its meaning within and in terms of a process of synthesis, a synthesis whose identity – and thus, whose subjectivity – is established precisely in terms of its (in this case, dialectic-teleological) negativity. So we find, continuing with the heterogeneity of the negative logic thus implied, that there must always exist some kind of 'excess' which slips past the mirrored-reflection of a positivity netted point-for-point against its oppositional distinction. And while this excess cannot be understood as a 'something', neither can it be understood as absolute ether or void. Indeed, this very concept of the excess-as-negation has only but a family resemblance to its more vacuous cousin, *le abysme.*

Why must this be the case? And, more to the point, what is implied, politically, ethically, not to mention theoretically, by claiming that it must be so?

Let's unravel these questions like this: if truth is no longer objective (or, perhaps more efficiently stated, if objectivity is no longer 'static' or 'fixed'); if, that is to say, we have indeed gone beyond Good and Evil as circumscribing the entirety of the field – precisely because there cannot be a point-for-point mimetic relation of fixed identity (since, without some kind of differentiation, identity would either become meaningless or one big indistinguishable lump, which in reality squares to the same thing) – then there must exist somewhere (logically, reasonably) a 'something' which is a 'not' (and hence, an excess) of that very identity relation. This, then, is to say, further and on the other hand, that this 'something-which-is-a-not' is utterly part and parcel of the is, standing neither outside nor inside. But it is to say, also (though not as 'addendum'), that because of this peculiar relation to the space (and time) of the outside or the in, which both contains the 'something-which-is-a-not' while simultaneously noting its necessary 'excessiveness' (to the very thing to which it's bound), this strange kind of negation situates any identity, indeed constitutes and establishes its meaning.

Think of a melody, any melody either real or imagined. The notes are arranged like so and so along the scale. Their distinction from one another is qualified in a number of ways, say for example with notes C and D, cast perhaps in a minor key of G. However complex or simple we wish to make our melody, none of it is meaningful if the breadth and width and timing does not at once also include the not-spacings between and amongst the notes in question, which, in all their multiple excessiveness, 'contours' and in that sense, [de-]limits, our song. But also and even though, this is a 'limiting' or 'contouring' – a 'defining' – it bears no self-reflexive interiorization, no indubitable certainty of an ego-I/self. Nevertheless, it 'makes sense'. Wittgenstein characterises it like this:

216. 'A thing is identical with itself.' – There is no finer example of a useless proposition... Does this spot ♣ '*fit*' into its white surrounding? – *But that is just how it would look* if there had at first been a hole in its place and it then fitted into the hole. But when we say 'it fits' we are not simply describing this appearance; not simply this *situation.*
'Every coloured patch fits exactly into its surrounding' is a rather specialized form of identity.

523. I should like to say 'What the picture tells me is itself.' That is, its telling me something consists in its own structure, in *its* own lines and colours. (What would it mean to say 'What this musical theme tells me is itself'?)

524. Don't take it as a matter of course, but as a remarkable fact, that pictures and fictitious narratives give us pleasure, occupy our minds...

527. Understanding a sentence is much more akin to understanding a theme in music than one may think. What I mean is that understanding a sentence lies nearer than one thinks to what is ordinarily called understanding a musical theme. Why is just

this the pattern of variation in loudness and tempo? One would like to say 'Because I know what it's all about.' But what is it all about? I should not be able to say... (Wittgenstein, n.d.: 84-5, 142, 143)[5]

To put the same point differently (and therewith perhaps say another thing altogether), this 'something-which-is-a-not', standing outside and inside exactly at the same time, all the time, in all time's varying dimensions, corruptions and decay, saddles also (and without taming) the disparate and oppositional distinctions; and it does so, whether hovering around a first, second, third, or fourth dimension (or more) or somewhere in between. But this is to say, also then, that in this kind of example, there is no *temporality* to the grammar of the 'that', ie, to the paradigm to which it points. '... [For] [t]hat connexion, a connexion of the paradigms and the names, is set up in our language', says Wittgenstein, '[a]nd [so] our proposition is non-temporal because it only expresses the connexion of [in an example he uses later around colours to appropriate "the fit"] the words "white", "black", "lighter" with a *paradigm*' (Wittgenstein, 1983: 76; #105).

We will return to this last remark momentarily. But for now, let us just say that with this strange little 'excess', we have here, then, an 'impossible' concept, existing and not existing exactly at the same time (or at a different time) all (or none) of the time in the *a-radicality* (the a-rootedness) of its spatial configurations. It is one which must, of necessity, escape the very sameness to which it is confined, and, in so escaping, contour – and, therefore, yes – 'define' the identity of the this, whatever that 'this' may come to mean.

But let us look at this 'escaping excess' a bit more carefully. For if there is neither inside nor outside *per se*; if that is to assert,

instead, we have before us a kind of mutant negation which slithers out from the land of the 'neither/nor' rather than from that of the 'either/or', how do we trace the *specificities* of its wanderings or movement, especially if that escape is cast as an excessive relation to that which has never existed 'as such' (or rather, as that which only exists in relation to an impossible negativity)? How do we express the particularity of this kind of negation, especially if it is neither configured as an eternal 'nothingness' stretching off to infinity and beyond nor as some form of nomadic positivity? A burdensome question, to be sure.

Several political philosophers, writers, artists and the like have attempted an answer. Bataille marks it as a kind of 'senseless sense' (Bataille, 1991)[6]; Blanchot, as 'dread' (later as 'passion') (Blanchot, 1978).[7] And Foucault, in a pretend dialogue he never had with either, as 'thought from outside', as a quasi-something (or quasi-nothing) 'setting its limits as though from without, articulating its end, making its dispersion shine forth, taking in only its invincible absence ... not in order to grasp its foundation or justification, but in order to regain the space of its unfolding, the void serving as its site' (Foucault, 1990: 15-16). In each case, it marks (by re-marking) the death of the Other – replacing what would have been cast as an infinite void

contrasted to the Something – now, rather, cast in terms of a contingent relation, a contingently negative relation, a relation contouring-yet-constituted-by the *distance* between the not and its other. Foucault names it as a *relation between the self and the self* (self, as future/past: other; and self as the present: and hence, impossible).[8] A kind of 'not-not-of the Other', or as Derrida would say, an 'ineluctable' multiplicity, a series of differences, the *de-de*-negation, *desistance* or 'supplementary re-doubling of negation...' (Derrida, 1989: 4).

It is a funny sort of excess, this not-not negativity, this multiplicity of the in-between (ie, the negative 'between-ness' of the not and its other). A kind of spiraling (or anyway, dizzying) interiority which regurgitates right *outside* the limit, and in that wake, constitutes it: neither/nor.

If we hold out for the negative along these configurations, three things become obvious – or, if not obvious, at least problematized. The first is that there exists several kinds of negation, the dialectical version of said negation being but one of many. The second is that, confining it only to a teleological (or for that matter, a transcendentalist) dialectic, infringes on the very suppleness of the kind of excess enlisted above, one that tends to smuggle in a whole set of assumptions around morality, politics and change, and in so doing tends to obfuscate rather than clarify the very problem (of identity/difference) it aims to resolve. It is precisely this (dialectical) version of negation which must be rejected, albeit (as Gramsci would say) 'with all honours due'. The third point is that, in groping awkwardly – maybe even blindly – toward some other a-systematic systemizing of negation, a peculiar elision comes to be established between the metaphoric and the metonymic, one that is a kind of 'struggle', as Kundera once said in his *Book of*

Laughter and Forgetting, 'of memory against forgetting' (Kundera, 1978/1980: 3). Let us now detail, more exactly, where these last few remarks may lead and why.

a time of forgetting /
a space to remember

As should be relatively clear by this point in our story (the story of negation), we have enlisted a kind of determinacy – of-the-not, that is to say, an *in-determinant* excess, as that which provides meaning, and therefore, as that which 'grounds' (as it were) any, and every, truth-game. Moreover, this is an indeterminancy which exceeds the very notion of eternal infinity; for it no longer adheres to a concept of homogeneous time nor one of empty space. Indeed, it could be said that it has more to do with a relation between some discrete, even deadly, form of rumination – ie, an odd, purposeless wandering – and the 'not' of that existence; a journeying somewhere different than within (or against) a metaphysics of the present; a straying on some other path neither inside nor outside the oppositional binaries of a positivity and its Other. Nietzsche characterises it in one word: forgetting. 'Consider the cattle, grazing as they pass you by', he says in his second untimely meditation, 'On the Uses and Disadvantages of History for Life':

[T]hey do not know what is meant by yesterday or today; they leap about, eat, rest, digest, leap about again, and so, from morn till night and from day to day, fettered to the moment and its pleasure or displeasure [they are] neither melancholy nor bored... A human being may well ask an animal: 'Why do you not speak to me of your happiness but only stand and gaze at me?' The animal would like to answer, and say: 'The reason is I always forget what I was going to say' – but then he forgot this answer too, and stayed silent: so that the human being was left wondering...

[Now] [i]magine the extremest possible example of a man who did not possess the power of forgetting at all and who was thus condemned to see everywhere a state of becoming: such a man would no longer believe in his own being, would no longer believe in himself, would see everything flowing asunder in a moving point and would lose himself in this stream of becoming: like a true pupil of Heraclitus, he would in the end hardly dare to raise his finger...

... Thus: it is possible to live almost without memory, and to live happily moreover, as the animal demonstrates; but it is altogether impossible to *live* at all without forgetting. (Nietzsche, 1983: 60-1) [Nietzsche's emphasis]

In short, in addressing this particular form of negation, we have landed in the undead realm of the present, that impossible – indeterminate and contingently negative – terrain which disappears at the very instant of its access and yet, without which, 'meaning', itself, cannot be sustained. Its 'un-historicality', as Nietzsche calls it in a later fragment, both side-steps and absorbs a past and future tense; and at the same time, makes that past or future 'decipherable', 'graspable'; that is to say, makes it 'possible'.[9] Indeed, in that sense, one could maintain that forgetting contributes to the making of 'what is' and becomes part and parcel of an *inventive* process, of the process – or rather processes (after all, there is no reason to assume that forgetting or indeed the paths to which it points remain anything other than multiple) – of making the 'that' alive, real.

In a peculiar way, then, and inasmuch as 'forgetting' is constitutive, it 're-members'. But what exactly is remembered? It cannot be experience: for in the land of the un-dead, there is clearly no room for *that*. And it cannot be rooted in an experimentation of any sort, for this would imply a sense of discovery, a sense of revelation (or a revealing) of some hidden truth or thing. But as we are speaking specifically of a (multiple) in-determinancy as the basis for a truth, there is nothing that can be concealed in here. Or to put this on a slightly different register, one *can* never discover the *content* of what has been forgotten. This is precisely what it is to forget; what has been forgotten has in its place: nothing. This does not mean to suggest or imply that forgetting can be identified with 'vacuum'.

As we play upon an impossible terrain of an indeterminate nothing, what is it that is *able* to be *re*-membered? It can only ever be the use of a thing; its technique; its custom, though we are speaking of use or technique or custom in terms other than 'lying to hand'. 'Does this mean', asks Wittgenstein, 'that I have to say that the proposition "12 inches = 1 foot" asserts all those things which give measuring its present point? No. [It simply means:] [t]he proposition is *grounded* in a technique [its use]' (Wittgenstein, 1983: 355; part VII, #1). But wouldn't this imply, we might want to ask, that there very well could exist someone who wished to use the proposition in some other (wrong) way, and that, therefore, a reliance on something as seemingly flimsy as the use of it might only encourage a chaotic nihilism (of sorts)? The possibility is entirely there: but the probability is not. For if there were no general commonality, no rule – a rule, in this context, meaning something quite different than *dictum* or *dogma* – the paradigm itself would disintegrate. 'The application of the concept "following a rule" presupposes a custom. Hence it would be nonsense to say', says Wittgenstein, 'just once in the history of the world someone followed a rule (or a signpost; played a game, uttered a sentence,

or understood one; and so on)' (Wittgenstein 1983: 322-3; part VI, #21).[10]

One could say, rather, and inasmuch as the [re-]membering of technique/application of a said rule has to do with establishing (inventing) the paradigm/framework of any truth game, that this [re-]membering plays a double function, albeit, let us not forget, in all its *negative indeterminancy*. On the one hand, it provides for a reproducing (repetition/imitation through *difference*) – of any proposition and therefore, of any paradigmatic structure; on the other hand, it provides for a kind of ground – now established without depth or width or speed or length (and yet encompassing all of that and more). We have in front of us, in other words, no greater (more securing or deeper) Ground to the ground than the indeterminate surface of the that; a surface 'indeterminate', but not, however, 'indefinitely homogeneous' or 'infinitely vague'. In Part VI of his *Mathematics*, Wittgenstein puts it like this:

> 31. ... The difficult thing here is not, to dig down to the ground; no, it is to recognize the ground that lies before us as ground. For the ground keeps giving us the illusory image of a greater depth, and when we seek to reach this, we keep on finding ourselves on the old level. Our disease is one of wanting to explain.
>
> [But] Once you have got hold of the rule, you have the route traced for you. (Wittgenstein, 1983: 333, part VI)[11]

In short, what seems to 'lie before us' is the possibility of accepting a non-existent 'excess' of indeterminancy (now placed in terms of an impossible place: to wit, the present) as the ground to any paradigmatic truth-game – a kind of fiction (rather than a lie) as Foucault will put it; a superficiality (of sorts), says Maurice Blanchot – one that has less to do with grammar (and the rhetoric thus implied), than it has to do with *techne*, custom, 'the way in which it is used'.[12] We are re-covering, then – in the fullest sense of that word (salvaging and accepting its invisibility) – the radicality of a fiction, a fictitious space herein epitomized by a contingent, anti-positivistic and non-affirmative 'excess'. Indeed, we are recovering perhaps more interestingly, still, an 'excess', an 'outside', an ever-effacing 'present' that seems to require not one whit of a dialectical logic or transcendental temporality to secure (as in 'invent') the horizon of its truth. 'Not reflection', says Foucault, 'but forgetting; not contradiction, but a contestation that effaces; not reconciliation, but droning on and on; not mind in laborious conquest of its unity, but the endless erosion of the outside; not truth finally shedding light on itself, but the streaming and distress of language that has always-already begun'. (Foucault, 1990: 22).

A shudder of disbelief! For who has not read their Marx, let alone their Heidegger! Who would wish to abandon time – and (seemingly) therewith history, not to mention, quite possibly, politics! Indeed and irrespective of where one might wish to stand on the question, who amongst us could fail to see the beauty inherent in the logic of the latter's *Identity and Difference*, precisely on this point (about forgetting and concealment, and the present and transcendence, not to mention time itself), wherein, among many, many other things, he reaches precisely the opposite conclusion: 'inasmuch', says Heidegger in his 'Onto-theology', 'as we are thinking of unconcealing and keeping concealed, of transition (transcendence) and of arrival (presence)' (Heidegger, 1969: 67). For we have, with Heidegger, the posing of an ontology rooted precisely in/on difference – a difference, of course, quite dislodged from its metaphysi-

cal suppositions – but one which nevertheless requires (or better put, must of necessity require) a re-thinking of the present as entailing or, rather, as being equivalent to, a transcendent temporality:

> The outward evidence of this (though of course it is merely outward evidence) is the treatment of Being as παρουσία or οὐσία, which signifies, in ontological-Temporal terms, 'presence' [*Anwesenheit*]. *Entities are grasped in their Being as 'presence';* this means they are understood with regard to a definite mode of time – the 'Present'... [Being is equal to no class or genus of entities, it pertains to every entity] ... Its 'universality' is to be sought higher up. Being and the structure of Being lie beyond every entity and every possible character which an entity may possess. *Being is the transcendens pure and simple.* And the transcendence of Dasein's Being is destructive in that it implies the possibility and necessity of the most radical *individuation.* Every disclosure of Being as the *transcendens* is transcendental knowledge. *Phenomenological truth (the disclosedness of Being) is veritas transcendentalis.* (Heidegger, 1967: 47, 62)

This is to say, then, that in order to capture the movement – ie, the non-fixity, dislocated, a-stasis of truth (identity, objectivity and so forth as radical individuation) – clearly, says Heidegger, there must be the facility to re-present the present, a [re-]presentation, which is, at one and the same time, ultimately 'impossible' and necessarily 'transcendent'. Its dis-location, 'movement', underwrites precisely what it is to be 'free'; a freedom no longer bound (if ever it was) to the exigencies of the spatial (why? because we are speaking here of a 'not'-location, a *dis*location), which, given the argument, can therefore only ever and by definition be established with respect to time and the (transcendent) [de-]structuration of the present. Or to say the same thing differently: if the possibilities of freedom are to be fully realised, they must primarily be established along the frontier or horizon of time, a frontier that would, *ipso facto*, maintain little or no room for the immovable, wholly sutured 'fixities' of life – a fixity (non-freedom) that would of necessity come under the rubric of, in a word, space.[13]

A dilemma. For we seem to be caught in the (not-so-delicate) web of an either/or division cast now in terms of a temporality quite distinct in its oppositional role from that of the spatial. Which is it to be, then: temporal over the spatial or spatial over the temporal? And does this require (in either case) some form of transcendence or not? These are not idle questions; for, as de Man very wisely surmises, '[i]t turns out that in these innocent-looking didactic exercises, we are in fact playing for very sizeable stakes' (de Man, 1979: 15). Indeed, we are.

I submit that there very well may be a way out of this impasse. And that is to take seriously the problem – no, the necessity – of pluralism itself. This requires, at the very minimum, an acknowledgement that 'indeterminancy' (and all we have said about it up to this point with respect to negation, forgetting, impossibility and so forth) is, in its most radical sense, paradoxical.[14] That is to say, this excess 'negation' – or, more to the point, its root, its 'division' or slash ['/'] – expresses that division (of difference) as always-already *incommensurably plural*. In any proposition, including that of contradiction, there is no fundamental unity (between a not and its other) or an ontological first, either as point of departure or as one of arrival.[15] We are speaking of a heterogeneic unity of the slash

['/'] itself; not the heterogeneity of that which falls on 'either side' of the cut. This is a radical composition, a radical multiplicity in all its negative dimensionalities; and it is precisely un-thinkable, in as much as it is neither paradigmatic nor syntagmatic; neither metaphorical nor metonymic; neither time nor space; neither true nor false. It is all of the above (and probably more) in all its fictitious, un-thinkable cohesive impossibility. We return to Wittgenstein:

> 200. Really 'The proposition is either true or false' only means that it must be possible to decide for or against it. But this does not say what the ground for such a decision is like. (Wittgenstein, 1974: 27e-28e)

> 205. If the true is what is grounded, then the ground is not *true*, nor yet false. (Wittgenstein, 1974: 27e-28e)

> 28. ... [Or to put it this way] [t]hat I can assume what is physically false and reduce it *ad absurdum* gives me no difficulty. But how to think the – so to speak – unthinkable?.. (Wittgenstein, 1983: 285; part V)

> 29. ... [Where geometrical illustrations cease to be *applications* of *Analysis*, they can be wholly misleading] ... The idea of a 'cut' is one such dangerous illusion. (Wittgenstein, 1983: 285; part V)

> 4. ... [Rather] [i]t might be said: *imagination* tells it. And the germ of truth is here; only one must understand it right. (Wittgenstein, 1983: 224; part IV)

Alright then, let us use our imagination. Let us imagine a different reading of the slash ['/'] as something other than the (seemingly) deep and ceaseless cut, dividing the something from its other. It no longer demarcates a site of departure (or arrival) with respect to any truth or certainty, dialectical or otherwise, and yet despite its fiction (or because of it), rewrites a truth. It is closer in description to a 'forgotten' homeland, a bleeding land as it were, whose very landscapes circumscribe the nomadic dislocation of the neither/nor – the multiplicities of which are wholly unthinkable without a radical reinvention/re-membering of space (as the de-de-negation) and of time (as its displaced movement). We have here a paradigm shift, axiomatic at the point of a non-dialectics. And yet, it is one that manages to address, as central, the problem of 'change', 'movement', and the 'probability of certainty', along the axes of an impossible ground, without recourse to a teleological unfolding or transcendentalist logic. Instead we have here an always-already fragmented web of journeying, of exile, contingent at its very limit; one whose 'existence' is, in all the plurality of a finite-infinity, opposite to nothing.

If we accept this proposition; if we accept that 'what tests the what' (to paraphrase Wittgenstein) is precisely the use of the rule itself and, therewith, re-enlist the fiction of an indeterminate negation in the fullest sense of its multiplicity; then we very well may have managed to have rescued (a not-) space from the ravages of time, without privileging one over the other. Indeed time itself, may have, finally also, been unhinged from the fixity of an eternal Time; re-configured in 'the now' as radically heterogeneic and in dispersion.[16]

But have we, in so accepting this radical neither/nor, space-time proposition – this *pluralism of the 'root'* – have we been able to avoid certain well-known problems of metaphysics (particularly around those that would seem to eradicate all forms of politi-

cal struggle)? Moreover, in accepting what may appear to be a pure relativity of the rule (or indeed, of custom), have we not forfeited our ability to demarcate an ethical proposition – any ethical proposition – managing to escape from metaphysics, dialectic or otherwise, only to fall prey to a kind of chaotic meaninglessness, a kind of 'radical nihilism', that 'whatever is' is, *ipso facto*, good?

The long reply follows in the next section. But the shorter one to both these questions, is that in re-thinking the problem of identity and difference in terms of a radical pluralism of indeterminate negativity at its 'core', one that is to say that, in its very 'exile', escapes and doubles (triples and, perhaps, quadruples) back to [re-]invent a contingent objectivity as such; in this movement there is no collapse into an always-already given 'truth' nor one that conceals or reveals or revels within an ethical void.[17] This is precisely because, political struggle, and indeed the political itself, becomes entirely central, placed exactly at, on, beside, over, and in terms of, an (imaginary) 'ground'. A ground of the bleeding land; a diasporic ground of space-time.

the a-moral interregnum

... I felt determined to transform the most simple details of life into so many insignificant words, that my voice, which was becoming the only space where I allowed her to live, forced her to emerge from her silence too, and gave her a sort of physical certainty, a physical solidity, which she would not have had otherwise. All this may seem childish. It does not matter. This childishness was powerful enough to prolong an illusion that had already been lost, to force something to be there which was no longer there. It seems to me that in all this incessant talking there was the gravity of one single word, the echo of that 'Come' which I had said to her; and she had come, and she would never be able to go away again. (Blanchot, 1978: 73)

The interregnum of this proximity and distance. It is fileted with the pathos of an imaginary beginning and, with it, the pathos of beginning an imaginary. We could have started our story anywhere: though just because there never has been, is, and never will be a 'first', should not imply, there never was a 'once upon a time' (as the storyteller might say) or a 'supposing that' (as the political economy variation, on storytelling, might say). No first causes; just beginnings/any beginnings/truncated beginnings: their weave produces the horizon (or is that a plateau, or a 'ground'?) of the start. In a way, it could be described as a tenuous weaving, threading together bits of memory, both dead and alive and somewhere in between, with the forgetting, the forgotten, the forgettable. For we take from 'what lies around us', to echo Wittgenstein, and we *use it*; we use the dreams, the nightmares, the incidental dinners, the laundromats to form our 'that'.

Indeed, and more specifically put, this struggle between and amongst memory and its forgetting produces the weave of a start – – of a that – which has already begun. There is no horizon of the either/or; no identity invented 'against' the Something *per se*. We have instead the creating of the imaginary, creating the imaginary 'as if' real; producing the curve around which the present movement unfolds – a curve which is no more (or less) or shorter or fatter than a series of dots or maybe just one long dot stretched to infinity. Imagination. No lie (nor truth): only the radical geography of a fiction, continuous in all its dis-continuity.

Is it so difficult, then, to see how every 'as if' always-already re-presents a way of life, selecting a bit of this and a bit of that; re-

presenting one's code of existence exactly at the same time as inventing it anew, and doing so 'as if' it were always eternally there 'beforehand' (or, at least remembering it as though it had been), in order to make the case that it now and forever always ought to be so? Foucault names this 'as if' as a popular memory; Derrida brings it forward (in honour of de Man's death) as a mourningful one; in either case its function is precisely to constitute the impossible terrain of the 'to be' in all its present and future tenses. Indeed, it could be said that every first year political militant knows about this kind of 'as if': for without some kind of 'picture' of 'what ought to be' based somehow and in some way in terms of the 'what have beens' of life – in all their varying memories, myth-makings and decay, (turning, as they must of necessity so do, between, with and against the exiled multiplicities of the 'what is' and the 'what lies before us') – without that picture, one has at best only a recipe for disaster, one that is out of reach, out of touch and utterly unsustainable.

But, this is also to say, simultaneously, that imagination, as powerful as it is (despite or perhaps because its profundity remains but skin deep) is only ever able to be inscribed – to become, that is to say 'institutionalised' along the surface of an impossible ground – on the basis of immense political struggles to make it so. It is a risk that we take, a risk we must take, in order to make change 'stick'. A risk taken at the very surface of the 'that'.

And yet, if we follow the logic through, we are left with a not-so-baffling, but for some, a conceivably dreadful, conclusion. By insisting on the radical political contingency of any social imaginary and the paradigmatic 'bleeding homelands' around which they turn, it is also to say, then, that the codes of existence – and, more to the point here, the moral and ethical truths implied by those codes – are only as solid as are the hegemonic expressions from whence they spring. For in exchanging a transcendental temporality (mixed metaphors and all) for the surface of the risk, we find at the end of the day, that the very ethics of the social have been exiled to the margins of an impossible spatiality; the measure of its truth journeying precariously (it might seem) along the soiled interregnum of the imagination, attempting to fight the good fight on the ever slimy battlefield of the political.

What is, conceivably, our picture then? The Hobbesian nightmare, *sans* the Leviathan, returning to a post-modern world in all its stunning brutality! And we, who have not the energy to struggle, are condemned to stand at the shore of a civilized Truth, forever waving a tearful farewell to the Good Life, our moral fibres cast away and adrift.

But I say: there is something wrong with this picture.

For this re-invention, this imagination, all born and bred and sustained precisely in the space of that indeterminate pause is a *social* ensemble. It no more falls from out of the sky than does language itself erupt from only one mouth. Indeed, this imagination marks by re-marking the history, custom, traditions of the immense variety of identities to which it is a part and from which it is most distant. Consequently, in that sense, not only does it [re-]mark the relation of itself to itself in all the ways we have described up to now; its meaning is established in the same way, exactly in the same way, as any sociality or law is established – be it scientific, civil, physical, theoretical or make-believe – to wit, in a (fantastic) relativity to the 'that' which lies around us. In this sense, too, then, its identity (meaning,

objectivity, truth) – already cast in relation to an (indeterminantly negative) plurality – is no more or less indefinite, no more or less whimsical, no more or less terrifying than is the statement E=mc².

'*Everything has its day*', as Nietzsche so eloquently reminds, musing on the prejudices of morality:

When man gave all things a sex he thought, not that he was playing, but that he had gained a profound insight: – it was only very late [and after the intervention of the feminist movement – I should like to add!] that he confessed to himself what an enormous error this was, and perhaps even now he has not confessed it completely. – In the same way, man has ascribed to all that exists a connection with morality and laid an *ethical significance* on the world's back. One day this will have as much value, and no more, as the belief in the masculinity or femininity of the sun has today. (Nietzsche, n.d.: 9; Book I, #3)

By insisting that the ethical is both somewhere afloat in the imagination and, perhaps more dramatically, that the kind of ethics understood as if a (neutral) expression of any epoch, ie, as the 'real' True Truth, is damning hypocrisy at best, have we squared the circle? For at the same time as exiling the ethical itself, we also want to say, for example, that this kind of democracy is *better* than that; that *this* kind of violence is *worse* than another. And we want to say it not just for any people, and not just for any time: but for now, and for us. Can we do this if we only insist on a presence that is not-here; or if we speak of an identity that is only ever difference captured in terms of some fractured impossible dimensionality called space-time; or if we insist on the radical pluralism of indeterminate negations as the core to any objectivity; or if we name the cut, the division, as bleeding homelands, ie as the exiled 'outside', reconfiguring the 'in'; or, finally, if we speak of an imagination collected from re-membering things which never were?

Yes. Yes, is the answer, and for precisely those reasons. For as it turns out, freedom is not the opposite of 'x' ('un-freedom' or immobility, as it were, for example); indeed, it is not an 'opposite' at all. It is a fiction in the best sense of that word; and we have a right to that fiction, not only in terms of accessing it, re-re-membering, institutionalizing it, but in terms of inventing it, playing with it and, yes, forgetting it too. And *that*, apart from everything else, is *exactly* an ethical proposition; an ethical proposition with no morals; no morals to this story of negation.

Which is to say one last thing. Supposing that we were never interested in anything anymore ever again; supposing that our senses were so dulled and flattened (for whatever reasons: drugs, over-whelming odds, boredom, torture, homelessness, too little money or too much) that we lay prone all day and night, forever, not even wiping away flies that might migrate over our noses and our eye-lids. We have a picture in front of us of utter dejection and hopelessness: the handmaidens to all things eternal, infinite and indistinguishable. But supposing that, on the other hand, we are to take seriously this problematic of a 'finite' infinity, ie, a pluralistic negativity. What would become *its* handmaiden? It cannot be the Truth or the Temporal or the Ethical or the Moral or the Dialectical, for the duties of this handmaiden are far too delicate to be handled by those giants of modernity.

I dare say, at its most modest point, it would be curiosity: the gentle muse, who, in 'supposing that' embarks upon the ever-impossible journey 'to find out'.

notes

* This essay was first delivered to the Department of Political Science, Yale University, April 1993, and to the Department of Comparative Literature, The State University of New York (Binghampton) in May of the same year. Later, it was given to the Ideology and Discourse post-graduate closed seminar, at Essex University. Accordingly, I would like to express my grateful appreciation to the scholars at all three places, and in particular, to Profs. Barry O'Neil, Chris Fynsk, and Ernesto Laclau, respectively.

1 M. Blanchot (1982: 24).

2 See, for example, Golding (1992: 56).

3 See, for example, G.W.F. Hegel (1977: 104-111).

4 My emphasis and brackets. Indeed, and continuing with this argument, he says:

> The force that shatters the appearance of identity is the force of the thing: the use of 'it is' undermines the form of that appearance, which remains inalienable just the same. Dialectically, cognition of nonidentity lies also in the fact that this very cognition identifies – that it identifies to a greater extent, and in other ways, than identitarian thinking. This cognition seeks to say what something is, while identitarian thinking says what something *comes under*, what it exemplifies or represents, and what, accordingly, it is not itself. The more relentlessly our identitarian thinking besets its object, the farther will it take us from the [actual] identity of the object. (Adorno, 1966b: 149)

5 Compare Nietzsche's remark: '255. *Conversation about music* – which, among other things makes "pictures" or rather "sees" music; knows its colour, etc.' (Nietzsche, n.d.: 145).

6 See, for example, where Bataille writes:

> Nothing exists that doesn't have this *senseless sense* – common to flames, dreams, uncontrollable laughter – in those moments

when consumption accelerates, beyond the desire to endure. Even utter senselessness ultimately is always this sense made of the negation of all the others. (Isn't this sense basically that of each particular being who, as such, is the *senselessness* of all the others, but only if he doesn't care a damn about enduring – and thought (philosophy) is at the limit of this conflagration, like a candle blown out at the limit of a flame.) (1991: 20)

7 See, for example, Blanchot (1978: 51) where he writes of the connection of the 'outside'/excess (as that of terror/dread) with the problem of 'memory' and 'forgetting':

So she came into this room, and what did she meet up with here? From me, the motions of a madman who did not recognize her; for her, a feeling of dread which had forced her outside with the thought that she had seen something she had no right to see, so that my name was the one she would most happily have banished from her memory. I will add that when she answered the question I asked – 'Why have you come?' – by saying, 'I've forgotten,' that answer was much more exact and more important (in my opinion) than the one this story holds.

This connection between memory and forgetting will be examined more thoroughly in the text.

8 This conceptual in-between-ness, is precisely the 'path', as it were, the 'distance' necessary to create/sustain any living (ie 'non-fixed') identity. Indeed, as Foucault puts it, it marks/contours/resuscitates the relation of the 'self to the self'. In his 'The Care of the Self', Volume III of *The History of Sexuality*, compare Seneca's remarks to Lucilius, quoted therein:

I do not wish you ever to be deprived of gladness. I would have it born in your house; and it is born there, if only it is inside you ... for it will never fail you when once you have found its source ... look toward the true

good, and rejoice only in that which comes from your own store [*de tuo*]. But what do I mean by 'your own store'? I mean your very self and the best part of you. (1988: 66-7)

9 Compare Nietzsche's sixth remark (within the same second 'untimely' meditation) regarding this point: '*If you are to venture to interpret the past you can do so only out of the fullest exertion of the vigour of the present* ... Like to like! Otherwise you will draw the past down to you ... When the past speaks it always speaks as an oracle: only if you are an architect of the future and know the present will you understand it' (1983: 94).

10 Compare Nietzsche's (now not so cryptic) remark on the importance of a rule in *Daybreak*, where he writes: '442. The rule. – "I always find the rule more interesting than the exception" – he who feels like that is far advanced in the realm of knowledge and is among the initiated' (Nietzsche, n.d.: 187).

11 Compare Nietzsche's remark on the error of dialectical logic: '474. The only ways – "Dialectics is the only way of attaining ... being and getting behind the veil of appearance" – this is asserted by Plato as solemnly and passionately as Schopenhauer asserts it of the anti-thesis of dialectics – and both are wrong. For that to which they want to show us the way does not *exist*' [Nietzsche's emphasis] (Nietzsche, n.d.: 196-97).

12 On the question of the 'lie' v. 'fiction' in Foucault and Blanchot, see especially, 'I Lie, I Speak' and 'Reflection, Fiction' in Foucault (1990: 9-13 and 21-6).

13 On this point, see, for example, Ernesto Laclau's crucial intervention on the matter, in his 'Dislocation and Capitalism', where he says in part:

Let us begin by identifying three dimensions of the relationship of dislocation...The first is that dislocation is the very form of temporality. And temporality must be conceived as the exact opposite of space... [Now] [i]f dislocation involves contingency, and contingency power, the absence of dislocation leads in the Platonic schema to a radical communitarian essentialism that eliminates the very question of power and thus the possibility of politics... [On the other hand] history's ultimate unrepresentability [eg, its dislocation, temporality] is the condition for the recognition of our radical historicity. (Laclau, 1990: 41, 69, 84)

14 Apart from the texts cited above, de Man speaks at length about the importance of the paradox. See especially his 'Conclusions: Walter Benjamin's "The Task of the Translator"' (de Man, 1986: 83ff.).

15 Compare Wittgenstein's remark, Part IV of the *Mathematics*, where he says, '56. Contradiction. Why just this one bogey? That is surely very suspicious' (Wittgenstein, 1983: 254).

16 This 'escape' of time from Time (whose route is aided and abetted by the imaginary 'not-space' of space), runs as a theme, certainly throughout the work of Proust (where time is invented/described as dead-time, real-time, living-time, memory-time and so forth) in his well-known and loved *Remembrance of Things Past* (Proust: 1983). Of course, it is taken up quite systematically by Walter Benjamin in *Illuminations*, particularly in his 'The Storyteller' (Benjamin: 97-106). But I am also thinking about different *dimensionalities* of time: as in the time of virtual reality. See, for example, *The Lost Dimension* (Virilio, 1991).

17 On the multiple uses of 'errance' as a politics of journeying, see de Man, 'Walter Benjamin's "The Task of The Translator"' (de Man, 1986: 91-105).

references

Adorno, T. 'Critique of Positive Negation' in *Negative Dialectics* (New York: The Continuum Publishing Company, 1966a).

Adorno, T. 'Cogitative Self-Reflection' in *Negative Dialectics* (New York: The Continuum Publishing Company, 1966b).

Bataille, G. 'A Story of Rats' in *The Impossible*, tr. Robert Hurley (San Francisco: City Lights Books, 1991) 11-82.

Benjamin, W. *Illuminations* (New York: Shocken, 1968).

Blanchot, M. *Death Sentence*, tr. Lydia Davis (New York: Station Hill Press, 1978).

Blanchot, M. 'Kafka and Literature' in *The Siren's Song*, tr. S. Rabinovitch (Sussex: The Harvester's Press, 1982).

Derrida, J. 'Introduction: Desistance' in P. Lacoue-Labarthe, *Typography: Mimesis, Philosophy, Politics*, ed. Christopher Fynsk (Cambridge, Mass.: Harvard University Press, 1989).

Foucault, M. and M. Blanchot *The Thought from Outside; Michel Foucault as I Imagine Him*, tr. Brian Massumi and Jeffrey Mehlman, respectively (New York: Zone Books, 1990).

Foucault, M. *The History of Sexuality: Care of the Self*, vol. III, tr. Robert Hurley (New York: Vintage Books, 1988).

Golding, S. *Gramsci's Democratic Theory: Contributions to a Post-Liberal Democracy* (Toronto: University of Toronto Press, 1992).

Hegel, G.W.F. *The Phenomenology of Spirit*, tr. A.V. Miller (Oxford: Oxford University Press, 1977).

Heidegger, M. *Identity and Difference*, tr. J. Stambaugh (New York: Harper and Row, 1969).

Heidegger, M. *Being and Time*, trs J. Macquarrie and E. Robinson (Oxford: Basil Blackwell, 1967).

Kundera, M. *The Book of Laughter and Forgetting* (London: Penguin, 1978, 1980).

Laclau, E. *New Reflections on the Revolution of Our Time* (London: Verso, 1990).

de Man, P. *Resistance to Theory* (Manchester: Manchester University Press, 1986) in the Theory and History of Literature series, vol. 33.

de Man, P. *Allegories of Reading: Figural Language in*

Rousseau, Nietzsche, Rilke, and Proust (New Haven and London: Yale University Press, 1979).

Nietzsche, F. *Untimely Meditations,* tr. R.J. Hollingdale (Cambridge: Cambridge University Press, 1983).

Nietzsche, F. *Daybreak: Thoughts on the Prejudices of Morality,* tr. R.J. Hollingdale (Cambridge: Cambridge University Press, n.d.).

Proust, M. *Remembrance of Things Past,* trs C.K. Scott Moncrieff and Terence Kilmartin (London: Penguin Books, 1983).

Virilio, P. *The Lost Dimension,* tr. D. Moshenberg (New York: Semiotext(e), 1991).

Wittgenstein, L. *Remarks on the Foundations of Mathematics* (Revised Edition), eds G.H. von Wright, R. Rhees, G.E.M. Anscombe (Cambridge/London: M.I.T. Press, 1983).

Wittgenstein, L. *On Certainty,* eds G.E.M. Anscombe and G.H. von Wright, trs D. Paul and G.E.M. Anscombe (Oxford: Basil Blackwell, 1974).

Wittgenstein, L. *Philosophical Investigations* (the English text to the Third Edition), tr. G.E.M. Anscombe (New York: The Macmillan Company, n.d.).

Hardly the draft for an article, and so different in tone and style from all the academic pieces I had written on Foucault, this text, in the flash of a moment, urged itself upon me with that brutal evidence of all confession. Perhaps the reason why I would like to see it published is that, in its simplicity, it surprised me with a question that I may not have been the only one to have avoided for too long a time: what is it that has kept us – that still keeps us – reading Foucault?

rudi visker

FASCINATION WITH FOUCAULT
object and desire of an archaeology of our knowledge

If we question Classical thought at the level of what, archaeologically, made it possible, we perceive that the dissociation of the sign and resemblance in the early seventeenth century caused these new forms – probability, analysis, combination, and universal language system – to emerge, not as successive themes engendering one another or driving one another out, but as a single network of necessities. And it was this network that made possible the individuals we term Hobbes, Berkeley, Hume, or Condillac.[1]

This passage expresses better than any learned commentary what was really at stake in *The Order of Things*: instead of a history of ideas or a history of opinions, an attempt to unearth the 'general system of thought' (OT,75) which made possible the interplay of simultaneous and apparently irreconcilable opinions. Buffon or Linnaeus, Turgot or Quesnay, Broussais or Bichat – once this system is found, all those antitheses which we ceaselessly try to reconstruct in our histories of ideas will seem to be mere ripples on the surface of what Foucault calls knowledge (*le savoir*), or, at most, antitheses which like the tines of a 'fork' – the expression is Foucault's own[2] – have a common archaeological ground. Which is why, for example, Foucault refused to take a position

in a debate such as that between structuralism and phenomenology – a debate which at that time held everyone in its clutches – for all he could see there were merely 'two *correlative* techniques whose common ground of possibility is formed by the being of language, as it was constituted on the threshold of the modern age' (OT, 299, my italics).

Perhaps it is this attitude to history – depersonalizing, distanced, and seemingly weaned of all pathos – which lies at the basis of the *fascination* as well as the *irritation* which Foucault provoked. Irritation of course with the iconoclasm with which the archaeologist seems to want to toss our history books into the paper shredder; irritation also with the air of superiority with which he dismissed as a 'tempest in a teapot'[3] what until then had seemed of highest importance. Fascination with that gaze which seemed to come from without, with that knowledge that seemed fundamental

113

and representative of a deeper wisdom because it appeared to have tapped the very source of knowledge itself. But also irritation in the fascination since Foucault, not wanting to place that source in our subjectivity, deliberately made it inaccessible. For the price of this knowledge, which describes with archivist's precision the law of what in previous epochs could be said, seems to be that it surrenders the validity of its own statements to 'an anonymous field whose configuration defines the possible position of speaking subjects' (AK, 122).[4] Irritating was not so much Foucault's idea that our knowledge had to be emancipated from the sovereignty of 'the' subject, but rather his message that even though our speech is only possible because it is grounded on a law which lays down 'what can be said' (AK, 129 – Foucault's most succinct definition of an 'archive'), we will always be denied access to that law, that 'archive'. For we might have been prepared to give up our sovereignty had someone only told us what our submission consisted in, what form that anonymous field had, and what position we occupied in it. But that was precisely what Foucault refused us: 'it is not possible for us to describe our own archive, since it is from within these rules that we speak' (AK, 130). Worse still, he applied that refusal to himself: 'I accept that my discourse may disappear with the figure that has borne it so far' (AK, 208). Wasn't it that, more than anything else, that he was going to be blamed for? Not only to have turned 'the subject' but even his own subjectivity into a position 'that may be filled in certain conditions by various individuals' (AK, 115) and then to have accepted that those conditions could not themselves be known? That figure of our knowledge which we call 'Foucault' – a figure who had every chance of becoming the new high priest of the meaning of our exis-

tence, who would finally reveal to us the outside and thus the significance of our significance, the meaning of our meaning – did not irritate us with his message about the death of man – that discussion was no more than the folklore of an existentialism which, as is well known, passed itself off as a humanism. What disturbed us was not the prediction that we would disappear and be washed away 'like a face drawn in sand at the edge of the sea' (OT, 387)[5] – it was just that possibility that fascinated us – but rather that Foucault, by denying us access to our own archive, did not grant us that disappearance. Foucault infuriated us because he confronted us with our fascination with what he revealed, and because he understood and named that fascination: 'they cannot bear (and one cannot but sympathize) to hear someone saying: '[d]iscourse is not life: its time is not your time; in it, you will not be reconciled to death ...' (AK, 211).

The death of the subject as something to which we cannot reconcile ourselves; death not as that long craved for disappearance but as its major impediment; and hence intolerable and irritating for announcing a de-centring in which the subject does not completely disappear – such was no doubt the proper meaning of the famous (post-) structuralist de-centring of the subject. And that is what is still at stake for us in Foucault who, as one will remember, never claimed that there was no subject. Instead of excluding 'the problem of the subject' (AK, 200), he tried to pose it by defining 'the positions and functions that the subject could occupy in the diversity of discourse' (ibid.). Showing such an 'anonymous field' at work in past epochs of knowledge, and highlighting the structure of those epochs without having recourse to 'the foundation of all knowledge and the principle of all significa-tion as stemming from the meaningful subject'[6], was what the examples from e.g. *The Order of Things* were aiming at. Examples which made apparent that, in spite of a certain de-centring, there was nonetheless still talk of subjects: though the one we call Marx might not represent the caesura in economic thought which he was so readily associated with, the fact is that it took a great deal of trouble for him to occupy a position which appeared in retrospect to be (merely) a different tine of the fork connecting him with Ricardo (OT, 260 ff.). Not that discourse thought for Marx; rather, that Marx was able to think is due to the fact that, in the field of knowledge, a position had come free which someone 'could occupy' (AK, 200, italics mine).

To link knowledge with an anonymous field, as Foucault has done, does not mean that the problem of knowledge or the problem of the subject is no longer taken seriously. On the contrary, for Foucault it seems to have been the only way of indeed taking those problems seriously. For if there is in fact something like discourse, which establishes 'the difference between what in a certain period can be said, and what actually is said'[7], and if such discourse is nothing other than a name for that difference, then the subject of knowledge seems subjected to a law which makes him speak just because he has no access to the content of that law. It is this inability to know the rules of his own archive which explains why there can still be, for Foucault, talk of such things as subjects. For a subject that would have a perfect insight into the structure of the archaeological ground on which it has to rest in order to make its statements, would have no more statements to make. Nothing would be worth the trouble any longer if we could be shown in advance, about our own epoch, what Foucault has shown us, for example, for the Classical epoch. There is, moreover,

nothing to be shown or known 'in advance' about one's own epoch, for the idea(l) of being granted a look into the structure of one's own epoch would turn discourse into a causality which could be realized without us. But Foucault denies this outright: there is no discourse without our knowledge, there is only knowing when *we* know, and yet this does not exclude that this knowledge seems to follow and to establish a law whose actual content is for the moment denied us.[8] It is that originary delay, that de-centredness which we have with respect to and within our own archive, which makes our speaking possible: it is that which *makes* us speak.

De-centredness is not, then, the disappearance of the subject, *but that which makes the subject unable to disappear*. To have the subject depend on a 'centre' (an 'anonymous field', an 'archive', etc.) in which (or against which) it occupies a position – to make it, in that sense, dependent or de-centred – does not mean denying it or making it the mere effect of something else.[9] That would be all too simple. A subject that would disappear completely in its de-centredness, that would be completely absorbed in something else of which it is only the dependent effect, would, in Heidegger's terms, definitively escape the 'burdensome character of Dasein'.[10] But this 'burden' arises precisely from the subject's not being permitted to disappear (in its dependence, in its de-centredness). The subject is that instance which is not there where it would like to be, which does not occupy the position of that centre which it thought it held, but which nevertheless cannot escape that centre's grip and attraction: centre which it does not know, key which it has 'lost', secret which retreats, and just for that reason, to cite Heidegger once more, '[can] more essentially concern [the subject] and can make a more intimate appeal [to the subject] than any other present thing which strikes or concerns [it]'.[11] De-centred, but not without centre: for this reason there is no subject without a desire, and without the possibility – and necessity – to comport to that desire. For this reason the subject is always a place where a fascination and an irritation intersect.

Hence, of course, *our own* fascination and *our own* irritation with Foucault's work, which on the one hand seems to have convinced us, by way of endless historical examples, that we are indeed not those sovereign subjects in the field of knowledge which we took ourselves to be; but which on the other hand refuses to tell us precisely what our decentredness would actually consist in, and which, while holding the key to our own archive, seems to withhold from us just what we most deeply desire: to gain access to the law of our knowledge, so that we would know at last the value and the ultimate meaning of our knowledge, or what is more likely: so that we would finally be capable – in light of the ultimate lack of value and meaning of our knowledge – of being relieved of a responsibility we no longer want to bear. For what could be more difficult than to be required to serve a truth which is no *index sui*, and whose ultimate meaning and value, for lack of that key, we can never know? Is not speaking the truth already demanding enough, and should one not be able to expect that the truth will be its own reward? But to have this reward postponed, and to be told that the ultimate meaning of our truth should only be visible to a gaze which is no longer our own – a gaze which would unravel, with the same cool aloofness that Foucault displayed in analysing the archives of past epochs, the laws of our archive and the *meaning* of the distinction we draw between true and false[12] – perhaps all this demands more of us than we are prepared to take on. And yet it was just that which was at stake in Foucault's

own fascination for the archival laws which time and again subjected our knowledge to another order of truth, and which time and again let us say other things and made us take other statements into consideration for the distinction between true and false. Henceforth we would have to speak without knowing if the truth of our speech shall ever seem relevant to the discourse which guides it; to speak without the assurance that it has any meaning for the archive whose rules it nonetheless follows; and to accept that this speech will have lost its meaning the moment that this meaning becomes completely visible from the standpoint of another archive with other criteria of relevance and another difference between what can be said and what, in fact, is said. The historicity of this distinction being no reason to give it up; the truth of our truth which lies enclosed in our archive being always denied us; and having, in spite of this, to conform ourselves to a law which we can never know in its full positivity – such are no doubt the reasons why the morals or the ethics – I would rather say: the ethos of truth Foucault might have to offer us, can only be '*une morale de l'incomfort*'.[13] Impossible after reading *The Order of Things* not to think of those lines in which Foucault, beyond the bickering of our time, encountered Merleau-Ponty:

> [A]ppreciate fully that all we perceive is only apparent when surrounded by a familiar and scarcely understood horizon, that all certainty is only certain when supported by a ground which is never explored. The most fragile instant has roots. Here there is an entire restless ethics of evidence, which does not exclude, far from it, a rigorous economy of the True and the False; *but which is not reducible to that*.[14]

'It is not reducible to that' – because the always receding object of our own archaeology lets us stand in a 'truth', without letting us ever seize the truth of our 'archive', of that which makes our truth true, and without letting us ever arrive at that point which would quell the desire to seize our truth. But there may well be an ethos by which or in which we can inhabit and learn to live that desire, without ever being able to appropriate it. There may well be a 'practice of the self' (Foucault) which can allow this wildness in us without renouncing it, but also without wanting to tame it, if only by making it the last in a long line of 'exotica'. By an ethos of finitude which, in depriving us of the comfort of a centre also deprives us of the comfort of a lack of centre (of a de-centred *en-soi*), perhaps is meant nothing more – but also nothing less – than this: learn to linger in the 'in-between' of the decentredness, learn that we must, with our appearing ('centre'), also let go of our disappearing, and that the real message about the death of the subject consists in the subject's having to go on living until further notice. In short: let death remain death, and not outstrip it of its alterity by always again 'anticipating' and desiring it. Or rather: in desiring that point where what we know and what makes us know will finally coincide, in this fascination for our own archive, to already catch a glimpse of that (law of) death which casts us as 'mortals' (Heidegger) and which leaves us alone with (and at) this distressing post: learn (not) to die.[15]

notes

1 M. Foucault, *The Order of Things: An Archaeology of the Human Sciences* (New York: Vintage, 1973) p63 (parenthetically quoted as OT, originally *Les mots et les choses* (1966) = MC; AK = *The Archaeology of Knowledge* (London: Tavistock, 1972)).

2 Contrary to what Ian Hacking suggests in his high-

ly recommended 1979 essay: 'a teasing device that I call Foucault's fork' (1979: 39-51). Cf. MC, 193 (OT, 181 mistranslates); OT, 299 and passim.

3 Cf. OT, 262: 'Their controversies may have stirred up a few waves and caused a few surface ripples; but they are no more than storms in a children's paddling pool'. Foucault is speaking here, in the heady days of Althusserianism, about Ricardo and ... Marx!

4 For example Habermas has interpreted Foucault as sacrificing validity on the altar of meaning – see Visker (1992: 15-22).

5 Cf. OT, 386: 'man is in the process of perishing'.

6 Foucault (1980: 3) and cf. AK, 54-5, 203.

7 Foucault (1968: 863).

8 I am thinking here of the following passages (among others): AK, 122 'discourse is not an "anonymous voice" but rather "the totality of things said" [etc.]', 127 'historical a priori in the sense of a condition of *reality* and not a condition of *validity*', 128 'nothing, therefore, would be more pleasant, or more inexact ...'.

9 'Structuralism or not, it seems to me that it is nowhere a question, in the field vaguely determined by that label, of the negation of the subject. It is a question of the dependence of the subject, which is quite different ...' – J. Lacan defends Foucault in the discussion subsequent to his 'Qu'est-ce qu'un auteur?' (1969: 104). The idea of a subject as a not-being-able-to-disappear is found also, in another context, in Lacan (1991: 199).

10 Heidegger (1962: 173). In making this reference to Heidegger I am presupposing what I developed elsewhere concerning Foucault/Heidegger. Cf. Visker 1991 and 1992.

11 'Was sich entzieht, kann den Menschen wesentlicher angehen und inniger in den Anspruch nehmen als jegliches Anwesende, das ihn trifft und betrifft' (Heidegger, 1985: 129).

12 On Foucault's relativism of *conditions* of validity,

fascination with foucault

see Visker 1991 (English trans. forthcoming from Verso).

13 Foucault (23-4-1979: 82-3).

14 Foucault (1979: 83, italics and translation mine).

15 The background is the following: if the death of Dasein is not a miserable perishing, then one can wonder if the authenticity of Being-towards-death must not be thought in terms of the experience of the inability to disappear and the *simultaneous* exposure to the temptation and fascination that seems to originate from such a desire. This 'simultaneous' may well be the only trace of death which we have, and Being-towards-death as a dwelling in mortality may well be nothing other than learning to live in this tension. The inevitable dramatization of our death (Bataille, Lacoue-Labarthe) is thus not a critique of that existential possibility designated by Being-towards-death, but rather its affirmation: the death which Heidegger speaks about is not that (factual) end which we try to imagine, but that end (*finis*) which attracts to the extent that it withdraws. The inaccessibility of death is, in a certain sense, the experience of death itself. Our mortality is not so much concerned with that black hole into which we will disappear, but with the experience of our not being permitted to disappear.

references

Foucault, M. Howison Lecture on Truth and Subjectivity (1), MS, Berkeley 1980.

Foucault, M. 'Pour une morale de l'incomfort', *Le Nouvel Observateur*, 754 (23-4-1979).

Foucault, M. *The Order of Things: An Archaeology of the Human Sciences* (New York: Vintage, 1973) (OT). Originally *Les mots et les choses* (Paris: Gallimard, 1966) (MC).

Foucault, M. *The Archaeology of Knowledge* (London: Tavistock, 1972) (AK).

Foucault, M. 'Qu'est-ce qu'un auteur?', *Bulletin de la Société Française de la Philosophie*, vol. 63 (1969).

Foucault, M. 'Réponse à une question', *Esprit*, vol. 36, 5 (1968).

Hacking, I. 'Michel Foucault's Immature Science', *Nous*, vol. 13 (1979).

Heidegger, M. *Vortrage und Aufsatze* (Pfullingen: Neske, 1985).

Heidegger, M. *Being and Time* (Oxford: Basil Blackwell, 1962).

Lacan, J. *Le Séminaire Livre VIII. Le transfert* (Paris: Seuil, 1991).

Visker, R. *Michel Foucault. Genealogie als Kritik* (Munchen: Fink, 1991) (English translation forthcoming: Verso).

Visker, R. 'Habermas on Heidegger and Foucault. Meaning and Validity in The Philosophical Discourse of Modernity', *Radical Philosophy*, 61 (1992).

Visker, R. 'From Foucault to Heidegger: A One-way Ticket?', *Research in Phenomenology*, vol. XXI (1991).

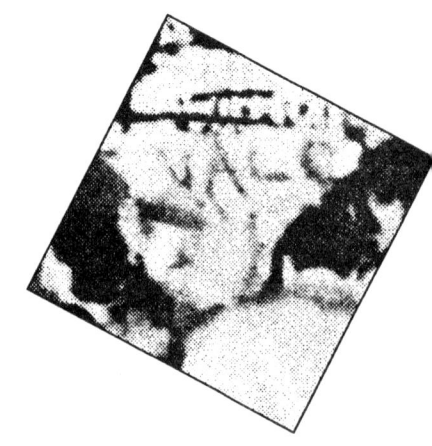

Granted this too is only interpretation – and
you will be eager enough to raise this objection? – well, so much the better ...
(Nietzsche, 1973 §22)

How are we to grasp Nietzsche as a political thinker? This question resonates
with overtones and arguments. Certainly we
cannot grasp Nietzsche's significance as a
political thinker without respect to the interpretations in which his name is encrusted.
Yet how should we interpret the political
appropriation of Nietzsche's name by the
ideologues of the Third Reich or, indeed, its
prior appropriation by anarchists, feminists,
socialists and conservatives?[1] And what significance does this question have for our
reading of Nietzsche as a political thinker?
This essay addresses the relationship
between these two questions in arguing that
the politics of Nietzsche's name discloses
two distinct modes of interpreting Nietzsche
as a political thinker (modes which we might
label 'master' and 'slave' interpretations).
Focusing on the moral and the epistemic
aspects of these modes of interpretation, I
will go on to draw out their implications for
locating Nietzsche as a political thinker by
attending to the forms of political activity
they exemplify. This reflective engagement
with the politics of interpreting Nietzsche
then acts to underscore an interpretation of
Nietzsche's thought as exemplifying an
understanding of the political as (site of)
contest, as *agon*, which accepts the self-referential implications of its activity as a political appropriation of Nietzsche.

politics and the
name of nietzsche

The history of Nietzsche-interpretation is
characterised by numerous tortuous and tor-
tured paths yet, if we address this history in
terms of the ontological politics of interpre-

david owen

AGONAL
THOUGHT
reading nietzsche
as political thinker

tation, two distinct modes of interpretation
reveal themselves in figurings of the interpreter as, on the one hand, lawgiver and, on
the other hand, poet.[2] The former is characterised by the identification of the *authentic*
Nietzsche – the 'truth' of Nietzsche as a person, as a philosopher, as a writer, as an out-
sider, etc. – and thus by the determination of
the standard against which all other
Nietzsche-interpretation is to be judged. The
latter is characterised by the disclosure of
multiple Nietzsche's and thus by the displacement of any determinate standard of
judgement by reflective standards of judgement which are the ongoing product of the
mutual contesting of specific (constellations
of) interpretations of Nietzsche. The distinction between these modes of interpretation is,
thus, that the former is committed towards
the idea that because there is a first word,
there must be a last word[3] – a final context
of contexts, whereas the latter suggests that

119

we have no warrant for making such a claim. Needless to say, these strategies of interpretation are characterised by mutual disdain insofar as the legislative mode of interpretation judges the poetic to be a nihilistic species of relativism[4], while the poetic situates the legislative as exhibiting a desparate desire to hold on to precisely that will to truth constitutive of the nihilistic condition.

The stakes raised by the confrontation between these two styles of interpretation are given particularly acute expression in the context of the Nazi appropriation of Nietzsche as a political thinker insofar as this appropriation calls out for judgement. Two questions emerge here. Is the Nazi interpretation justified? Are the ideologues of the Third Reich entitled to acquire Nietzsche in a proprietary act of interpretation? What is notable about much of the often acrimonious debate which characterises this topic is the way the relationship between these two questions is played out. Thus the attempt to posit an immanent relationship between Nietzsche's thought and Nazi ideology – for example, by specifying both as forms of an anti-modernist irrationalism[5] – is contested *either* by the claim that Nietzsche is an anti-political thinker[6] and, therefore, any political use of Nietzsche is necessarily abuse *or* by the claim that Nietzsche's philosophy discloses a politics radically at odds with Nazi ideology insofar as, for example, Nietzsche is both a pro-European anti-nationalist and a harsh critic of anti-semitism.[7] A further possibility within this arena of contest is to radically separate Nietzsche's political claims from his philosophical arguments[8]; this strategy allows potentially for the idea that while the Nazi appropriation of Nietzsche's politics is appropriate, the use of his philosophy is not. What all of these strategies share, however, is the commitment to the idea of an authentic Nietzsche – it is this idea which underpins and motivates the debate – and, concomitantly, *an identification of the question of the justification of the Nazi interpretation and the question of proprietary rights to Nietzsche's corpus.* In other words, each of these interpretations collapses the issue of justification with that of exclusivity. By contrast, the poetic mode of interpretation teases apart the question of justification and that of proprietary rights in order to repose their relationship; this is apparent if we reflect on the commitment to reflective judgement embodied in this strategy of reading in which standards of judgement are the ongoing outcome of the contest of interpretations. Thus, the question of the justifiability of the Nazi interpretation of Nietzsche is a matter of contestation (insofar as we recognise the contingency – but not arbitrariness! – of our standards and, thus, acknowledge the situated character of our judgements), while the question of proprietary rights is ruled out – since there is no 'true' interpretation of Nietzsche, it makes no sense within this perspective to claim exclusive rights to his corpus.[9] The costs of taking up this stance are immediately apparent: one cannot rule out a priori any interpretation of Nietzsche (however unpleasant or terrifying). In other words, to put the same point in a more positive fashion, no voice can be excluded from the arena of contest (this does not imply, however, that all voices speak with equal authority). Thus, this perspective entails that *to interpret Nietzsche as a political thinker is to engage in the struggle of political interpetations of Nietzsche.* At this juncture, let's pause and prepare to reflect back on these strategies of reading Nietzsche in terms of the moral and epistemic positions they manifest. To prepare for this act of reflection, I want to offer a brief reading of Nietzsche's essay '"Good and Evil",

"Good and Bad"' in which he sketches out two distinct modalities of morality: an art of superabundance and an art of hunger (Nietzsche, 1974 §370).

Nietzsche's delineation of the two forms of morality begins with his naming of them as *master* morality and *slave* morality, and continues in an analysis on the conditions of emergence and logical form of these moralities – I shall concentrate of the latter aspect as significant for our immediate concerns. The distinctive features of master morality is the affirmation of the relationship between the self (as embodied agency) and the world (as sensuous totality) in which it is situated. This morality denotes as 'good' those activities which enhance the situated embodied agents' experiences of themselves as autonomous agents able to determine and achieve goals, that is to say to 'give style' to their existence (Nietzsche, 1974 §290), and as 'bad' those activities which undermine this art of autonomy. By contrast, slave morality is predicated on a creative nay-saying, a denial of the relationship of the self and the world in which it is situated that expresses itself through the fictioning of another (non-sensuous) world, the 'real' world, which reinscribes the 'true' self as disembodied *soul* and posits an intrinsic moral order, where *order* operates either as a verb – '[a]n ultimate command is treated as the basis of morality. The command may emanate from a god or a law of nature or a transcendental subject presupposed by every person who acts rationally' (Connolly, 1993: 34) – or as a noun – 'an inherently harmonious design to which things may be predisposed or toward which they tend when they are on the right track' (Connolly, 1993: 35). In this context, the term 'good' denotes simply that *action* which conforms to the intrinsic moral order. We should note immediately that each of these modalities of morality

entails distinct epistemic commitments. On the one hand, the morality of the slave is predicated on the idea of a disembodied and disinterested soul which disavows (and suspends) the affective and situated aspects of agency. As such this morality manifests itself in the attempt to formulate a God's-eye view which specifies determinate rules of moral action (e.g. Kant's categorical imperative) and, concomitantly, entails a commitment to the epistemological project of specifying abstract (and eternal) standards of truth. It is with respect to this epistemological position that Nietzsche comments:

> [L]et us be on guard against the dangerous old conceptual fiction that posited a 'pure, will-less, painless, timeless knowing subject'; let us guard against the snares of such contradictory concepts as 'pure reason', 'absolute spirituality', 'knowledge in itself'; these always demand that we should think of an eye that is completely unthinkable, an eye turned in no particular direction, in which the active and interpreting forces, through which alone seeing becomes seeing *something*, are supposed to be lacking. (Nietzsche, 1969 III §12)

And again:

> [T]o suspend each and every affect, supposing we were capable of this – what would this mean but to *castrate* the intellect? (Nietzsche, 1969 III §12)

By contrast, the ethics of the noble is predicated on an account of selfhood as embodied and situated agency. This ethics points to the formulation of exemplars – which recognise the contextual character and affective investments of agency – through the contestation of ethical positions and finds its cognitive correlate in Nietzsche's commitment to perspectivism:

> There is *only* a perspectival seeing, *only* a

perspectival 'knowing'; and the *more* affects we allow to speak about one thing, the *more* eyes, different eyes, we can use to observe one thing, the more complete will our 'concept' of this thing, our 'objectivity' be. (Nietzsche, 1969 III §12)

In other words, this ethics involves the claim that there is no epistemically pure standpoint and as such our 'objectivity' consists in 'the ability to *control* one's Pro and Con and to dispose of them, so one knows how to employ a *variety* of perspectives and affective interpretations in the service of knowledge' (Nietzsche, 1969 III §12).[10]

Let us now return (prepared) to our reflection on the moral and epistemic aspects of the legislative and poetic strategies of interpretation. We can now note that the relationship between poetic and legislative modes of interpretation, and that between master and slave modalities of morality are *structurally isomorphic*. On the one hand, the poetic and the noble are characterised by a commitment to contextualism which recognises that scholarly/political standards of judgement are the *reflective* (ongoing) outcome of the contestation of interpretations/perspectives which are radically situated and necessarily partial. On the other hand, the legislative and the plebeian are characterised by a commitment to transcendentalism which holds that scholarly/political standards of judgement are the *determinate* outcome of the 'proper' (authentic/true) interpretation/perspective which is both radically abstract and necessarily total. To draw out the distinct forms of political activity exemplified by these modes of interpretation and modalities of morality, I will contrast Kant's political moralism (legislator/slave) with Nietzsche's political aesthetics (poet/noble) through a focus on, firstly, the categorical imperative in relation to the doctrine of eternal recur-

rence and, secondly, the ways in which these thinkers tie their criteria of, respectively, moral and aesthetic probity to specific understandings of the political.

difference, distance and politics

Our primary concern is with the moral and extra-moral (aesthetic) conceptions of politics disclosed by these imperatives, however, I will also include within this discussion a consideration of the status and authority of these rules – for if we are concerned with what these positions say, we are also concerned with what they *show*.[11] As a route into this topic, let's begin by formally stating Kant's and Nietzsche's respective positions: (i) *act always according to that maxim you can at the same time will as universal law* (Kant) and (ii) *act always according to that maxim you can at the same time will as eternally returning* (Nietzsche).

For our purposes, the salient distinction between the categorical imperative and the thought of eternal recurrence *qua saying* is that while both exhibit a universal form, the categorical imperative presupposes the universalizability of contents whilst the thought of eternal recurrence 'provides the form of universality only in the act of returning, whereas what returns (the actual content) and is willed to be returned cannot be universal, since each life (each becoming) is unique' (Ansell-Pearson, 1991: 198). It is this distinction which leads to the charge that whereas Kant's thought leads to a moral politics (and a conception of politics as morality), Nietzsche's thought engenders an immoral politics (and an understanding of politics as immoral). After all, we might cry, Kant's categorical imperative entails respect for human beings as ends-in-themselves and, thus, presents us with an ethic of duty which is also an ethic of respect, whereas

Nietzsche's thought of eternal return places only an aesthetic constraint on the form of agency insofar as it demands of (intellectual) conscience only that, like the brushstroke on canvas, the action can be affirmed by the artist/actor as integral to the totality of one's life/work of art (Nietzsche, 1974 §341). Does not Nietzsche comment that what is needful is to give style to one's character and that '[w]hether this taste was good or bad is less important than one might suppose' (Nietzsche, 1974 §290)? And doesn't this stance potentially allow a figure such as Hitler to affirm their actions? The heart of this charge lies in the claim that the categorical imperative requires that we acknowledge the claim to dignity of all human beings insofar as all human beings are free, that is, can act morally, and the thought of eternal return involves no such requirement. However, we may note, in response, that the law of artistic probity which Nietzsche terms the thought of eternal recurrence does require that we acknowledge the dignity of all human beings insofar as they are free, that is, can give style to their existence. This follows if we consider that the idea of eternal recurrence grounds the meaning and value of one's existence in its constitution of itself as a work of art; as such to recognise one's own claim to dignity as grounded in one's capacity to make one's life a work of art presupposes that one recognise the claim to dignity of others who have this capacity (i.e. all human beings) however different the works of art they may (or may not) produce of themselves. In other words, *just as perspectivism entails that any perspective must acknowledge the claim to knowledge of any other perspective, so too the doctrine of eternal recurrence entails that any person must acknowledge the claim to dignity of any other person.* We should also note though that just as perspectivism does not entail

that all perspectives speak with equal epistemic authority, the thought of eternal recurrence does not entail that all persons speak with equal artistic authority; while Kant's thought commits us to the view that all persons speak with equal moral authority, Nietzsche's perspective points us towards an artistic agon in which the authority of a given person is contingent on their capacity to constitute a community of judgement.[12] Perhaps the simplest way of expressing the distinction between Kant and Nietzsche, to summarise the above, is to say that Kant provides a rule which grounds our dignity in our *being what we are* and seeks to legislate the form of our actions as rational agents, while Nietzsche provides a rule which grounds our dignity in our *becoming what we are* and seeks to legislate the form of our agency. Thus, the difference between Kant and Nietzsche is not that Kant provides a ground for dignity which Nietzsche's account lacks, but that each provides a different account of what constitutes the dignity of persons and Nietzsche's account, unlike that provided by Kant, is capable of embracing difference (this should not surprise us since Kant's moral reflections seek to abstract from the bodily and situated character of agency, whereas Nietzsche's thought seeks to embrace the embodied and contextual character of agency).[13] Consequently, to return to our opening question concerning the conceptions of the political disclosed by these moral and extramoral stances, we can note that, for Kant, the political is the (site of) consensus of sameness (insofar as we are our true, rational – noumenal – selves, we are identical), while, for Nietzsche, the political is the (site of) contest of difference. Kant identifies the political with the moral which exhibits itself in the idea of a kingdom of ends characterised by the equal authority of persons, whereas Nietzsche identifies the political with the extra-moral which manifests itself in the idea of an *agora* of ends characterised by an order of rank (authority). If these are the notions of the political as moral and extra-moral revealed by the *saying* of Kant and Nietzsche as political thinkers, the question remains as to the notions of the political disclosed by their *showing*. To address this topic, we need to turn to the questions of the status and authority of the categorical imperative and the thought of eternal recurrence.

For Kant, the categorical imperative is the maxim through which the moral law of freedom which governs the noumenal realm is rendered comprehensible; it is the synthetic a priori judgement of practical reason. As such the status of the categorical imperative is unambiguous, it is a transcendent command, it knows no boundaries in time or space (which are simply forms of intuition), and presents us with a determinate standard for judging moral conduct.[14] For Nietzsche, by contrast, the doctrine of eternal recurrence is a very specific imperative addressed to the needs of a culture plunged into nihilism. To explicate this point, we must return to the first essay of *On the Genealogy of Morals* in which Nietzsche argues that the ability of the nobles to affirm the relationship between themselves and the sensuous world is predicated on the *pathos of distance* by which Nietzsche refers to that capacity for goal-directed agency constituted through the pre-reflective internalisation of social distance (i.e. the social order of rank). It is to this which Nietzsche refers when he comments that 'a concept denoting political superiority always resolves itself into a concept denoting superiority of the soul' (Nietzsche, 1969 I §6). The inability of the slaves to affirm the relationship between themselves and the world is similarly

grounded in their lack of distance; it is this which motivates the slave-revolt in morality as the construction of a *metaphysical distance* which enables the slaves to experience themselves as goal-directed agents. The dilemma posed for modern agency by nihilism involves the recognition that, on the one hand, the capacity for reflective engagement with the world bred under the aegis of Christian asceticism rules out the possibility of constituting the pathos of distance through the unreflective internalisation of social distance and, on the other hand, the self-undermining of the will to truth characteristic of Christian asceticism entails that the pathos of distance can no longer be constituted by reference to metaphysical distance. It is in this context that we can grasp the doctrine of eternal recurrence as an attempt to constitute the pathos of distance through the reflective construction of artistic distance. Consider for a moment the following passage:

The greatest weight. What, if some day or night a demon were to steal after you into your loneliest loneliness and say to you: 'This life as you now live it and have lived it, you will have to live once more and innumerable times more; and there will be nothing new in it, but every pain and every joy and every thought and sigh and everything unutterably small or great in your life will have to return to you, all in the same succession and sequence – even this spider and this moonlight between the trees, and even this moment and I myself. The eternal hourglass of existence is turned upside down again and again, and you with it, speck of dust! (Nietzsche, 1974 §341)

Having set the scene, Nietzsche poses the question of how well-disposed one would have to be to affirm the eternal recurrence of one's life. What is noticeable about this doc-

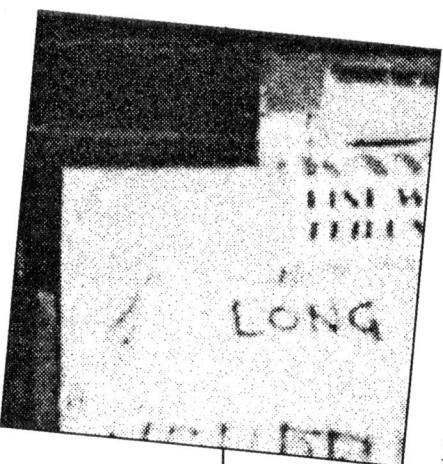

trine as it is expressed in this passage is that it presents the idea of one's life as potentially exhibiting the self-referential structure of a work of art in which parts and whole are insepa-rably entwined such that to (desire to) alter a single moment is to (desire to) alter the whole. Thus, Nietzsche presents the idea of eternal recurrence as a reflective rule through which to constitute artistic distance and it is this *artistic distance* which reconstitutes the pathos of distance requisite to the formation of autonomous goal-directed agency (we should also stress that artistic distance, like social distance but in contrast to metaphysical distance, involves the affirmation of the relationship of self and sensuous world of becoming characteristic of noble morality). In contrast to Kant's timeless injunction to will that maxim which we could at the same time will as universal law, then, Nietzsche presents us with a culturally and historically specific imperative designed to facilitate our overcoming of nihilism and our formation of ourselves as autonomous agents.

Moreover, we can continue by noting that whereas the categorical imperative presents us with a determinate rule, the doctrine of eternal recurrence is a reflective rule whose status is tied to that of the perspective of Herr Nietzsche and the diagnosis of nihilism disclosed by this perspective. In other words, whereas the authority of the categorical imperative is grounded in the transcendental subject presupposed by every person who acts rationally, the authority of the doctrine of eternal recur-rence is grounded in the affective community constituted by Nietzsche's writings. Consequently, we can conclude our reflections on the status of the categorical impera-tive and the doctrine of eternal recurrence by stating that the former presents itself as a transcendent command whose authority is a necessary presupposition of rational agency, while the latter presents itself as a historically and culturally specific imperative whose authority is grounded in the 'community of judgement' formed by Nietzsche's genealogi-cal portrayal of our modernity as nihilism.

If we reflect on these points concerning the status and authority of the categorical imperative and the thought of eternal recur-rence in terms of the ideas of the political they exemplify, we can note that Kant pre-sents us with a conception of the political as the timeless site of a single universal author-ity to which all are subject, whereas Nietzsche offers an understanding of the political as the historically and culturally shifting site of the contest of multiple author-ities. Moreover, if we relate these reflections on the idea of the political *shown* by Kant and Nietzsche to our early reflections on their *saying*, it is apparent that Kant's polit-ical moralism reveals itself to be caught between an understanding of the political as the site of the consensus of equal authorities and as the site of obedience to a single tran-scendent authority[15], whereas Nietzsche's notion of the political as the site of contest, as *agon*, is common to his saying and show-ing. The significance of the mutuality of

agonal thought

Nietzsche's *saying* and *showing* is that his texts serve as exemplary instances of the agonal politics which they seek to elaborate.

nietzsche's contest

On the reading offered in this paper, Nietzsche's thinking is thoroughly political insofar as it exemplifies his understanding of the political as contest. Nietzsche's perspectivism, for example, is not simply a response to Kantian epistemology; it is an exemplification of the noble ethic and the agonistic ethos which characterises Nietzsche's understanding of the political as the site of contest of difference. Thus, Nietzsche cannot (and does not) claim any a priori privilege for his voice; as the quotation which opens this paper reveals, Nietzsche accepts the self-referential implications of his position. On the interpretation I have sought to elaborate, an interpretation which recognises and accepts itself as one intervention within the *agon* of Nietzsche-interpretation, Nietzsche's political thought is both modest – it does not command us to ignore other voices and listen to its song alone – and provocative – it calls for our attention and seeks to disclose a world to us. In other words, insofar as Nietzsche's work has authority, it is because we endow it with this authority. Here a comment of Max Weber's is appropriate:

> [T]he values to which the scientific genius relates the object of inquiry may determine, i.e., decide the 'conception' of a whole epoch, not only concerning what is 'valuable' but also concerning what is significant or insignificant, 'important' or 'unimportant' in the phenomena. (Weber, 1949: 82)

If we live in a Nietzschean age, it is because the charisma of Nietzsche's thought, his portrayal of our modernity as nihilism, draws us into his evaluations of ourselves and our contemporary condition. Yet Nietzsche's thought in recognising the contingency of its own reflective judgement also calls on us in a further sense – Nietzsche calls on us to contest with him, to struggle and quarrel and argue; he calls on us to enter the arena. As Zarathustra remarks to his disciples:

> *I now go away alone, my disciples! You too now go away and be alone! So I will have it.*
>
> *Truly, I advise you: go away from me and guard yourselves against Zarathustra! And better still: be ashamed of him! Perhaps he has deceived you.*
>
> *The man of knowledge must be able not only to love his enemies but also to hate his friends.*
>
> *One repays a teacher badly if one remains only a pupil. And why, then, should you not pluck at my laurels?*
>
> *You respect me; but how if one day your respect should tumble? Take care that a falling statue does not strike you dead!*
>
> *You say you believe in Zarathustra? But of what importance is Zarathustra? You are my believers: but of what importance are all believers?*
>
> *You had not yet sought yourselves when you found me. Thus do all believers; therefore all belief is of so little account.*
>
> *Now I bid you lose me and find yourselves; and only when you have all denied me will I return to you.* [16]
> (Nietzsche, 1961 I 'Of the Bestowing Virtue')

notes

I would like to thank Keith Ansell-Pearson, Samantha Ashenden, Charlie Blake, Howard Caygill and Joanna Hodge for their comments on an earlier draft of this paper.

1 A brief but interesting discussion of these prior appropriations of Nietzsche is given in Hinton Thomas (1983).

2 This contrast between the poetic and legislative modes is explored more fully in Owen (1993).

3 I am grateful to Tracy Strong for this phrase.

4 A contemporary version of such an argument generalised to apply to all Nietzschean positions is presented by Habermas (1987).

5 This is the position taken up by Lukács (1979).

6 This stance is exhibited in Kaufmann (1974).

7 This case is made in Ansell-Pearson (1990).

8 This stance is elaborated in Warren (1988).

9 Derrida (1979) offers an example of this strategy of reading.

10 An interesting elaboration of this reconstituting of objectivity which has influenced my own reading is Conway (1993).

11 I use this distinction between saying and showing in a straightforwardly Wittgensteinian sense.

12 A similar claim to this is made by Strong (1989).

13 The question of the embodied and contextual character of agency has been of central concern to recent feminist theorists such as Iris Marion Young, (Young, 1987). This topic is taken up with respect to Nietzsche and feminism in Conway (1993) and Owen (1993).

14 For a consideration of Kant's political thought, see Riley (1982).
    Kant's clearest elaboration of the categorical imperative can be found in Groundwork of the Metaphysic of Morals.

david owen

15 It should be noted that I do not address the question of Kant's third Critique in this essay and it might reasonably be pointed out that the reflective/determinate judgement distinction which I deploy is drawn precisely from Kant's Critique of Judgement. This observation deconstructs the Kant/Nietzsche distinction presented here and reconstructs Nietzsche as rewriting the Critique of Judgement. I am grateful to Howard Caygill and Keith Ansell-Pearson for bringing this to my attention.

16 Zarathustra's comment concerning falling statues seems particularly appropriate to much of the angst-ridden interpretation concerning the relation of Nietzsche and, more recently, of Heidegger to Nazism.

references

Ansell-Pearson, Keith 'Nietzsche the Rebel', The Jewish Quarterly, 139 (1990) p27-32.

Ansell-Pearson, Keith Nietzsche Contra Rousseau (Cambridge: CUP, 1991).

Connolly, William The Augustinian Imperative (London: Sage, 1993).

Conway, Daniel 'Das Weib an sich: The Slave Revolt in Epistemology' in Nietzsche, Feminism and Political Theory, ed. P. Patton (London: Routledge, 1993) p110-129.

Derrida, Jacques Spurs. Nietzsche's Styles, tr. B. Harlow (Chicago: Chicago University Press, 1979).

Habermas, Jürgen The Philosophical Discourse of Modernity (Cambridge: Polity, 1987).

Hinton Thomas, Richard Nietzsche in German Politics and Society 1890–1918 (Manchester: Manchester University Press, 1983).

Kant, Immanuel Groundwork of the Metaphysic of Morals, tr. H.J. Paton (New York: Harper and Row, 1964).

Kaufmann, Walter Nietzsche. Philosopher, Psychologist

and Antichrist (New Jersey: Princeton University Press, 1974, 4th ed.).

Lukács, Georg *The Destruction of Reason* (London: Merlin Press, 1979).

Nietzsche, Friedrich *Beyond Good and Evil*, tr. R.J. Hollingdale (Middlesex: Penguin, 1973).

Nietzsche, Friedrich 'On the Genealogy of Morals' in *On the Genealogy of Morals/Ecce Homo*, tr. W. Kaufmann & R.J. Hollingdale (New York: Random House, 1969).

Nietzsche, Friedrich *The Gay Science*, tr. W. Kaufmann (New York: Random House, 1974).

Nietzsche, Friedrich *Thus Spoke Zarathustra*, tr. R.J. Hollingdale (Middlesex: Penguin, 1961).

Owen, David 'Nietzsche's Squandered Seductions: "Woman", the Body and the Politics of Genealogy' in *The Fate of the New Nietzsche*, eds K. Ansell-Pearson and H. Caygill (London: Avebury Press, 1993).

Riley, Patrick *Will and Political Legitimacy* (Cambridge, Mass.: Harvard University Press, 1982).

Strong, Tracey 'Nietzsche's Political Aesthetics' in *Nietzsche's New Seas*, eds M.A. Gillespie and T.B. Strong (Chicago: Chicago University Press, 1989) p153-74.

Warren, Mark *Nietzsche and Political Thought* (Cambridge, Mass.: MIT Press, 1988).

Weber, Max *The Methodology of the Social Sciences*, tr. E.A. Shils & H.A. Finch (Glencoe, Ill.: The Free Press, 1949).

Young, Iris 'Impartiality and the Civic Public' in *Feminism as Critique*, eds D. Cornell and S. Benhabib (Cambridge: Polity, 1987) p56-76.

I

Rorty's work is significant in its attempt to recover some of the strongest arguments in a rather neglected strand of Anglo-American philosophy – arguments dealing with the central issues of modern philosophy. He returns, in particular, to the work of Charles Peirce, William James, and John Dewey, who developed the school of thought known as pragmatism. For Rorty, a reconsideration of the work of this school is one way of coming to see the error of the 'gradual return [in the last two decades] to systematic attempts to solve traditional [philosophical] problems' (Rorty, 1991: 3). The attempt to solve these traditional problems involves looking for a foundational theory, securing, in the first instance, our claim to knowledge. Taking the work of Michael Dummett as representative, Rorty notes Dummett's insistence that philosophy identify a foundation in something transcending the contingencies of our discourse and our set of practices (1991: 3), and, following this programme through, Rorty notes his attempt to identify how statements can be said to be 'determinately true or false independently of our knowledge or our means of knowing' (1991: 145). Pragmatism has, since Peirce's work first appeared in 1868, generally supported a form of anti-foundationalism (although Peirce, for one, was not entirely consistent in this respect (cf. Habermas, 1987a, chapter VI)). Rorty draws upon this to identify the questionable assumptions made by modern forms of foundationalism, borrowing very selectively from Peirce, James, and Dewey.

In what follows I will try to give a sympathetic presentation of Rorty's reconstruc-

michael reid

RORTY'S PRAGMATISM
argument and experience

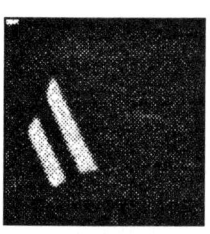

tion of a consistently anti-foundationalist pragmatism. My criticism concerns the way in which Rorty's pragmatism leaves us with the idea of apparently free-floating language games. The problem does not concern the loss of metaphysical realism (the loss of the idea that our discourse grasps things as they are in themselves independently of our contingent ways of talking about them). The problem concerns the relationship between language, or more specifically, theory, and experience. This problem goes back at least to Kierkegaard's complaint that the predominant notion of truth has become divorced from a passionate engagement with things in the world, setting up a split between argument and lived-experience – between facts and values, the latter being categorised as merely subjective. However, to support my discussion of the link between argument and experience I will refer not to Kierkegaard but to Adorno.

The problem with the content of Rorty's pragmatism is also evident in the form of his work. A striking feature of both Rorty's writing and his oral presentations is their detached and rather irreverent tone. Reading his articles one is struck by what he himself describes as the 'air of light-minded aestheticism' he adopts towards traditional philosophical questions (Rorty, 1991: 193). In *Philosophy and the Mirror of Nature* he makes the history of Western metaphysics sound as if it rested on nothing more than an unfortunate choice of metaphors, rather than upon something historically more substantial. He writes as if all philosophical problems boil down to a conflict of metaphors. Thinking about this trivialisation we might recall the manner of Rorty's oral presentations, and his manner of responding to questions from passionate students. Listening to him, one is likely to be struck by the ease with which he shrugs his shoulders. The gesture has a certain stiffness, a certain tiredness, and yet it would like to be carefree. The shrug aims to brush off questions from earnest students concerned about an emphatic notion of truth – questions from students concerned that there is something in the world that we need to take seriously and respond to. The shrug accompanies repeated affirmations of the Jamesian notion of truth as what is 'expedient in our way of thinking' (Rorty, 1991: 127). It is part of a rhetoric aimed at making it seem as if we should rest content with an instrumental notion of rationality and with an idea of discourse as a playful weaving and re-weaving of sets of beliefs. The objection that needs to be raised concerns the way in which Rorty appears to close our discourse off from anything that might call for a response. The latter would be something that we could not be ironic about. Rorty, however, sees no limit to what we can or should be ironic about since 'anything can

be made to look good or bad by being redescribed' (Rorty, 1989: 73). The shrug of Rorty's shoulders and his affectation of a light-minded aestheticism are animated by this idea.

Rorty insists that the 'air of light-minded aestheticism' he adopts toward traditional philosophical questions has a moral purpose behind it:

> Like the rise of large market economies, the increase in literacy, the proliferation of artistic genres, and the insouciant pluralism of contemporary culture, such philosophical superficiality and light-mindedness helps along the disenchantment of the world. It helps make the world's inhabitants more pragmatic, more tolerant, more liberal, more receptive to the appeal of instrumental rationality...
>
> ... Moral commitment, after all, does not require taking seriously all the matters that are, for moral reasons, taken seriously by one's fellow citizens. It may require just the opposite. It may require trying to josh them out of the habit of taking those topics so seriously. (Rorty, 1991: 193)

We do not have to have a pathological aversion to being playful to feel bound to take issue with Rorty's expressed moral purpose. We do not need to take up a stance against all forms of levity. The problem does not concern levity in general; it concerns the levity evident in Rorty's approach to the problem of truth, or the way in which Rorty takes irony to be disclosive of the 'true' status of all our beliefs. His pragmatism aims to persuade us to drop an emphatic notion of truth, and, although Rorty does not put the matter in these terms, that emphatic notion includes the idea of something that calls for us to think, something that requires a response from us, requiring that we take it seriously. The emphatic notion of truth that needs to be defended is one referring to a level of experience, a response to the world that engages our thinking by disclosing something that needs to be thought about and articulated. What I want to take issue with in this paper is the systematic exclusion of this experiential engagement by Rorty's treatment of traditional epistemological problems. A lot of what he has to say against traditional attempts in philosophy to come up with a metaphysical support for our claims to knowledge hits the mark. However, his positive position leaves our 'language games' disturbingly idle, closed off from what could engage and call forth our thinking.

II

In his reconstruction of the pragmatist position, Rorty's overriding philosophical concern involves trying to get us to drop the ideas of knowledge as representation, and truth as correspondence. In other words, he wants to persuade us to drop the traditional philosophical interest in metaphysical realism – the interest in arguing that one particular way of thinking about things corresponds to the way things are in themselves. Often the interest in vindicating a metaphysically realist position is a response to a scepticism about the ability of our beliefs to 'hook up' to a mind-independent reality. If we take such scepticism seriously we will end up trying to assuage the fear of error by trying to vindicate a form of metaphysical realism. Modern epistemology – the project at the centre of modern, post-Cartesian philosophy – takes the problem posed by the sceptic seriously, and it tries to argue that our thoughts do connect up somehow with a reality independent of our thinking. Cartesian rationalism, for instance, resorted to a story about God to establish the veracity of our

foundational intuitions; and Lockean empiricism relied upon the idea of unmediated sensory inputs from an external world.

Rorty, in common with many others, thinks that, instead of trying to solve the sceptic's problem we should try to dissolve it. Rather than accept the problem as set up by the sceptic we must question its assumptions. Scepticism is not innocent. It makes some very question-begging assumptions. It assumes, for instance, that knowing is something that must be achieved by minds standing quite apart from reality. Furthermore, it assumes that the cognitive relation is something entirely independent of any prior practical interest. Cognition is assumed to be the achievement of a purified, disembodied, asocial, and contemplative intellect. It assumes what has been called a spectator theory of knowledge (Quinton, 1977). The pragmatist critique of this view of knowledge recalls the dependence of our cognitive relation upon a prior practical interest in the things around us. Peirce's reflections upon natural science, (leaving aside his relapse into Scholastic realism), recall the way in which the objectification of reality under its scientific description is grounded in the behavioural system of instrumental action. As Habermas puts it, that behavioural system is 'the transcendental framework which establishes the conditions of objectivity of possible statements about the real' (Habermas, 1987a: 126). In other words, the categories of natural science only make sense, and only appear to be valid, in relation to the experimental situation – the situation in which predictions are tested and singular events are taken to represent universal effects. It is only because we engage practically with our world in this way that it makes sense for us to theoretically construe reality in terms of universal causal laws. The important point here is that the cognitive relation is contingent upon a prior practical objectification of our world. At the forefront of pragmatism is this notion of the priority of our practical concerns.

Rorty, following Dewey, suggests that we see 'beliefs as adaptations to the environment rather than quasi-pictures' (Rorty, 1991: 10). This completely undermines the way in which the sceptic sets up the problem of knowledge. Once we recall the behavioural system that grounds the way in which we theoretically construe reality 'there is no room for the sort of wholesale slippage between organism and environment which the Cartesian notion of "inner representation of the environment" is capable of producing' (ibid., 10). Once we recall the broader context of practices that situate us in the world we lose the idea of a radical disjunction between our ideas about the world and the way the world is.

On the pragmatist account, reality is always something objectified by our practices, i.e. something objectified under a description determined by those practices. Those practices determine what we see things as – they determine the 'as' of perception. If a sceptic were to ask again whether the way we see things corresponds to what they are in themselves, we would reply that we cannot make sense of that notion of a thing in itself, at least as a possible object of knowledge. If knowledge is only possible for us in a context of practices that make it appear valid for us to objectify reality in one way rather than another, we cannot make sense of the idea of knowing something purely and simply as it is in itself. Again, instead of trying to answer the sceptic, attempting to meet the demand for metaphysical realism, we dissolve the problem. The re-description of the phenomenon of knowledge attempts to undermine, firstly, the sceptic's assumption that knowledge would be something achieved by a disem-

bodied contemplative intellect, and, secondly, the project of trying to abstract ourselves in thought from our practices to get a grip on things as they are in themselves. Hence Rorty's suggestion that 'questions which we should have to climb out of our own minds [or, rather, practices] to answer should not be asked' (Rorty, 1991: 7). Instead of trying to argue that our knowledge corresponds to a metaphysically real state of affairs, we need to reflect upon what makes it valid for us to objectify reality in one way rather than another. Such a reflection would have to comprehend the practical context in terms of which it makes sense for us to 'see' things under a certain description.

Instead of trying to get outside of our practices one might try, following Kant, to work from within them to come up with a transcendental ground for some particular set of categories. Dropping the idea of transcendental or metaphysical realism, Kant, in his first Critique, sought to establish the universal validity of the particular set of categories employed by modern science. He tried to argue that those categories were necessary for any knowledge of reality (an empirical reality which is, for Kant, transcendentally ideal since the categories and their schematism are intellectual constructs and not the things themselves). Rorty's version of pragmatism, however, implies that Kant failed to establish that there was any necessity involved in our employment of one particular set of categories or one manner of schematising them. Kant established that our cognitive activity must always assume some particular set of categories, but he did not establish that only one set was valid. There are different ways of objectifying reality, the validity of which is contingent upon a prior practical orientation to our world. If this is so we must drop the idea that our particular way of looking at things – of disclosing things – has some universally valid basis, or some claim to objectivity transcending the contingencies of our particular set of practices. Although 'we must, in practice, privilege our own group ... there can be no non-circular justification for doing so' (Rorty, 1991: 29).

The argument against Kant would be continuous with the argument Rorty uses against Descartes. He refers to 'the Cartesian fallacy of seeing axioms where there are only shared habits, of viewing statements which summarise practices as if they reported constraints enforcing such practices' (Rorty, 1991: 26). The Cartesian assumes that purely intellectual categories necessitate one particular way of relating to reality. Kant's addition of the schematism does not significantly alter this assumption. Kant still assumed that our theoretical construal of reality could be dealt with independently of our practical situation. The Rortian pragmatist recalls that it is only because we have a prior set of practical involvements with things in our world that it makes sense for us to talk about reality in one way rather than another.

III

Up to this point, Rorty's version of pragmatism seems to me to be defensible. What I want to take issue with is what Rorty has to say about experience in relation to the notion of truth. Although he does not discuss this at length, he deals with it in his critique of the ideas of truth as correspondence and of knowledge as representation.

As noted, his approach to these ideas involves persuading us to give up the idea of our beliefs as pictures of a problematically mind-independent reality. Re-interpreting beliefs as ways of coping with reality, and recovering the priority of practice, the fear of radical slippage between thought and being, so crucial for scepticism, need not arise. The problem that remains, however, concerns Rorty's instrumentalisation of our practical engagements. He one-sidedly emphasises the activity through which we determine the way in which we construe reality. Hence the ease with which Rorty can begin to talk about irony in terms of the 'realisation that anything can be made to look good or bad by being redescribed' (Rorty, 1989: 73). What is missing here is any acknowledgment of the way in which we can be engaged by reality, being called upon to respond to our situation – an engagement that discloses something as important and as something we must address. To further define this problem we need to say more about how Rorty's pragmatism abstracts argument from experience, leaving an idle weaving and re-weaving of beliefs.

Having dropped the idea of truth as correspondence Rorty affirms the idea of truth as coherence. This requires some qualification since Rorty, at one point, refuses any theory or definition of truth. A theory would imply that there is some antecedent prescription of the way in which we should talk about reality. Rorty's 'anti-representationalist strategy' drops the idea of constructing a theory, appealing instead 'to what we do as a resolution of familiar representationalist problems' (Rorty, 1991: 156). The familiar representationalist problem in question concerns doubts about the veracity of a belief. Following Davidson, in this case, Rorty refers us back to what we actually do to establish the veracity of a belief. Here, Rorty refers us back, not to a prior behavioural system, but to the contingent structure of our language game, i.e. the way we commonly deal with mundane claims to knowledge. Rather than refer to something antecedent to which our belief might correspond, we try to back up our belief with arguments. In other words, we draw upon other beliefs. On Rorty's reading of Davidson, 'his "coherence theory" of truth says that only evidence – that is, other beliefs, as opposed to experience, sensory stimulation, or the world – can make beliefs true' (1991: 153). Irrespective of what makes it valid for us to 'see' things in one way rather than another, knowledge, on this account, has to do with argument, not experience.

As Rorty notes, the attempt to define truth in terms of the coherence of beliefs leaves room for a familiar sceptical response. It leaves room for doubts about whether any coherent set of beliefs are actually true. What Rorty suggests is that we leave 'true' unanalysed, and so take it as primitive (1991: 153). In effect, Rorty disarms the sceptic by taking the sceptical response as simply a reminder that in our set of linguistic practices 'true' has a cautionary use – the use evident in such remarks as 'Your belief may be perfectly justified, but perhaps not true' (1991: 128). This refers us back to what we do – to how we use the term 'true'. Rorty takes this sort of move to be characteristic of the pragmatism he seeks to promote. Again, this pragmatism consists 'simply in the dissolution of the traditional problematic about truth, as opposed to a constructive 'pragmatist theory of truth' (1991: 127).

Although Rorty refuses to pin down the notion of truth, he leaves us, when we are not being sceptical, establishing the truth of beliefs by referring to other beliefs. The problem here concerns the way in which beliefs, and the question of their veracity, are held apart from experience. A thin notion of discourse – our practice of talking and theorising about the world – gets lifted out of a deeper notion of our experiential involvement with the world and our being in it. The relevant notion of experience is not that of

something that is absolutely first – it is not the notion of an input from a mind-independent reality. Our experience of the world is mediated by our understanding of ourselves, which is in turn mediated by our personal history. The mediating practices will involve the use of language, and our understanding of our situation will involve a great deal of theoretical knowledge of what is going on around us. However, the experience in question is one that calls forth our thinking and which our thinking can follow as it becomes progressively more theoretically sophisticated. As something that our thinking follows it has to be acknowledged as something that our truth claims depend upon.

When we talk about our situation – about our world – the sense or the rational force, and, above all, the importance of what we say depends upon our experience – a sense of what matters and how it should be addressed. Similarly, in such talk we necessarily refer or appeal to the experience that others have or are capable of. This experience is what we try to articulate when we discuss our world, and in trying to find concepts to express it and identify what it is that actually engages us we have to acknowledge that it is not identical with those concepts. Experience, in this sense, is what our thinking aims at, but is not identical with its discursive construal. This is not experience in the sense of empirical data or something objectified in an experimental situation. It is rather our lived-experience.

Rorty would treat such a reference to experience as another slide into representationalism. His dismissive references to experience assume that it will be treated as something to which our discourse about the world will be said to correspond. If it is somehow antecedent to the relevant beliefs how can we say anything about it? It would seem to be another one of those metaphysical things that we would have to climb out of our set of linguistic practices to identify. How can it possibly make any of our beliefs true if it is only through our discursive constructs that we can say anything about it? But we can accept that our lived-experience can only become an object of knowledge for us by being worked up through the available concepts, and we can accept this while maintaining that it is our prediscursive experience that we are trying to put into words. Rorty's approach would close the world of discourse off from its relation to what is not identical to it, leaving only the intentionality of thoughts to account for the relation of language to reality (Rorty, 1991: 150).

What Rorty terms Davidson's and Wittgenstein's 'holism' involves the claim that our grasp of the meaning of what we say is entirely a function of our grasp of the inferential relationships between the sentences we are able to use (1991: 145). Rorty's pragmatism is holistic in this sense. To try to tie meaning to something given independently of those sentences is to epistemologise meaning – it is to hark back to the old subject-object dualism presupposed by the problem of epistemology. That epistemology assumed that it made sense to try to say something about reality as it is independently of our discursive construal of it. But we do not have to make that assumption when we insist that our thinking follows an experience that goes beyond, and is not identical with, any particular set of discursive constructs. We can think of the non-identical as something which our thinking follows. It is something we need to articulate. It has a

truth value insofar as it discloses a world for us which we believe to be one others can recognise. It is because of that belief that we strive to find ways of conceptualising that world. Through that conceptualising activity we are not idly solving intellectual puzzles, but trying to get to grips with something that weighs upon us. Once we acknowledge this phenomenology we can see that our reference to experience does not presuppose the sort of metaphysical subject-object dualism to which Rorty rightly objects. Our lived-experience is not something we would have to try to climb out of our language games to appreciate, rather it is something that gives to our linguistic activ-

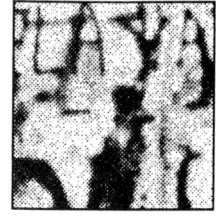

ity its urgency, import and relevance.

What is missing in Rorty's account is an acknowledgment of the expressive dimension of our cognitive activity. His account leaves us talking about the world, forgetting our ability to talk out of a particular historical situation, disclosed to us partly through our lived-experience of it. Reflecting upon his own approach to traditional problems in philosophy and social theory, Adorno insisted that '[w]e are not to philosophise about concrete things; we are to philosophise out of these things' [Nicht über Konkretes ist zu philosophieren, vielmehr aus ihm heraus] (Adorno, 1973: 33; 1982: 43). Adorno acknowledges that he writes out of, and appeals to, a spontaneous resistance to the hegemonic contemporary practices (the key practices being the extension of commodification and the development of the productive process as an end in itself, both of which exclude a non-instrumental concern for the well-being and the development of human subjects and the qualities of their worlds). Critical theory is inconceivable without an experience of the negativity of contemporary practice – the negativity of those practices which, as Habermas put it, accord authority to those steering mechanisms functioning independently of the spontaneity of human subjects (Habermas, 1987b). The systematic exclusion of that spontaneity, and its marginalisation in a politically irrelevant and increasingly pre-fabricated domestic sphere, is what Adorno chiefly reacts against.

The truth claim raised by his work relies upon an appeal to a similar felt reaction in us. 'Direct communicability to everyone is not a criterion of truth' [Kriterium des Wahren ist nicht seine unmittelbare Kommunizierbarkeit an jedermann] (Adorno, 1973: 41; 1982: 51). We do not ascertain the truth of our discourse by standing back to judge whether a consensus is developing. We have to remain in our situation and judge whether what is being said enables us to make sense of that situation. What we rely upon, and what we try to develop is an experientially grounded way of seeing things, not an experience-independent argument tailored to be vindicable by someone not already engaged by the situation to which we are trying to address ourselves. We do not do justice to the truth about that situation by identifying it with an objectifying discourse, i.e. one that systematically excludes the expressive moment. The objectivity Adorno's writing aims at 'needs not less subjectivity, but more' [bedarf ... nicht eines Weniger sondern eines Mehr an Subjekt] (Adorno, 1973: 40; 1982: 50). This would be a subjectivity not idly expressing its fancies, but passionately engaged by contemporary reality, and able to discriminate between what is and what is not important and timely. As engaged, subjectivity is not whimsical or arbitrary, even

though it remains contingent, and, perhaps, only the privilege of those who have escaped the predominant forms of social conditioning. Here, 'where the subject feels altogether sure of itself – in primary experience – it will be least subjective [or arbitrary]' [wo das Subjekt seiner selbst ganz gewiss sich fühlt, in der primären Erfahrung, ist es wiederum am wenigsten Subjekt] (Adorno, 1973: 39; 1982: 50).

At one point Adorno adds that primary experience is not the truth (1973: 40 & 50). What is at issue here is the importance of developing a reflective comprehension of the object of our experience. The primary experience is, for Adorno, an experience of the hostility of the predominant practices, i.e. their hostility with respect to the spontaneity of the subject. It is in this experience that the untruth of the prevailing system is disclosed. Although, in one sense our primary experience is not the truth, we still have to acknowledge its cognitive, its disclosive, significance. But to limit ourselves to this experience we could say nothing more than that something has gone terribly wrong. So when Adorno says that primary experience is not the truth he means that we need to conceptualise it, to comprehend discursively what has been disclosed to us. We need to develop a more reflective understanding of the prevailing practices, drawing upon some highly theoretical work. But in order not to lose sight of what is really at stake in the situation we are trying to comprehend we continue to depend upon that primary experience. Its disclosive function continues to be crucial.

Elsewhere Adorno speaks of our thinking 'following' an experience of what is at stake in our situation, of what, above all else, needs to be addressed (Adorno, 1973: 168; 1982: 170). Incidentally, this reference to our thinking following a guiding experience rules out a decisionistic interpretation of the relevant notion of engagement, differentiating Adorno's understanding from that of, for instance, Sartre. Later we read:

[T]here actually is a mental experience [geistige Erfahrung] – fallible indeed, but immediate – of the essential and the unessential, an experience which only the scientific need for order can forcibly talk the subjects out of. Where there is no such experience, knowledge stays unmoved and barren. (Adorno. 1973: 169-70; 1982: 171-2)

This experience, dependent upon our capacity for suffering and happiness, which both moves and calls forth our thinking, is the key to our ability to distinguish what is really at issue in the matter to be discussed. It guides our thinking in a way that, in part at least, helps to disclose what we need to think about – what, above all else, we should be addressing ourselves to.

Rorty's talk about the weaving and re-weaving of webs of beliefs leaves thinking idle. Thinking appears to be unmoved and barren, lacking any passionate awareness of something that needs to be said, something that needs to be put into words. Thinking appears to have gone on holiday – as so much academic philosophy appears to have done. The problem here is twofold. Firstly, Rorty's conception of knowledge is impoverished – it simply forgets what calls for and orientates thinking at its best – thinking that is, at least, not idle. Secondly, this conception of knowledge is complicit with a set of social practices that sytematically exclude the spontaneity of the subject, handing over their guidance to topic-neutral steering mechanisms. It implicitly affirms the degradation of subjectivity into something to be enjoyed in our 'free time'.

IV

There is an internal connection between Rorty's approach to the problem of truth and his political allegiance. The engagement – the sense of solidarity – that guides Rorty's work, and that grounds his defence of the status quo, is his solidarity with the 'hopes of the North Atlantic bourgeoisie' (Rorty, 1991: 198). These hopes aim at a notion of private fulfilment – a notion of the good life that depends upon a certain understanding of a split between the public and the private domains. On this interpretation the problem of meaning is to be limited to the private sphere (Rorty, 1991: 183), leaving the public sphere to be dominated by instrumentally rational considerations. This is in accordance with Rorty's avowed moral purpose of making us more 'receptive to the appeal of instrumental rationality' (1991: 193). Regarding the problem of truth, the disengagement of the realm of discourse leaves us with an idea of the extradiscursive as merely a field for the discursive constitution of theoretical objects. Of course there is more to life than theory, but as far as the question of truth is concerned Rorty's account does not acknowledge anything to which our thinking is indebted. Rorty's account of irony is particularly illuminating since it shows Rorty collapsing the real into the circuit of our descriptions, losing the moment of non-identity. The forgetting of this moment of non-identity is consistent with, and it lends support to, a rampant instrumental rationality.

Rorty's engagement is with a form of life that confines the expressive moment to the private sphere. This excludes the recognition of something that we feel called upon to respond to publicly, appealing to a public sense that something ought to be done. According to Rorty's liberalism, the expressive moment is to be confined to private acts of self-creation. Hence his refusal of the intended public significance of the works of Nietzsche, Foucault, and Derrida – all of whom were or are concerned with issues of public importance, despite the difficulty of finding a public with ears to hear what they feel needs to be said (cf. Rorty, 1991: 64-5 & 83). Rorty would leave the works of these writers as simply ports of call on our private odyssey, completely ignoring the way in which they open up matters for public discussion, matters of public significance. This is consonant with his exclusion of experience as something that can open up an issue for us, directing our theoretical activity. Confining the expressive moment in this way involves excluding our concern for the good life as a matter of public priority. Such confinement hands over the public realm to impersonal steering mechanisms and forms of instrumental rationality.

The insistence that the good life must be pursued privately pulls the shutters down tight, cutting off the possibility of a more open response to the fate of the subject in contemporary society. There is a deathly rigidity in Rorty's insistence upon the public-private split, despite his affectation of a light-minded aestheticism. The response orientating Adorno's critical theory draws upon, as he says, our capacity for happiness and suffering. We are not told simply to seek our happiness in private. We read instead of a life experienced as damaged by the practices Rorty endorses. This is a life whose capacities for happiness and suffering are engaged by what occurs within the public sphere. That engagement is cognitively significant – it registers that there is an issue here that we should address, that we should think about, understand, and address practically. It is not simply the expression of a preference – an idle emotivism. Adorno opens this matter up for discussion, if it was

not already a burning issue for us, whereas Rorty simply rules the matter out, with the blunt assertion that 'there is no way to bring self-creation together with justice at the level of theory' (Rorty, 1989: xiv).

Adorno, of course, is not trying to bring together private self-creation and justice at the level of theory. He is simply responding to the actual marginalisation and deformation of subjectivity as it is fenced into little pockets of free time – time which is increasingly organised by advertising and the leisure industry. On the basis of such a response we can begin to talk about the thinness and the meaninglessness of the sort of selfhood that Rorty sets up as his highest concern, and of the threat posed by the practices that Rorty talks of as if they did not thoroughly orchestrate the lives of individuals but simply leave them to realise their autonomy.

Rorty's confinement of any meaningful engagement to a private project of self-creation holds such engagement apart from its cognitive significance – its importance for our public discourse about what our priorities should be and how we should delimit and incorporate forms of instrumental rationality. The problem is not that Rorty fails to acknowledge that things can engage us – he does not (cf. Rorty, 1989: 37) – nor is the problem simply a matter of any lack of the 'horror of finding oneself a copy' (cf. Rorty, 1989: 29). The problem is that Rorty holds apart this account of our experience from our publicly and cognitively significant discourse, and thus from our publicly significant practice. However, for this particular paper, the most fundamental problem concerns, not the prescriptions of Rorty's reading of liberalism, but the dichotomy between argument and experience entailed by his treatment of traditional epistemology. Despite the strength of Rorty's critique of metaphysical realism, his positive position leaves the reflection upon the truth of our beliefs disconnected from a reference to our lived-experience. Without that basis in experience our thinking risks becoming idle – an unreflective parroting of the prevailing consensus – and it risks losing the ability to discriminate what really needs to be addressed.

references

Adorno, Theodor W. *Negative Dialectics*, tr. E.B. Ashton (London: RKP, 1973).

Adorno, Theodor W. *Negative Dialektik* (Frankfurt am Main: Suhrkamp Verlag, 1982).

Habermas, Jürgen *Knowledge and Human Interests* (Cambridge: Polity Press, 1987a).

Habermas, Jürgen *The Philosophical Discourse of Modernity* (Oxford: Basil Blackwell, 1987b).

Quinton, Anthony 'Inquiry, Thought, and Action: John Dewey's Theory of Knowledge' in *John Dewey Reconsidered* (London: RKP, 1977).

Rorty, Richard *Contingency, Irony, and Solidarity* (Cambridge: Cambridge University Press, 1989).

Rorty, Richard *Objectivity, Relativism, and Truth: Philosophical Papers Vol I* (Cambridge: Cambridge University Press, 1991).

To start our inquiry into the radically contingent articulation of the 'floating signifier' 'democracy', in the context of the precarious contemporary situation following the demise of Communism, we shall quote one of E. Laclau's illuminating observations. According to Laclau:

[A] signifier like 'democracy' is essentially ambiguous by dint of its widespread political circulation: it acquires one possible meaning when articulated with 'anti-fascism' and a completely different one when articulated with 'anti-communism'. (Laclau, 1990: 28)

Indeed, one is almost tempted to say that the word democracy does not have the same meaning in the West and in the East. The aim of our examination is to draw out some of the implications of this observation by way of linking the East European process of democratization with Lefort's notion of 'democratic invention'. One possible way of addressing this issue is to adopt what we might call the 'Kantian point of view'.

The past decade has been witness to a powerful resurgence of interest in Kant's later writings on politics and history, which was partly instigated by the debate between modernists and postmodernists and their conflicting interpretations of the Enlightenment. The implications of modernist and postmodernist readings of Kant's political writings are obviously too complex to be dealt with in the present paper. For our purposes it suffices to focus on one aspect of these readings: it is significant that both modernists (H. Arendt in particular)[1] and postmodernists (M. Foucault and J.-F. Lyotard)[2], describe the articulation of a political event (the French Revolution of 1789) with a theoretical one (the Enlightenment) – the articulation which marked the beginning of modern democracy

jelica sumic

rado riha

THE REINVENTION OF DEMOCRACY IN EASTERN EUROPE

– in terms of Kant's ambiguous distinction between actor and spectator. In the same way, the debate about a new definition of democracy, put on the agenda by the so-called East European 'democratic revolutions of 1989', also suggested the viewpoint of the 'spectating public' as appropriate for the assessment of the contemporary East European transformations.

To open our discussion on the relevance of the Kantian approach for analyzing political changes in Eastern Europe, it should be noted that, although the opposition between actor and spectator enjoys a growing appeal among modernists and postmodernists, it also raises a set of embarrassing questions that need to be addressed. One of the crucial questions at stake in this debate is not, as one would expect, how to create a common framework for reconciling the standpoints of actor and spectator. Rather, it is the question of justifying the primacy that both sides of debate attribute to the spectator's viewpoint. The modernists (H. Arendt, for example) ground the spectator's 'supremacy' in the autonomy and impartiality of his/her judgement. It is the spectator's external position that secures his/her impartiality, his/her 'capacity to rise above the parochial limits of local community', as D. Ingram puts it (Ingram, 1992: 119). By contrast, the postmodernists (J.-F. Lyotard in particular) insist on the idea of indeterminacy of judgement, on the irreducible conflict of standpoints, rejecting entirely the possibility of impartiality. For postmodernists, the very notion of impartiality is erroneous as it is grounded in a highly questionable assumption of a universal community of rational agents aiming at the attainment of rational agreement.

Clearly, the postmodernist critique of the modernist universal ideal of rational community, in which the modernist model of the spectator's judgement is grounded, provides some salient points. Still, the rejection of the modernist model does not in itself account for the postmodernist conception of the spectator's viewpoint, as we shall demonstrate presently. It does suggest, however, that, contrary to modernists, postmodernists do not base the primacy of the spectator's standpoint in his/her *better* insight into an event.

We believe that the best starting-point for addressing the postmodernist conception of the spectator's primacy is provided by Foucault's reading of Kant's essay *Conflict of the Faculties*. Following Foucault's reading we wish to focus principally on disturbing aspects of the above-mentioned primacy.

As is well known, Foucault pays most attention to the fact that for Kant the French Revolution only acquired the significance of a *historical event* as a result of the way the 'uninvolved public, looking on' perceived it (Kant, 1979: 157). A public which openly

supported the revolutionary events, but did not directly participate in them, indeed followed them 'without the least intention of assisting' (Kant, 1979: 157). According to Foucault, Kant's reflections on the French Revolution teach us that in history it is not the so-called 'great' historical events themselves that are significant, but something quite different, which at first sight is of only secondary importance: the enthusiasm with which the public responded to them. The 'wishful participation that border[ed] closely on enthusiasm' (Kant, 1979: 153) indicates, according to Foucault, that what was happening in the 'heads' of spectators, the 'way the revolution was depicted' (Foucault, 1984: 37) was much more important than the noisy revolutionary drama itself.

Foucault's interpretation of Kant therefore suggests to us that a judgement as to the historicity of actual events is not made by those *immediately involved in* the events – who experience them *from within* – but by mere 'spectators', those who have an *external relationship* to events. From the 'Kantian point of view' the history-creating act, which gives actual events their 'true' significance, is not 'active' involvement; it is, rather, a subsequent, 'passive' interpretation of events, an interpretation which is entirely external to and contingent upon events.

In an attempt to explain the primacy of the spectator's standpoint we could say that, for Foucault and modernists likewise, it is the spectator's exclusion from events which justifies it. Yet, having both accepted the exteriority as crucial, they remain devided in their respective efforts to account for it. Whereas the modernists perceive the exteriority of the spectator's position as guarantee of *better* insight into the events, it would be misleading if not false to maintain the same of Foucault. It would be misleading for two reasons. Firstly, the assumption of a better insight involves a comparison, which in turn presupposes a common ground and criteria for comparing different, conflicting interpretations of an event, which is probably irreconcilable with Foucault's understanding of the genealogy and overdetermination of an 'episteme'. Secondly, by privileging the epistemological dimension over the ethical one, this interpretation of the spectator's primacy distorts the real issue of Foucault's reading.

The issue at stake here is that, irrespective of the adequacy of the insight in an event, the historicity, the true meaning of an event, depends entirely on the spectator's judgement. However, this thesis could be upheld only if we assume that, for Foucault, the role of the spectator is to confer the meaning of an event, even though the event taking place may appear at first sight as messy and meaningless. In Lacanian terms we could say that, for Foucault, the function of the spectator is to transform chaotic, 'lawless' events into a 'lawlike', orderly sequence of symbolic reality.

To explain this spectator's role, we may find the Lacanian matrix of the intersubjective communication helpful. Slightly accommodating it for our purposes, we could say that the spectator is assigned the task to decide the true significance of an event only if s/he is identified with the 'guarantor of meaning', in short, only if the spectator is situated in the role of the Other. Clearly, the spectator's duty, seen from the Lacanian perspective, that is, as 'responsibility' for conferring the historic meaning retroactively upon the event, for reintegrating it into the symbolic reality, is not grounded in his/her effective capacities but in the paradoxical, self-reflexive signifying structure.

According to Lacan, one of the crucial features of a signifying structure is the retroactive presupposition of meaning. In the context of a signifying structure the meaning is always already there. Moreover, it is embodied in a specific subjectal position: the 'subject supposed to know'. The primacy of the spectator's standpoint, perceived as a position that incarnates the very possibility of meaning, is therefore one of the possible interpretations of the 'subject supposed to know'.

This situating of the spectator in the role of the 'subject supposed to know' – due to his/her 'detached', 'passive' attitude towards actual events – might well in itself be indisputable. However, we shall focus on its problematic aspects, as we shall explain in three steps.

Regarding the East European reinvention of democracy, it is no doubt tempting to adopt this position of the spectator-judge. Instead of trying either to justify or to reject it, we shall start by examining what implications can be drawn from positioning the Western 'spectators' in the role of the 'subject supposed to decide' the true historical significance of the East European 'revolutions'.

Second, on the level of the emergence of nationalism, a constitutive element of the new East European reality, we shall investigate a variety of ways in which the spectacle of nationalism involves the mere 'spectator' of the event and corrupts his/her impartial, detached attitude.

Third, we acknowledge the merits of 'the Kantian and/or Foucauldian approach' and accept fully its clearly subversive impact on the traditionally conceived oppositions: inside-outside, interpretation-action, passivity-activity. Yet, we shall try to show its limits. We believe – and this is the basic assumption of our investigation – that one essential element of the East European democratic reinvention nonetheless remains beyond the grasp of what we propose to call the 'Kantian-Foucauldian point of view'. This element is, in our view, constitutive of both the event and its interpretation. In addition, it is an element which, by definition, remains either suppressed or overlooked. On the level of the history-creating act we situate this overlooked constitutive element in the blind spot of the interpretation, as it is embodied in the subject of the enunciation. On the level of the process of democratization, we locate this suppressed constitutive element in the nonsymbolized, in fact, unsymbolizable radical particularity. To expose this blind spot and to excavate this 'kernel of the real', which is another name of the radical, irreducible particularity, we shall turn for help to Lacanian psychoanalysis.

Let us examine first the explanatory force of the 'Kantian-Foucauldian' opposition 'actor-spectator' in the context of the East European democratic reinvention. The profound political and social changes in the East were, at first sight, clearly the work of those who were actively involved in them, the East European *actors*. That this was the case is evidenced not least by the surprise, bordering on consternation, with which the Western 'audience' greeted the collapse of 'really existing socialism'. The active role of East Europeans in, on the one hand, the dismantling of 'really existing socialism' and, on the other, the reconstruction of democracy, was obvious from the beginning. Much less clear, however, was whether their activity, for all its undisputed impact on current political relationships in Europe, and indeed throughout the world, *constituted a significant novelty*. To put it differently, the East European democratic reinvention was supported right across the political spec-

trum. But despite this fascination, this 'wishful participation', there was an unease in the political and intellectual response of the West to this transformation: quietly harboured doubts as to whether the events in Eastern Europe were *historical* in the true sense of the word, whether they constituted *truly new historical events*.[3]

This unease was elaborated in an article by F. Furet, published in the magazine *Le Débat* at the end of 1990. Furet's answer to the question of the historicity of the East European revolutions, that is, whether they were historically new events, consists of – somewhat simplified – two theses. What was most striking about the collapse of 'really existing socialism', he writes, was its speed and the fact that it could not have been predicted. 'If the collapse had been better anticipated it would not have undermined our analytical habits and political schemata in the way that it did' (Furet, 1990: 265). But – and this is Furet's first thesis – there was something else that was really surprising, indeed quite enigmatic, about the collapse of Communism: that, as it were, Communism dissolved – before our eyes – *into nothing*. After having existed for seventy years it will apparently leave nothing behind: no positive legacy, 'no institutions, principles or traditions, not even a history' (Furet, 1990: 168).

This brings Furet to his second thesis. However many forms the disintegration of Communism took in the various states of the former Communist bloc, in each state one essential element was present: a regressive historical movement, a movement backwards to ideas, practices and institutions which once constituted the starting-point of Western democracy. 'It appears', writes Furet:

[T]hat nothing positive or even usable will survive the historical Communist experience. Not one idea or law has remained. The peoples who have been through the Communist historical experience seem to be obsessed with completely negating the system in which they lived; obsessed, that is, with a passion for restoration: the restoration of the constitutional state; the restoration of freedom; the restoration of elections; the restoration of private property; and the restoration of the free market economy. (Furet, 1990: 169)

To summarize: insofar as the process of social and political transformation in Eastern Europe is characterized by two basic elements – a rejection of Communism and a turning towards the achievements of the Western democratic invention – then the result of this process can be described as a *double void*. On the one hand the massive structure of the 'Communist invention' – its state apparatuses, ideological practices and daily rituals – dissolved into *nothingness*. On the other hand the whole East European thrust towards democracy appears to be an *empty repetition* of an earlier historical experience, a sort of return from the dead end of history to the historical 'mainstream': that is, an unhistorical experience *par excellence*.[4]

It is against the background of this double void – which appears to be the first original achievement of the East European democratic reinvention – that we can understand the unease these changes have occasionally aroused in the 'visitor from the West'. This unease can be regarded as an initial indication of the fact that in the 'revolutions of 1989' – as in the case of the French Revolution – the historical significance of the actual events did not lie in the misery and splendour of the 'revolutionary spectacle' itself, but in the way in which it was perceived by mere 'spectators'. In the 'revolu-

tions of 1989' the historicity of the events obviously also had to be determined from the viewpoint of the Western 'spectators', or 'visitors', who followed these events with undisguised excitement, almost enthusiasm, 'without the least intention of assisting'.

We would like now to turn to close examination of the following question: What was the object of the Western fascination? The answer to this question is – because of its self-reflexive structure – rather complex. The revolutions of 1989 exerted attraction for the fascinated Western gaze to the extent to which the Western spectator recognized their truth to be a return to the origins of democratic experience, that is, to the extent to which these events were seen to constitute an answer – *one already realized* in the West – to the fundamental question of democracy. The West thus saw in the East the confirmation of its own truth. But it saw its own truth in a very specific way.

What fascinated the West was by no means the simple return to democratic ideas and institutions.[5] The West is only too familiar with all the failings and dead ends of 'really existing' liberal democracy to be fascinated by it. Rather, in his spontaneous ideology, the attitude of the Western spectator towards some of the legal, social and political aspects of the democratic welfare state is ironic, even cynical. The object of the West's fascinated gaze was thus not the reinvention of democracy as such. Rather, what really fascinated Western 'spectators' was the imputed fascination of the East European actors with – their naive belief in – Western democracy. By means of this imputed fascination of the East Europeans with democracy, the Western spectator was thus able to see the truth of

the reinvention of democracy
in eastern europe

democracy in its 'pure' form, free of distort-
ing empirical circumstances, disillusions and
mistakes. In other words, having been a witness to the re-birth of democracy in the East,
the West could, as it were, return to the
unsullied origins of democracy.

At first sight, therefore, the 'revolutions
of 1989' seem to confirm the Kantian-
Foucauldian thesis maintaining that the historicity of an event lies in its subsequent
interpretation. But if we examine somewhat
more closely the issues which the 'democratic revolutions of 1989' give rise to, it quickly becomes apparent that the question, to
whom the historical truth of the event
belongs – to the actors involved in it or to
the spectators observing it from a distance;
to the internal or to the external standpoint
– remains undecided.

To address the problem of this undecidability which, in our view, is not contingent,
on the contrary, it is grounded in the very
structure of 'two mutually fascinated gazes',
to use Žižek's term (Žižek, 1990: 20), we
need to pay closer attention to the complexity of the Western spectator's response to
the East European democratic reinvention.

At a certain stage of the East European
democratic revolutions, mostly at the point
when they seemed to have been successfully
completed, the mutual interplay of fascinated gazes was unpleasantly interrupted. The
initially harmonious picture of the Eastern
democratic reinvention was gradually
replaced by a new reality in the former
Communist states: nationalist populism,
xenophobia and racism on the one hand; a
decline in democratic political practices, tolerance and liberal political culture on the
other. It is not surprising that the Western
spectators, who perceive themselves as heirs
and bearers of the cosmopolitan and universalist tradition of the Enlightenment, soon
rejected these phenomena as historically

regressive – after all, some East European
actors also fought against them.

Yet, it appears that this rejection under-
scores once more the function of the 'spectating public' as the creators of history.
Paradoxically, one could say that the East
European events appear to be historical precisely to the extent to which they belong to
the Other (the spectator that is sympathetic
to them), not to the subject (the actors
involved in them). And the obverse is true:
at the point when the events practically
belong to the actors themselves – when they
are 'national' events – they lose their historical character.

Our aim in what follows is to argue that
this new element, the emergence of nationalism, radically transformed the structure of
identification. Whereas the East European
democratic reinvention, perceived as a
return to the origins of democracy, provided
a basis for symbolic identification (that is,
by means of the imputed fascination of the
East European actor with democracy, the
Western spectator reached a point of self-
transparency and thus self-recognition), the
'irruption of irrational nationalist hatred'
provided a new framework in which the
Western spectator no longer recognized
him/herself in the Eastern actor. To put it
differently, while the imaginary interplay of
two fascinated gazes enabled the Western
spectator to see him/herself through the eyes
of the Eastern actor in the form in which
s/he likes to be seen (Lacan, 1979: 268), the
emergence of nationalism dispelled this
mutual fascination.

To explain this disillusionment we would
turn our attention to the 'blind spot' of the
Western spectator, and would argue that the
blemish in the picture which appears to the
spectator as meaningless nonetheless indicates his/her presence in the picture –
although s/he does not recognize it as such.

In this context, the case of the former Yugoslavia is instructive.

It is worth noting that the Western spectator has never been so fascinated by events in Yugoslavia, the 'Slovenian Spring' included (which was a sort of model of the Yugoslav democratization process), as it was by the struggles of the Hungarian and Polish opposition, by the fall of the Berlin Wall, or by the Czechoslovak 'Velvet Revolution'. On the contrary, Yugoslavia soon began to represent the epitome of all that was negative about – the distillation of all the faults of – the East European thrust towards democracy. In this sense we would say that Yugoslavia came to represent *the stain* in the West's harmonious picture of the Eastern democratic invention.

Yet, it was not the most obvious phenomenon – the outbreak of war amongst previously united, 'brotherly' peoples – that makes Yugoslavia such a perfect negative example. It is, rather, something which – to use Foucault's words – appears at first sight to be 'insignificant and without value': a radical division between the actors' understanding of the events in which they took part and the way in which these events were interpreted by their spectator. The same phenomenon – a strong national(ist) mobilization in all parts of former Yugoslavia – was given two completely incompatible interpretations. The spectator on the outside interpreted it as outbreaks of nationalism. Those being mobilized understood it as a struggle for independence founded on the right of the people to self-determination. What both official European policy-makers and many European left-wing intellectuals rejected as a *particularistic* 'short cut', historically doomed to fail-

ure, the actors in Slovenia, for example, regarded as an essential element of their *universalism*, of their existence as Europeans.[7]

At this point we will interrupt our argument and return to the problem of the double void: the void into which Communism disappeared and the void produced at the end of the process of democratization in the East. For Furet this void is a *simple negation*.[8] It indicates that the emancipation in Eastern Europe did not achieve anything that was *historically new*. But if we read Furet's reflections on the situation in Eastern Europe in terms of Claude Lefort's political philosophy[9], we can draw a different conclusion from the existence of this void; and one which, in our opinion, is just as well founded.

One of the crucial aspects of Lefort's political philosophy is the *positive function* he attributes to *radical negativity*. As a result of the democratic invention, which had dissolved all landmarks of certainty, the structure of modern democratic society is, according to Lefort, marked by an irreducible lack, the 'empty space of power'. Modern democratic society is therefore, in Lefort's words, a 'completely social society', that is, a society lacking an ultimate legitimation and guarantee.[10] One of the consequences of positing democracy as pure discursive effect, moreover, of reducing it to an 'empty form', is that modern democratic societies remain by definition open to a plurality of conflicting, even anti-democratic options, that is, they are 'exposed to a radical indeterminacy' (Mouffe, 1992: 229).

This theoretical approach allows us to explain a whole set of positive effects resulting from a pure negativity which we have dubbed 'the void of the East

European democratic revolutions'. We can thus draw the following conclusion from Furet's analysis: what was new about the Eastern struggles for democracy – their *genuine historical achievement* – was precisely this void in which they ended. Indeed, if there is a *trait unaire* justifying the parallel between the democratic invention and the 'democratic revolutions of 1989', it should be situated in this discovery or, rather, exposure of radical negativity.

However, this interpretation of the void as pure negativity is still insufficient to explain the East European democratic reinvention. Although the void is, as we pointed out above, a positive historical achievement of the 'democratic revolutions of 1989', it is never present as such. On the contrary, its presence is concealed, distorted by what we called the double blemish. And it is a double blemish in the literal sense, since it applies to both, the 'objective' level of events, and the 'subjective' level of interpretation.

Let us try and explore the above more precisely by employing the 'Yugoslav case'. The events in Yugoslavia – which almost from the outset were diagnosed as a case of *'acute nationalism'* – exemplify what happens when the fascination in the gaze of the 'uninvolved public, looking on' fades. We will proceed in two stages.

We will begin with what appears at first sight to be a disputable assertion, namely, that the diagnosis of nationalism, made by the Western spectator, was inadequate to the 'thing itself'. Clearly, it would be absurd to deny that there is nationalism in the former Yugoslavia. In Slovenia, for example, the process of democratization was strongly marked by nationalism and xenophobia, in Serbia, on the other hand, the massive mobilization turned into 'blood and soil' nationalism. But despite this actually existing

nationalism we maintain that what the Western spectator saw in Yugoslavia was not the nationalism that was actually tearing apart the country. The nationalism which the Western spectator – both official European policy-makers and left-wing opinion – believed to recognize in all conflicts in the former Yugoslavia existed only in the European gaze, confirming in this way Hegel's thesis that the *evil is in the gaze* not in the object observed.

The nationalist mobilization of the masses is without doubt one of the numerous 'ills' that are a product of the specific political conditions in Yugoslavia. But this ill became a real 'evil' only when the allegedly neutral European policy-makers saw in Yugoslavia *nothing but* nationalism. In other words, nationalism became a real 'evil' the moment when the European gaze transformed the nationalism as a discursive effect into a substantive entity: to be a Slovene, a Croat or a Serb – in short, to be Yugoslav – meant, from now on, simply to be (a) nationalist.

It is no surprise that European policy-makers have today seen their diagnosis of nationalism confirmed; after all, these policy-makers did everything to give life to these political tendencies. To put it differently, the nationalism in Yugoslavia is, at least partly, a result of the West's efforts to realize their own fantasy of a centralized, unified Yugoslavia, without paying attention to the actual economic, social and political interests of the parts constituting ex-Yugoslavia – as a result of which Yugoslavia, which a few years ago could still have become a confederate state, today no longer exists. They tried to treat and to suppress unresolved political contradictions indiscriminately – as a result of which these contradictions were heightened to such an extent that – still unresolved – they made possible the Serbian war of conquest. With unparalleled stupidity[11] and

150

arrogance they dismissed as separatism all demands for autonomy – as a result of which Yugoslavia really did disintegrate into its constitutive parts.

The Western diagnosis of nationalism has therefore very little to do – or only very indirectly – with actual political circumstances and actual nationalisms in the former Yugoslavia. The 'Yugoslav nationalisms' diagnosed by the West are an illusion and as such have more to do with the spectating audience itself: that is, with political relations of power in a Europe in the process of unification; with the tension between the process of European universalization and European local particularities; and with the imaginary world of the European Left, for which Yugoslavia always represented something 'more than Yugoslavia itself': workers' self-management, independence from the superpower blocs and so on.

This illusion of Yugoslavia created by the Western spectator thus concealed a double distortion: the imaginary 'Yugoslav nationalisms' are a distorted picture of the nationalism that is *constitutive of actual political and social relations* in the former Yugoslavia; and they are also a distortion of what we might describe as *the Other* in European universalist democratic culture: everything from the pluralilty and diversity of the local particularisms through to alternative, and utopian, ideas and projects which surpass the *status quo* of *Realpolitik*.

But what is the standard by which one can measure the inappropriateness of the Western interpretation of events? By the inappropriateness we do not mean simply an incomplete, distorted depiction of a real state of affairs. Our conception of this inappropriateness clearly does not imply that there is something that might be called the 'true' depiction. Equally, it does not imply that, behind the depiction, there is, although hidden, the thing itself. We mean, rather, that the depiction is by necessity inappropriate, not only because events themselves are unclear, fragmented and ambiguous – 'formless', as Kant would say. It is inappropriate because the thing itself is nothing but a retroactive reconstruction.

Yet, the depiction made by the Western spectator is inappropriate in a different sense: it is inappropriate because it measures particularistic, conflicting claims against a universalistic standard. By opposing particularistic nationalism to universalistic democracy, that is, by tacitly identifying democracy with universalism and anti-democracy with particularism, the Western spectator thus turned a blind eye to the way in which this very universalistic position incited an increase in particularisms and anti-democratic politics; in the blossoming of a national-socialist regime; in the disintegration of Yugoslavia; and in a war that is still raging today.

Nationalism – this stain that becomes manifest in the West's initial fascinated gaze – is thus the point at which the roles of the *actor* who makes history and the *spectator* who creates history are reversed. In the 'Yugoslav example' the Western spectator, a mere observer passing judgement from a distance, gradually becomes an actor in the most literal sense of the word: someone who, like an active participant in the historical drama, is unaware of its own real significance and so constantly discovers that what s/he *has actually done* is quite different to what s/he *wanted to do*, to his/her *proclaimed intentions*. At the same time, the actor becomes more and more of a spectator: that is, someone who does not take part in the action and, for that reason, bestows meaning upon events; someone who, as it were, is in charge of the historicity of events. Is it not the Bosnian Muslims who – irrespective of their involvement in the war – are today playing the structural role of the 'spectating public'? It was they who, to the end – as the Yugoslav army prepared for the blood bath that was to come by surrounding Sarajevo with tanks, trenches and artillery emplacements – held on to the idea of Yugoslavia; it was they who advocated a pluralistic democracy of citizens, not of ethnic monads; it was they who, in contrast to all the other peoples of Yugoslavia, did not secretly arm themselves but, faced by an armed Serbia, continued to pursue an active policy of peace. Paradoxically, it was precisely to the extent to which the Bosnian Muslims adopted the 'way of thinking' and standards of the Western spectator that their project was necessarily doomed to failure.

This brings us to the second stage of our attempt to define the void of the East European democratization process as something positive. To use a formula of Kant, we can say that the spectator's version of events was appropriate precisely in its inappropriateness. It was appropriate insofar as it made clear how the spectator, by merely observing events from a distance, was in fact literally 'wishfully' incorporated in the scene s/he was observing, that is, s/he was part of what was being neutrally observed.

Our main thesis is that it is essential for liberal democratic theory to be able to situate the subject of modern, formal democracy – the 'Western spectator' in our case – at the level of those 'stains in the picture'. Or to put it in other words, it is precisely in these stains that we have to look for the truth of the subject of democracy, which is in our case embodied in the ambiguous figure of the Western spectator. These stains are more than just pathological phenomena. As a 'blind spot' of democracy they represent a condition of possibility of its normal functioning; an element of democracy *in*

action, constituting at the same time the only substance that the empty democratic subject, that is, the subject who achieves his/her identity only by means of differentiation, can achieve.

To see what this identification of the Western spectator, the subject of democracy, with these blemishes, these senseless stains that resist interpretation means, we should reconsider the diagnosis of nationalism. At first sight it is a typical example of a *process of delimitation* constitutive of the object of the diagnosis but even more so of the subject who is making the diagnosis. It could be understood as a device which makes it possible for the Western spectator or, rather, for the subject of democracy to avoid facing, recognizing his/her own presence in the spectacle s/he merely observes by simply opposing a universal, European democratic way with the other, the non-European, represented by the separatist, particularistic nationalism in Yugoslavia.

The role which the diagnosis of nationalism has played for the Western public in the 'Yugoslav example' now makes it clear why we said that the presence of the subject in the picture is to be looked for precisely in the picture's 'blemishes': the subject does not and in fact cannot recognize him/herself in his/her own distorted image as represented by the stains and blemishes because s/he occupies that blind spot where s/he can no longer see nor understand anything or, to put it differently, the subject does not and can not see anything because there is nothing to see, nothing but a void. In Lacanian terms we would say that the spectator's gaze, trapped in the picture's blemishes, disorganizes it, disfigures it. Yet, these stains in the picture, which trigger the spectator's interpretative delirium, exist nowhere but in his/her and for his/her gaze. In so far as the spectator is identified with the subject of desire we could say that with its picture, the West was actually *staging a production*, a specific, deluded production of its own political point of view.

The fascinated gaze is thus nothing but a way of avoiding the void of modern democracy, its lack of substance, its formal emptiness. In this respect one could say that the chimera of nationalism is a discursive device whose principal function is to prevent the confrontation with the other side of this lack of substantiality: a paradoxical substantial moment that cannot be universalized. Paradoxical precisely in the sense that it is generated by the formal and 'empty' nature of democracy itself. Yet, this element, to the extent to which it is a remainder, a leftover of the process that constitutes modern democracy and its subject by obliterating all their concrete, material, specific features, does not and can not disappear. On the contrary, it haunts democracy and its subject in the form of or, rather, as the image of the hostile Other.

It should now be clear why one of the *enjeux* in democratic discourse should be the identification with the stain that is exemplified in the case of former Yugoslavia by nationalism. This of course does not mean that the democratic subject is to be identified with the nationalist. The real issue is something different. The issue at stake here is not the acknowledgement that the process of differentiation and exclusion is constitutive of political discourse as such – and democratic political discourse is no exemption in this respect – as is more than sufficiently demonstrated by the attitude of the West in the 'Yugoslav example'. It is rather the recognition that democracy as an 'empty form' – precisely in its formality and emptiness – always contains something particular irreducible to empty form, in short, has 'content'.

And it is precisely this substantial moment functioning as an internal condition of the modern, democratic process of universalization that corresponds to that void that characterizes the East European process of democratization. Paradoxically we could say that this void, this absolute negativity, is in itself something positive; it is also something historically new – in as much as it not only demands a fresh definition of democracy, but also makes it possible for us to determine, in this new definition of the democratic invention, in what way something undefinable and unthinkable even is inherent in the democratic invention essence.

In this respect one could say that nationalism is not something absolutely strange to democracy and its subject. On the contrary, nationalism is one of the (im)possible ways of compensation for the irreducible deficiency, original lack, which characterizes the nature of modern democracy. If we are to follow C. Lefort, modern democracy conceived as an 'empty form' is not something given in advance but, rather, the effect of discourse, a result of operations of abstraction, purification. But this process of purification or universalization, this constitution of democracy as universal political form is never complete. There is always an irreducible leftover, a remainder of particularity that cannot be universalized. If nationalism haunts contemporary democracy, especially in Eastern Europe, it is precisely because nationalism, in the context of the process of East European democratization, is nothing but a name of this residue that cannot be integrated into the structure of democracy, a residue that is, paradoxically, produced by this very process of democratization.

It is therefore not enough to identify the 'democratic reinvention' with a contingent, discursive effect marked by radical negativity. It is not enough to say that the democratic experience is a result of the inner impos-

the reinvention of democracy in eastern europe

sibility of democracy to achieve its final suture. Democracy is, rather, the experience of this impossibility as something positive: the experience that the radical negativity of democratic discourse is embodied by a non-discursive moment, the real. It is one thing to confront the democratic principle of equality with actually existing inequalities, to recognize in them the lie, the manifest untruth, in the principle of democracy. But it is another matter to try to situate in the universalistic discourse of democracy that eradicates all differences and particularisms a moment of radical particularism, the real, which has been produced by, but at the same time is not reducible to, this universalist democratic discourse. Liberal-democratic theory will only be up to its task when it succeeds in shedding light on that heterogeneous, other nature of democracy, and demonstrating in what way it is a condition of possibility of contemporary democracy. Liberal-democratic politics, on the other hand, could be defined as a politics that consists of a certain '*savoir-faire*' in relation to this radically contingent 'substantial' moment of formal democracy, which always transgresses and evades its normal framework.

notes

1 See her posthumously published *Lectures on Kant's Political Philosophy*.

2 See M. Foucault (1985) and J.F. Lyotard (1989).

3 A typical example of this attitude is a report published in the German magazine *Kommune* in 1988, during the democratization process in Slovenia, with an extensive and accurate description of the political and social struggles of the so-called 'Slovenian Spring'. The author concludes his report with these words: 'As a visitor from the West one sometimes asks oneself if the ideology of the eighteenth century is not being mixed up with the political and legal structures of the nineteenth and twentieth centuries. Typical of the peculiarly anachronistic, early bourgeois Enlightenment approach' (Köhler, 1988: 9).

4 A rejection of this point, though it may be tempting, is far from satisfactory. It cannot be denied – to return briefly to the above mentioned report in *Kommune* – that it would be inaccurate simply to describe the democratic struggles in Eastern Europe as a simple repetition of the past: they were, after all, characterised in part by the broad spectrum of social and political demands made by the 'new social movements'. There were also numerous contacts between Eastern social movements, oppositional groups or dissidents and various political parties and social movements in the West, contacts from which the 'visitor from the West' was certainly able to learn something new. Furthermore, Furet's powerful thesis that Communist institutions dissolved into nothing could also be empirically modified. However, a more scrupulous depiction of *empirical reality* in the former Communist states would not, in our opinion, discard the *historical truth* of the Eastern democratic experience as articulated by Furet.

5 For a detailed elaboration of the ideological function of this fascination, see S. Žižek (1990).

6 Paradoxically, one could say that, at first, the Western gaze was fascinated by precisely those events in Yugoslavia that marked the beginnings of a new totalitarianism which combined elements of both communist and nationalist ideology. Quite a few left-wing West European intellectuals, for example, saw Milosevic's so-called 'anti-bureaucratic revolution' as a grassroots and democratic people's movement and counterpoised it to the 'egotistical' nationalist movement in Slovenia.

7 We base our argument here on the analysis developed in our paper 'Nationalisms and the Disintegration of Yugoslavia', presented at the colloquium 'States, Nations and Ethnic Identities' at the European University Institute, Florence, in March 1991.

8 There was a 'pure and simple negation', a 'void in the true sense of the word, a pure negation, a systematic *tabula rasa*' (Furet, 1990: 175-178).

9 See, above all, the two collections *L'invention démocratique* and *Essais sur la politique (XIXe-XXe siècle)*.

10 The positive functioning of the lack, as expressed concisely in the notion of the *empty space of power*, can be described briefly as follows: the democratic revolution establishes *the people* as the ultimate origin of political power. Yet, one of the immediate consequences of positing the people in the role of the sovereign is its division: on the one hand, the people (or, rather, the People) are the source of the legitimation of power; on the other hand, they are all subjects subordinate to power. The people is, therefore, a contradictory entity. Whereas it no doubt exists as collection of atomised individuals, as symbolic authority, it clearly does not exist, or, rather, it exists only as 'fiction' in relation to which the society constitutes itself. The consequence of this division is that the space of power remains by necessity *empty*; that is, it is a space that no-one, no representative of the people, can claim as his own, nor can legitimately occupy in his own name, which is why any attempt to incarnate this absent, impossible entity, the People, leads to totalitarianism.

11 We mean here stupidity in the Kantian sense. Kant uses the word to denote weak judgement, that is the inability to apply general rules to concrete examples:

> A physician therefore, a judge or a statesman, may have in his head many admirable pathological, juridical or political rules ... and yet in his application of these rules, he may very possibly blunder – either because he is wanting in natural judgement, and while he can understand the general *in abstracto*, cannot distinguish whether a particular case *in concreto* ought to rank with the former; or because his faculty of judgement has not been sufficiently exercised by examples and real practice ... Deficiency in judgement is

properly that which is called stupidity; and for such a thing we know no remedy. (Kant, 1943: 98-9)

bibliography

Arendt, Hannah *Lectures on Kant's Political Philosophy* (Chicago: University of Chicago Press, 1982).

Foucault, Michel 'Kant. Was ist Aufklärung?', *Magazine Littéraire* (1984).

Foucault, Michel 'What is Enlightenment?' in *The Foucault Reader*, ed. Paul Rabinow (London: Penguin, 1985).

Furet, François 'L'Énigme de la déségrégation communiste', *Le Débat* 62 (1990).

Ingram, David 'The Postmodern Kantianism of Arendt and Lyotard' in *Judging Lyotard*, ed. Andrew Benjamin (London: Routledge, 1992).

Kant, Immanuel *Conflict of the Faculties* [1789] (New York: Abaris Books Inc., 1979).

Kant, Immanuel *Critique of Pure Reason* (New York: Wiley Book Co., 1943).

Köhler, Erich 'Laibacher Frühling. Ein Porträt der slowenischen Reformbewegung' (Ljubljana Spring. A portrait of the Slovenian reform movement), *Kommune. Forum für Politik-Okonomie-Kultur* 11 (1988).

Lacan, Jacques *The Four Fundamental Concepts of Psycho-Analysis* (London: Penguin, 1979)

Laclau, Ernesto *New Reflections on The Revolution of Our Time* (London: Verso, 1990).

Lefort, Claude *L'invention démocratique* (Paris: Fayard, 1981).

Lefort, Claude *Essais sur la politique (XIXe-XXe siècle)* (Paris: Seuil, 1986).

Lyotard, Jean-François 'The Sign of History' in *The Lyotard Reader*, ed. Andrew Benjamin (Oxford: Basil Blackwell, 1989).

Mouffe, Chantal 'Democratic Citizenship and the

the reinvention of democracy in eastern europe

Political Community' in *Dimensions of Radical Democracy*, ed. Chantal Mouffe (London: Verso, 1992).

Žižek, Slavoj 'Eastern Europe's Republics of Gilead', *New Left Review* 183 (1990).

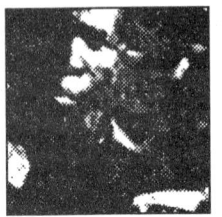

introduction

[H]ome: n.,a., & adv. OED 1.n. Dwelling-place; fixed residence of family or household ... 2. Native land of oneself or one's ancestors, esp. Britain (*sic*). 3. Place where thing is native or most common ... come ~ to, become fully realised by...

In April 1994, with the singular, unrepeatable event of the election, South Africa once again has come to occupy a space in the imaginary of the West which is both unique and exemplary.[1] In a world torn apart by ethno-nationalist struggles, in the absence of the stabilising influence of the Cold War, South Africa almost effortlessly moved from being a pariah state, to becoming a symbol of hope and unity, of what can be achieved in the name of democracy. However, reading this event from the standpoint of the spectator alone, will not do. For the election not only reaffirmed that which the West desired but also, and perhaps more importantly, it instituted a new imaginary, a horizon within which for the first time, a fluid, open South African identity became a possibility for all those denied it before.

institution

The election acted as the moment of institution of a new social imaginary, signifying a beginning, an origin, as well as a completion. That is to say, the delineation of the horizon within which a newly articulated South African identity originated, also prefigures the space of its own fulfilment. What is instituted as radically new, serves as an always already given origin, marking out the space of the possible. Such is the paradox of all beginnings. However, this is not to say, in Hegelian fashion, that such beginnings are determined by developments to follow. To

aletta j. norval

THE POLITICS OF HOMECOMING?

contending identities in contemporary south africa or identité à venir

the contrary, the element of paradox on which I want to focus here emphasises the contingency and impurity of all beginnings which, while far from determining its forms of identification, cuts out a space open to contestation and subversion, at the same time as it sets limits to that identification.

In South Africa, the radical institution of a new imaginary happened before our very eyes:

> The abiding image of the day that South Africa began to become one nation, all together, was in the orange, autumn sun rising over a new country teeming with extraordinary, renewed people. It rose over a country with a new flag, a new anthem, a new map, and a profound new human mood. When the people began to form those lines they became a new people, spontaneously and unintentionally. The tiny seed first glimpsed on the national peace day last year, giving life to the otherwise lifeless political

157

the politics of homecoming?

slogan 'non-racial', burst into resplendent flower. Black South Africans learnt what whites already knew: how to vote. White South Africans learnt what blacks knew: how to wait. They did it together, in marvelous straggly multi-coloured queues... (Johnson, 1994)

The question remaining to be addressed in this respect is the following: how do we think this moment of institution? The most obvious candidate for this in the tradition of political theory is, of course, the social contract tradition which attempts to theorise the moment of inauguration and establishment of society. The paradox we encounter here is well known: in order to institute society, we already need to have in place that which can only be brought about as a result of the very act of institution. As Connolly (1991: 465) argues with reference to Rousseau, '[f]or a general will to be brought into being, effect (social spirit) would have to become cause and cause (good laws) would have become effect'. As we know, Rousseau resolved this problem in an interesting fashion. He argued that the legislator, being unable to employ either force or argument, 'must have recourse to an authority of another order', must claim his own contingent wisdom to be that of the Gods (Rousseau, 1968: 87). In order to establish the purity of the law, the lawgiver in fact has to resort to the impure mechanism of deception. In this sense, Rousseau not only 'solves' his own problem, but sets into place a radical argument for the 'ignobility of all origins', even that of the law, so introducing an ineliminable element of arbitrariness into political life.

This act of institution is always *retroactively* realised, constituted after the fact. Analogously, it could be argued that the real constitution of the South African nation took place not so much in the actual act of

queueing, as in the retrospective viewing of that act, emphasising the moment it entered the gaze, making the actor simultaneously spectator of her own acts. And in this very moment of elation, of birth, was enacted the contractual paradox: it foreshadowed the very thing which would make the nation possible. It established a South African *identité à venir*. It provided a vision of tolerance, of fusion, and one might say, of precarious unity, which everyone knows is patently absent in the present.[2] To put it differently, the very conditions of possibility for democracy were instituted in a context scarred by their very absence.

empty spaces, barred subjects

While the act of institution always contains a paradox, this does not mean that the paradox is eradicated with the full institution of a democratic social order. As I have pointed out earlier, there is an ineliminable element present in the ignoble, arbitrary moment of institution, which continues to mark the political space. In order to understand why this is the case, we need to look more closely at two further dimensions of this institution: that of the space itself, and of the subject of democracy. Let us start with the former.

> [D]emocratic society could be determined as a society whose institutional structure includes, as part of its 'normal', 'regular' production, the moment of dissolution of the symbolic bond, the moment of the irruption of the Real: elections. (Žižek, 1989: 147)

In his seminal work on the democratic imaginary, Lefort argues that in a democratic society the place of power is an *empty* one (1988: 17). That is, democracy involves the institutionalisation of the markers of uncertainty. What is sacrificed here is precisely the possibility of a given

158

and certain content filling, without question, the place of power. But with this sacrifice, as with all sacrifices, something crucial is gained. The empty space of power, in fact, secures in its very nature, the space of contestability. Far from being a safe and merely bourgeois phenomenon, democracy shows the radical incompletion of all forms of identification.

The third dimension of the paradox of this institution concerns the nature of the subject to complement this empty space. We can ask with Žižek, 'who is the subject of democracy?' The answer? The subject of abstraction, 'the empty punctuality we reach after subtracting all the fullness of particular contents' (Žižek, 1991: 190). As both Laclau and Žižek, following Lacan, have argued, the important point here is not simply the empty point of reference, the 'all people *without regard to...*' which forms the preamble to every democratic credo (Žižek, 1991: 190). Rather, what is crucial is the fact that the non-substantiality of subjectivity, or to put it in Lacanian terms, the subject of a constitutive lack, the barred subject, inaugurates the need for *identification*.

However, here the further paradox, or perhaps *the* paradox of democracy emerges. For democracy, in order to be democracy at all, has to be anti-humanistic in that it has to abstract from specificity. Yet, it also has to engender acts of identification which will always threaten the very moment of abstraction itself, which will 'smear' democracy with particularity (Žižek, 1991: 192). This is the very space in which the recent debate between liberals and communitarians is constituted, with liberals focusing exclusively on the abstraction of the subject from all context – exemplified in the Rawlsian 'veil of ignorance' – while communitarians, in what had to amount to anti-democratic gestures, tended to solidify the subject, cementing it

for ever in the bonds of community. Neither of these options will do, and while it is not possible here to discuss the matter in detail, it is necessary to signal our disquiet with these 'either-or' options, both of which misrecognise the complexity as well as the essential finitude, not only of the subject, but of the very space of democracy itself.

minimal remainders

Instead of seeing this 'smearing' of democracy with singularity as a disaster, it is necessary to recognise that democracy arises in the very *tension* of this empty space. Or perhaps, it could better be designated as a non-full space, a space marked forever with a radical impossibility. As I have argued elsewhere, the questioning of forms of universality by the emerging particularisms of our time should not lead to a simplistic reassertion of universality as such.[3] It is in the terrain of the tension between the emptiness of universalism, and the particularistic smearing of the democratic space, that we will be able to renegotiate not only spaces for the democratic recognition of particularity, but also for the revalorization of quasi-transcendental universalisms. We will return to the theoretical nuances of this phenomenon. However, in order not to be accused of excessive theoreticism, let us address these issues in the concrete-historical setting of the transition we are witnessing in South African politics.

closures

It is a truism to say that changes in the political imaginary structuring South African politics are taking place against the grain of developments in world politics. It is almost *passé* to remark that since 1989, with the end of globalising ideologies, we have

the politics of homecoming?

entered the realm of a vicious proliferation of particularistic forms of identification. In the absence of a single principle of division of international frontiers, with the present undermining of universalistic forms of thought, the new South Africa appears almost as an anachronism, out of place in the contemporary world. But precisely for this reason, South Africa now also acts as a crucial signifier in the imaginary of the West. In contrast to its earlier pariah status, it is now a site invested with the most extreme of hopes. We will explore this dimension further in a moment. However, let me consider the role played by 1989 in the South African context, for it is in the precise manner of its articulation that its significance is to be found. It is of course well known that the February 2, 1990 FW de Klerk speech, unbanning the ANC, SACP and other political organisations, very much took its cue from the series of events marked by 1989:

> The year 1989 will be known in history as the year of the death of Stalinist communism. The effects of these events for Europe are unpredictable, and they will also be of decisive importance for Africa... The implosion of the Marxist economic system of Eastern Europe stands as a warning against all those who want to persevere with this in Africa. (Hansard, 2 February 1990, col. 3, my translation)

Thus, the scene was set for the reconstruction of South Africa, for the creation of a 'just political order in which everyone will have equal rights ... [and] opportunities' (Hansard, 2 February 1990, col. 2). It is important that the moment of the death of 'Stalinism' and 'Marxism', coincides with the death of apartheid.

This, of course, does not come as a surprise. Indeed in the contemporary international political context referred to earlier,

the end of grand narratives inevitably had to mark the project of apartheid. Lest we forget, let us reflect for a moment on the nature of this project. Elsewhere I have characterised the *logic* of apartheid as an identitary logic, one in which the closure and purity of identity was primary.[4] The complicated vicissitudes of this project should not be allowed to obscure the centrality and specificity of its logic in the shaping of the South African political landscape. I will not dwell on the nature of apartheid here. However, I would like to reflect briefly on the lingering effect this discourse of closure may have on the longer term prospects for a democratic settlement in South Africa. Three areas of identity formation are crucial in this respect. They are, the struggles around Inkatha and the Zulu monarchy; the question of coloured identity, and the role of the far right.[5]

What I would like to do here, is to focus on the third: the grouping of forces aligned around the far-right Afrikaner Volksfront and the Freedom Front under the leadership of General Constand Viljoen.[6] The reasons for this choice are the following. Literature on these groupings is scant and largely journalistic, written either by sympathisers or scaremongers. Academic accounts are few and far between and tend to subscribe to simplistic views of history, locating the re-emergence of the radical right in the 1980s and 1990s as a straightforward continuation of a certain tradition of 'Afrikaner nationalism'.[7]

Very little attention has been given to the precise *imaginary* feeding into the constitution of these groupings. It has been all too easy to pigeonhole these groupings in a rather simplistic fashion as just one more manifestation of the sort of extreme racist discourse which informed segregation as well as apartheid, resulting, once again, in a left impotent in front of the values espoused by these forces.

160

This evaluation may not be entirely out of place here, especially as the Afrikaner Volksfront makes no effort to conceal the overtly racist criteria of inclusion and exclusion contained in their conception of the 'Afrikaner *volk*'.[8] The situation with regard to the Freedom Front, however, is complicated by the precise articulation and contextualisation of the demand for a *volkstaat*. Here is articulated for a second time what seems, at first glance, a tragic enactment of apartheid discourse, a yearning for a territorially sovereign state where the 'Afrikaner people' can be at home. However, it is important not to proceed too quickly here. We need to investigate more closely what and who exactly is designated by the notion of the 'Afrikaner *volk*'. In this respect, it is necessary to investigate the functioning of '1989' in the discourse of the Freedom Front (FF), and the role it plays in the distancing of their discourse from that of traditional apartheid.

This distancing occurs in the discourses of most of the far-right groupings organising themselves around the notion of a *volkstaat*. Across most of the spectrum of far-right discourses, apartheid is not regarded as the saviour-ideology of the Afrikaner. Rather, it is seen as that which ruined their case for a territorially sovereign state. It is argued that while much has been written on 'the effects of apartheid on Africans, Coloureds and Indians, on the ecology, white rhino (*sic!*) and whatever else', no study has been done of the effects of apartheid on the Afrikaner *volk* (Bruwer, 1992).[9]

Apartheid, here reduced to an ideology which entrenched white privilege on a racial basis, is regarded as 'the opium of the masses' in that it created a false illusion that the Afrikaner had a 'land of its own' (Bruwer, 1992), blinding them to the 'blackening' (*verswarting en verbruining*) of 'white South Africa'. In fact, apartheid's legacy for the 'Afrikaner people' is that it left them in the position of 'a people without a country', a homeless people. Moreover, by conflating the retention of political power and the uplifting of the *volk*, apartheid created a nation of servile civil servants, particularly vulnerable to any change in regime. It stripped the Afrikaner *volk* of its territorial basis and work ethic, leading to moral and territorial decay.[10]

Already, then, it is clear that the contemporary right cannot be seen as a simple continuation of the extreme, dogmatic forms of Afrikaner nationalism. However difficult to swallow politically, it must be emphasised that there is a certain distancing from apartheid which makes it untenable to conflate it with earlier forms of right-wing ideology. Simply to regard the right as a spent force, built on outdated and discredited ideological structures, would be a mistake, both in theoretical and political terms, for the rearticulation effected in their discourse may have far-reaching and unforeseen resonances in a changed international context.

This brings me to the signifying force which the post-1989 world has in the discourse of the *volkstaat* ideologues. The most sophisticated version of this articulation is to be found in the analysis of the Freedom Front, also making it a 'milder' version of the argument, compared for example to the position of the Afrikaner Volksfront. Distinguishing between the illegitimate racial basis of apartheid, and legitimate ethnic forms of identification in our contemporary world, it is argued by Corne Mulder –

constitutional expert of the Freedom Front – that South Africa's problems are not unique.[11] As in the rest of Africa, colonial boundaries created artificial entities; in the case of South Africa, the non-existent 'South Africans'.[12] Having left the *uhuru* phase behind, Africa is now in a 'democratising' phase. For Mulder, what is important to remember in this context is that emerging demands for 'ethnically' based democracies cannot be separated from the increasing globalisation of the world economy. Economic interdependence is coupled everywhere with demands for territorial separatism. Here, once again, the current ideologists of the right are distancing themselves from the tradition of Afrikaner separatism, as it was, for example, found in the early SABRA demands for 'total apartheid', which meant apartheid both in the political and economic spheres.[13]

Such demands for a sovereign Afrikaner territory can be pursued in two ways: via conflict or via constitutional settlement. Referring to the recently won 'self-governing status' of Palestine, the Freedom Front holds that their struggle today, far from being anachronistic, is wholly in step with developments in our contemporary world. While Palestine acts as a positive referent here (and it is interesting to note that Palestine has replaced the role given to Israel by apartheid ideologues), the former Yugoslavia serves as the negative pole. This is especially the case for the Afrikaner Volksfront which holds that it is simply biding its time. On this reading, the theory and practice of non-racialism will fail in South Africa – witness Inkatha – and the far right will be ready to step in at the point at which the conflict in South Africa reaches Bosnian proportions.[14] In keeping with the rest of the world, South Africa is bound to disintegrate into separate ethnic territories.

In contrast to the Afrikaner Volksfront, the Freedom Front is, for the moment, intent on pursuing the constitutional path to achieve its goals.[15] In this respect, it is important to note that they are already working on what is called the 'internationalisation' of the Afrikaner question', and have embarked upon a programme of establishing contacts with senior members of the United Nations (Boutros Boutros-Ghali), the Commonwealth, and the Organisation of African Unity in order to create the climate in which the 54th independent state in Africa may be created via constitutional means. Shortly before the election, General Constand Viljoen negotiated a deal to the effect that the issue of self-determination be written into the constitution. The 34th (34.1) constitutional principle entails that the

> right of the South African people as a whole to self-determination, shall not be construed as precluding, within the framework of said right, constitutional provision for a notion of the right to self-determination by any community sharing a common cultural and language heritage, whether in a territorial entity within the Republic or in any other recognised way.

This concession is described by the Freedom Front as 'wrenching open a door for the continuation of ethnic politics in South Africa' (Vryheidsfront, 'Beginsel 34 en die Volkstaatraad', 1994). Article 34 further states that self-determination may be established should there be substantial support from within the particular community for such a form of self-determination.[16]

This, of course, immediately raises the vexed question as to who the members of such an 'Afrikaner *volk*' might be. While members of the Afrikaner Volksfront (and presumably also other far-right organisations affiliated to them) are quite clear about the need for a racial component to this identity, the Freedom Front is less forthcoming on this point. They insist on the fact that the Vryheidsfront is a 'non-racial' organisation (simply not taking 'race' as a criterion of qualification) and that it is therefore quite at home in contemporary South Africa (Mulder, 1994). However, when pushed on the issue, they argue that the '*volk*' will have to decide the issue of membership, thus leaving the door open to racial politics.[17] This suspicion is further reinforced by the emphasis in their discourse on 'nonartificial', that is 'organic', forms of ethnicity and community (Mulder, 1994), as well as in their open denial of full citizenship rights to 'others' who may find themselves within the boundaries of such a *volkstaat*.[18]

Situated then in the double context of the failure of apartheid and the emergence of ethno-nationalism in our contemporary world, the far right continues the tradition of identitary politics found in its most extreme form in apartheid. It remains to be seem whether their strategy of distancing themselves from apartheid will succeed. For our purposes, however, it is important to stress the ever-present dimension of closure and exclusivity articulated in this discourse. A discourse in which identity can be seen to pretend to be fully at home with itself, coinciding with itself, externalising all difference into otherness, indeed, quite literally, externalising difference beyond the borders of the *volkstaat*.

tensional openings

Exactly how out of step this discourse is with the instituted myth now animating the discourse of a new South African identity becomes clear when it is contrasted with the discourse of non-racialism. Non-racialism, of course, has an illustrious and venerable history in South Africa, informing generations struggling against apartheid, and is perhaps captured best in Mandela's oft-quoted words, spoken during his 1964 trial:

> I have fought against white domination and I have fought against black domination. I have cherished the ideal of a democratic and free society in which all people live together in harmony and with equal opportunities. (1990: 217)

It is a theme which has continued to structure and inform the voice of the African National Congress, becoming more and more infused with a discourse on national reconciliation during the 1990s, and which reached its most eloquent expression in the Presidential inaugural address of the 10 May 1994:

> Out of the experience of an extraordinary human disaster that has lasted too, too long, must be born a society of which all humanity will be proud... The time for the healing of wounds has come... We have, at last, achieved our political emancipation. We pledge to liberate all our people from the continuing bondage of poverty, deprivation, suffering, gender and other discrimination... *We enter into a covenant* that we shall build the society in which all South Africans, both black and white, will be able to walk tall, without any fear in their hearts ... – a *rainbow nation* at peace with itself and the world... Never, never and never again shall it be that this beautiful land will ever again experience the oppression of one by another... (Mandela, inauguration speech, 10 May 1994, reproduced in *The Star*, 11 May 1994)

Or as a more irreverent commentator put it: 'Miracle-man Mandela' is now president of all South Africans: 'the bald-headed and the bearded, housewife and servant, capitalist and unemployed, archbishop and squatter ... white and black... (Breytenbach, 1994, my translation). However one puts it, in Mandela's words is contained a vision which is constitutive of the new imaginary which will shape the identities of generations to come, a vision of a 'rainbow nation', one nation constituted of many cultures. While this may hold up a positive vision of a new 'nationhood' or South African identity, much depends on exactly how the relation of identification is understood and is given concrete expression.[19]

As I have argued elsewhere, if it is simply a matter of a recognition of the plurality of the South African population, it is possible that the discourse of non-racialism may reproduce identitary logics.[20] On this reading, the bringing together of the African, white, Coloured and Indian groups, presumes the existence of differential and homogeneous communities. While the need for a discourse on unity is clearly urgent in the current South African context, the question at stake here is exactly how that may be thought. If non-racialism is understood on the model of a unification of pre-existing homogeneous communities, then several problems may arise in terms of the institution of a democratic form. The most important of these would be precisely the tendency to treat differential communities as internally homogeneous, thus obliterating more complex forms of identification which may arise. In its turn, this may lead to difficulties in constructing a South African identity, for if positive identification is attributed to the level of the group, it is difficult to see how an 'overarching' identity will be construed, an identity which will of necessity make competing claims to identifcation.

Quite the reverse may of course also take place. The fact that so much emphasis is placed on 'reconciliation' and 'nation-building' may very well lead to stifling discourses on the 'unity' of the nation. However, it is my contention that the tension inherent in the discourse of non-racialism, with its simultaneous recognition and subversion of a certain category of 'race', will make this very unlikely. This brings me to another possible reading of the discourse of non-racialism, namely, one which has as a project the articulation of a terrain of a tension. This can be understood most clearly if one focuses on the problematisation and weakening of discourses of 'racialism' inherent in non-racialism. In positing the problematics of race as a question, thus not attempting to suppress it – as has been the case so often in 'progressive' politics – non-racialism subverts all naturalising discourses on race. In addition, the form of identification which is to be characteristic of South African identity, does not function at the level of a positive specification of a set of elements. Rather, it tends to emphasise the negative. Put differently, 'South African' identity is given precisely in the problematisation of the racial as an ordering principle.

Here I would like to focus for a moment on the question of a negatively constituted identity. This would entail that no positively specified set of elements in principle can exhaust the content of an identity. In fact, one may put it even stronger and argue that such a form of identification recognises the fact that an identity can only be formed in the process of differentiating itself from something else. The essence of an identity is thus not given in positive characteristics, but in and through the moment of exclusion, in what it externalises as other. In the case of non-racialism, the role of the other is taken by naturalising discourses on race, of which apartheid is the exemplary case. Non-racialism thus articulates itself in this field of the denial of the other; it recognises the absence of a natural community of identity, and consequently the need to construct a community as a project.[21] This project animates an identity never quite at home with itself.

Inherent in this discourse is thus the possibility of coming to terms with the contingency and fluidity of forms of identification, of taking the non-closure of identity seriously. This, of course, takes us directly back to our earlier remarks on the nature of the subject appropriate to the democratic form. Following Žižek, I have argued that the subject of democracy has to be a non-substantial subject. However, before proceeding any further, a number of further specifications, not made by Žižek, have to be added. The problem of remaining at the level of addressing the question of a democratic subjectivity by reference to the 'empty subject', is the following. The lack inherent in all identity inaugurates the *general* need for identification. But, and this cannot be over-emphasised, there is *nothing* in the form of lack as such, which in and of itself will lead to a 'democratic' form of identification. To put it differently, nothing can be read off from the subject of lack.

What then is one to make of my remarks concerning the discourse of non-racialism and its 'negative', non-substantial form? Here the notion of non-racialism which has been articulated in the South African context has to be fleshed out in greater detail. Two remarks in terms of its relation to a discourse on democracy are particularly pertinent here. The first is that this signifier acted as a nodal point in the discourses of resistance, 'stitching' together many other signifiers, of which the demand for democracy was one of the most central. The discourse of non-racialism thus acted as a signifier designating a whole series of demands. But secondly, and more to the point, is the fact that the discourse of non-racialism, though it is a negatively formulated discourse, is nevertheless

'smeared' with a certain particularity. That is to say, it is not simply a discourse emptied of all concreteness. It articulates itself precisely in a *context*. It is marked by this context. It cannot be absolutely abstracted from this context. And it is this 'stain', the fact of its non-total emptiness, that in the final instance allows for its articulation to a democratic project. While holding off essentialist and identitarian conceptions of identity with its emphasis on the negation of racism, non-racialism nevertheless contains a certain contextual particularity which gives a democratic content to forms of identification. It opens and delineates a certain space of identification. The combination of these two elements – the holding open of a space of identification in principle on the one hand, and the provisional filling of that space on the other – is what characterises the democratic space, and makes identity always to an extent an *identité à venir*.

spectral desires

At this point, it is necessary to return to the wider context in which this imaginary has been instituted. The events sparked off by the unbanning of the African National Congress, the South African Communist Party and other proscribed  organisations in February 1990, also played an important role in the imaginary of the West in the post-1989 context. South Africa has become a signifier of hope in an international political landscape which is increasingly torn apart by ethno-nationalist struggles. Against such violent and aggressive particularisms, the formation of a new South Africa,

165

the politics of homecoming?

a country for 'all its peoples', stands as a reminder of the power of the universalism or 'anti-humanist humanism' of discourses of democracy. In this sense, the new South Africa acts out what is lacking in the 'post-historical' West itself: a sense of optimism, engagement and hope. This investment by the spectating West, however, is not without its difficulties, for it could involve a refusal to come to terms with some of the problems which may be created by an unabashed universalism in the South African context.[22] Moreover, the colonial legacy has to make one somewhat suspicious of the 'good intentions' of the other.

This problem can be discussed, metaphorically, through the imminent return to South Africa of the collection of artworks 'contre/against apartheid'.[23] This collection of works took the form of a travelling exhibition to be presented as a gift to the first democratically elected government of South Africa.

As is well known in the wake of Derrida's writings on the subject, the structure of the gift is a dual one: indicating both a giving without demand and the possibility of a poison (Derrida, 1985: 246). What is at stake here then are the various dimensions and implications of this gift to the new South Africa: the gift as recognition of the accomplishments of generations struggling for a democratic settlement in the country which has become the signifier of oppression in the international world; the gift coming home, to its original place; the effects of this homecoming, of the coming to rest of a moving, fluid exhibition; the gift poisoning the present...

But it is also that God who, in the action of his anger ... annuls the gift of tongues, or at least embroils it, sows confusion among his sons, and poisons the present. (*Gift-gift*) (Derrida 1991: 246)

We can only touch upon some of these dimensions. For our present purposes, it is perhaps most important to concentrate upon what is given in the gift of the 'contre/against apartheid' exhibition. To do this, one has to clarify what this exhibition signified in the first place. It had to serve as a reminder in the world at large of the presence of the heinous crime of apartheid. Lest we forget.[24] In addition, it also had to serve as a signifier of hope. The exhibition would travel the cities of the world until such time as it could return home to take its rightful place in a democratic South Africa. That time is now. But, a question remains. This question concerns the homecoming of the exhibition. What could it possibly mean for an exhibition to come home to a place where it never was at home, to a place which never was its native land, to take up its birthright, its residency, in a dwelling-place foreign to it? Moreover, could an exhibition, born to dwell restlessly, come home, come to rest? Would that signify its 'full realization'?

Different possibilities are opened up here. One would certainly be to argue that this exhibition, insofar as it signifies an abhorrence of the thing itself, of racism as such, and insofar as it therefore carries a significance far wider than the historically existent state of apartheid, should never come to rest. Not in South Africa. Not anywhere. Lest we forget. It should continue to circulate in the capitals of the world. Especially now, when we are faced with the full horrors of an explosion of ethno-nationalisms and fundamentalisms in a post-Cold War world.

Another possibility would be to argue that it *should* come to South Africa, for South Africa now is the place where it belongs. But to repeat the questions raised earlier: how can something whose very nature was conceived as being in movement, come to belong anywhere? Would it not be better to leave it as a signifier of racism in general? Again, various possible modes of thinking 'belonging' are possible. The most common-sensical and most dangerous (poisonous) would be simply to argue that since apartheid has come to an end, has been superseded once and for all, that the rightful place of the exhibition is inside the geographical boundaries of the new South Africa. Such a rendering of 'belonging' would, to my mind, be completely out of touch with, and against the ethos of, the exhibition; it would force it to rest, force it into a definitive mould. Moreover, such a definition, a location, a placement would signify politically that it is possible to end completely, to create an absolute and unequivocal break with the past. It is precisely that which has to be problematised, for such a rendering would simply reinforce identitary logics once again.

deferred homecomings

What then are the alternatives? Another way of conceiving of the exhibition would be neither to deny its legitimate place in South Africa, nor confine it to that geographical space, but to combine its specific and universal value, its necessary content and that which escapes all content. Indeed, one could think it along the lines of a never-ending movement, or space of identification proper to the democratic space, and its articulation in the discourse of non-racialism. That is, the exhibition 'contre/against apartheid' could be argued to have the character of the negative attributed to non-racialism earlier. In that case, a break with apartheid will not be able to function as an absolute one, not yet, in any case. Apartheid, for the time being, will remain its other. It will keep open the democratic space. Its homecoming will always be a radically delayed one. A deferred homecoming. A coming home which never quite reaches home. The tension characteristic of the democratic space will be replicated there. To conclude: if it could find its home, once and for all, if the gap between identity and identification could be closed, 'society would have found its final form and democratic interaction would be impossible. It is because the gap cannot be filled that society can be constructed as that political management of its own impossibility that we call democracy' (Laclau 1994: 12).

notes

1 This argument is elaborated in Norval (1994b).

2 The extent of the intolerance characterising the South African political landscape, most recently, has been visible in the extreme violence in the PWV-region as well as in kwaZulu-Natal. Other indicators can be used here as well. For example, a survey of the Western Cape region showed that 61% of Africans and 45% of Coloureds would not allow a political party they oppose to make political speeches on their home turf (Collins, 1994). Shortly before the elections, voter education programmes were reportedly being thwarted in kwaZulu-Natal by both the Inkatha Freedom Party and the African National Congress. Several incidents in the rest of the country were reported where speakers were violently prohibited from addressing political meetings. These more recent indicators should, of course, not overshadow the fact that the political history of South Africa as a whole can be described as a severely intolerant one.

3 This problem is discussed further in Norval (1993b).

4 My argument concerning the logic of apartheid is elaborated in Norval (1994b).

5 The struggles between Inkatha and the ANC are well documented and analysed in the existing litera-

ture. This is not the case with reference to the question of Coloured identity and the far right. I have discussed some of the problems with regard to the former in Norval (1994c).

6 The Freedom Front (*Vryheidsfront*) was formed in March 1994 when General Constant Viljoen decided to break away from the Afrikaner Volksfront, and to participate in the April elections. A considerable amount of overlap in terms of membership affiliation continued to exist between the two organisations.

7 See, for example, the recent study by Van Rooyen (1994) on the 'hard right' where he argues that 'as the NP expanded its narrow ethnic origins to incorporate a broader white nationalism in the 1960s and 1970s, and an even broader territorially based South African nationalism in the late 1980s and early 1990s, it was left for the right wing to take up the cause of Afrikaner nationalism' (1994: 3). Van Rooyen's account leads him into two difficulties. The first is the tendency to assume the existence of an 'Afrikaner ethnicity', even if he tends to emphasize its non-homogeneity insofar as it is expressed in Afrikaner nationalism. Drawing on Horowitz in this respect, Van Rooyen assumes a highly questionable naturalistic account of the 'psychological tendencies inherent in ethnicity', such that ethnic conflict should be understood in terms of the collective drive by ethnic groups to obtain or maintain social status and power (1994: 201). The second is that, in spite of his emphasis on disunity within Afrikaner nationalist circles, he ends up affirming a continuist view of history which holds that the right can only be explained as a continuation of that tradition. Such a simplistic affirmation of continuities is precisely what, I would argue, is questionable if we are to understand the contemporary right in South Africa today.

8 An Afrikaner Volksfront spokesperson, for example, suggested that the issue of membership of the *volk* may easily be decided by applying the 'd/jakkals' test (Aucamp, 1994). Should a person pronounce the Afrikaans word 'jakkals' on its 'standard' pronunciation ('jakkals') then s/he clearly is a member of the *volk*. Should it be pronounced 'djakkals' instead, such a person is excluded from membership. This racist 'test' is clearly designed to exclude Coloured Afrikaners from the *volk*, and is reminiscent of the various tests employed in the early apartheid years to establish a person's 'race'.

9 The series enumerated here reads like the one Borges allegedly took from a Chinese dictionary. Its principle of intelligibility is well-nigh unintelligible to us.

10 Here one already sees the 'moralism' of the far right emerging. It has to be stressed that, in this case, it is also coupled with a clear anti-semitic thrust.

11 Contrast this with the *ad nauseam* argument by apartheid ideologues on the uniqueness of the South African situation!

12 The debate on the existence or not of 'South Africans' is a long one. I have discussed this in a historical context in Norval (1994c).

13 During the late 1950s and early 1960s, the issue of 'total' versus 'partial' apartheid was a key debating point in Afrikaner nationalist circles. The concern primarily was whether apartheid should be enforced only on the political terrain, or whether it also had to be brought about in the economy. Elements within SABRA (Suid-Afrikaanse Buro vir Rasse Aangeleenthede) came out in favour of 'total' apartheid, as the only 'moral' form which apartheid could take.

14 The Afrikaner Volksfront seem to hold an apocalyptic belief in the eventual failure of the discourse of non-racialism. In this sense, their 'strategy' is simply to bide their time, and to continue to foster alliances with forces which may, under such circum-

stances, act as allies in the search for territorial autonomy on 'ethnic' grounds (Aucamp, 1994).

15 It is a well-known fact that the Freedom Front can muster considerable military and para-military forces behind them. These forces, in contrast to those of the Afrikaner Weerstandsbeweging (AWB) who were responsible for the battle for Boputhatswana, are highly trained and disciplined. For the moment, however, they remain loyal to General Constand Viljoen and the strategy of constitutional negotiation.

16 The question of how this support is to be tested is a vexed one. During the election it was suggested that the share of the regional vote gained by the Freedom Front would act as a fair indicator of their support. Regionally this vote ranged from 6% in the Freestate and Northern Cape to 0.5% in Natal. However, the more serious issue concerns the determination of those eligible to participate in the decision for/against a *volkstaat*, since a considerable proportion of 'Afrikaners' would under no circumstances associate themselves with the 'Afrikaner *volkstaat*' and the Freedom Front.

17 Here, of course, it is clear that the real issue concerns the position of Afrikaans-speaking Coloureds. The Freedom Front, in line with its distancing of itself from the racialism of apartheid, have great difficulty in dealing with this question. They seem to want to have it both ways: an ethnic 'Afrikaner' community which nevertheless does not include Coloureds. Thus, the strategy of not making pronouncements on their stand on the 'race'-issue, leaving it to the 'members' of the *volk* to decide. It is, moreover, interesting to note that 'democracy' does not feature prominently in their discourse, if at all. However, legitimacy as to the 'membership' of the group is to be bestowed by 'democratic' decision-making procedures – as if that would make the result any more palatable!

18 Further problems arise from the very idea of a *volkstaat*, should one take seriously their principles as stated in their 'Core Manifesto'. Whilst maintaining that the *volkstaat* should exist within a broader non-racial South Africa, no concessions are to be made as to the inalienable and 'fundamental right of the Afrikanervolk ... to self-determination', including the right 'to govern themselves in their own state'. This immediately raises the issue of the extent of the limitation of the rights of 'others'/'non-*volk* residents' in such a state.

19 Much depends here on the concrete expression given to non-racialism and the extent to which it will, of necessity, be limited with respect to the application of 'affirmative action' programmes. For a fuller discussion, see Norval (1994a and 1994c).

20 This possibility has been discussed in greater depth in Norval (1993a).

21 This may amount to an overestimation of the extent to which the African National Congress in fact views this community as contingent. Some would argue that it rests on the basis of 'given' and 'common humanity'.

22 See Norval (1993b).

23 This moving exhibition came to 'academic' public knowledge with the publication in *Critical Inquiry* of Derrida's piece originally written for the catalogue accompanying the exhibition.

24 I treated the complicated question of the role of the memory of apartheid today in Norval (1994a).

references

Aucamp, P. 'Personal Interview' (Afrikaner Volksfront), Pretoria, 19 May 1994.

Bruwer, P. 'Die droom van 'n Afrikanerland', *Vrye Weekblad*, 182 (1992).

Breytenbach, B. 'Kraglyne, Kaplyne', *Die Beeld* (7 May 1994).

Collins, G. 'Political Intolerance High', *The Weekly Mail* (31 March 1994).

Connolly, W.E. 'Democracy and Territoriality', *Millenium*, vol. 20, 3 (1991).

the politics of homecoming?

Derrida, J. 'From "Des Tours de Babel"' in *A Derrida Reader*, ed. P. Kamuf (New York: Harvester Wheatsheaf, 1991).

Freedom Front 'Beginsel 34 en die Volkstaatraad', Election pamphlet, 1994a.

Freedom Front 'Core Manifesto', Election pamphlet, 1994b.

Johnson, S. 'All Together unto One Destiny', *The Star* (April 29, 1994).

Laclau, E. 'Georges Sorel, Objectivity and the Logic of Violence'. Paper presented to the 'Politics and Passions' conference, Oxford, 24-6 June 1994.

Lefort, C. *Democracy and Political Theory* (Oxford: Polity Press, 1988).

Mandela, N.R. 'Address to Rally in Cape Town, 11 February 1990' in *Nelson Mandela. The Struggle is My Life* (London: IDAF Publications, 1990).

Mandela, N.R. 'Inaugural Speech', *The Star* (11 May 1994).

Mulder, C. 'Personal Interview' (Freedom Front), Pretoria, 19 May 1994.

Norval, A.J. 'Decolonisation, Demonisation and Difference. The Difficult Constitution of a Nation'. Paper presented to the 'Societies of Southern Africa in the 19th and 20th Centuries' seminar, Institute of Commonwealth Studies, University of London, October 1993a, mimeo.

Norval, A.J. 'Minoritarian Politics and the Pluralisation of Democracy', *Filozofski Vestnik*, vol. XIV, 2 (1993b).

Norval, A.J. 'Memories of Babel: Language and the Politics of Identity'. Paper presented to the 'Politics of Identity, Secular Criticism, and the Gravity of History: The Work of Edward Said' conference, University of Warwick, 4-6 March 1994a, mimeo.

Norval, A.J. 'Social Ambiguity and the Crisis of Apartheid' in *The Making of Political Identities*, ed. E. Laclau (London: Verso, 1994b).

Norval, A.J. 'Vote the Beloved Country. Notes on the 1994 South African Elections'. Paper presented to the Department of Government Seminar, University of Essex, 15 June 1994c, mimeo.

Rousseau, J.J. *The Social Contract* (Penguin Classics, 1968).

Van Rooyen, J. *Hard Right. The New White Power in South Africa* (London: I.B. Tauris, 1994).

Žižek, S. 'Formal Democracy and its Discontents', *American Imago*, vol. 48, 2, p181-98.

J acques Rancière works in the field of political philosophy, analysing the nature and forms of democracy, identity and subjectivation, the frontiers of philosophy and its relation to literature and social science. His most recent publications include *Aux Bords du politique* (1990), and *Les Mots de l'histoire* (1992). In this interview, done in conjunction with the journal *Acta Philosophica*, questions on the relation between politics, philosophy and our contemporary political condition are explored.

Let us begin with a paradox. You say there is no political philosophy. Yet a large part of your work concerns politics and also political philosophy.

Jacques Rancière: The central idea animating my work is that there is no political philosophy or that political philosophy is the name of a misunderstanding. This idea can be clarified in terms of the present situation: the end of the Soviet system appears to spell, on the one hand, the end of the only political alternative to democracy and, on the other, the end of the Marxist alternative to the tradition of political philosophy. It seems that the fall of the Soviet system definitively legitimated democracy as the end of political history, and also re-established political philosophy as the only legitimate reflection on societies and their governments.

But I approach this coincidence from the other side: if the collapse of the Soviet system liberated a discourse of self-satisfaction on the part of governments, which is presumed to coincide with the self-satisfaction of democracy, this actually corresponds to a void in practical politics, even in the practice of what is called formal democracy. Similarly, the political philosophy that is supposed to be liberated by the collapse of the Marxist hypothesis often entails no more

POST-DEMOCRACY, POLITICS AND PHILOSOPHY
an interview with jacques rancière

than academic commentaries on a few canonical authors or grand declarations that politics has come to an end, both of which could be argued to be not much different from the discourse and aims of ordinary politicians.

I begin from this conjuncture, where a presumed liberation of politics and political thought opens up onto a void, in order to reflect on the specificity of politics, on the difference between the political act and the rules by which the state functions on the one hand, and that between democracy as a system of practices and democracy as a constitutional form or as a state of the social, on the other.

Equally, I try to think the difference, maybe internal and unperceived, of the concept of political philosophy. In fact, the platitude of a political philosophy supposedly restored to its rightful place may indicate that the relationship between philosophy and politics is one of conflict. And it is from

post-democracy

this point that I try to return to the origins of what we call political philosophy, to reveal in its founding texts the sign of a disagreement or fundamental misunderstanding between the objectives followed by philosophy and by the political process as I understand it.

Given that the notion of political philosophy is problematic, the question arises of whether politics, and especially so-called democratic politics, can do without philosophy. In other words, is there a link, a necessary relation, between poltics and philosophy?

J.R.: There is in fact an encounter between philosophy and politics in its democratic form, a meeting where, in some sense, it is the misfortune of philosophy always to arrive too late. Politics, in the form of democratic politics, is there before philosophy. This is the whole problem of equality for Plato and Aristotle. For them there is arithmetic equality, the equality of exchange, and there is geometric equality, which is the proportion in terms of which each group must be given its share according to the principle it embodies. But the problem is that the equality of citizens, the equality of Athenian democracy, is implied in neither of these two categories. The scandal of politics for philosophy turns on this equality: it is a 'bad' equality for Plato, a 'formal' equality for the Marx of *the Jewish Question*. Politics exists because there is an equality which is not a 'true' equality, a paradoxical measure of incommensurables.

So there is a kernel of concepts which directly instituted a relation of disagreement between philosophy and politics, an interweaving which is always at the same time conflictual. So, for me the term 'political

philosophy' is one of denial. It supposes that the right concept or the right measure of incommensurables has been found which would permit the deduction of the political community – as it is in the specific case of formal democracies – from the philosophical idea of the common good. I try to show that the kernel of illusion lies in the way this notion of the common good is treated as if it unified in some way the demands of philosophy and politics.

It is usual to distinguish between 'politics'

[la politique] and 'the political' [le politique]. But the way you interpret the idea of 'police' suggests quite a different distinction.

J.R.: Classically, when one tries to think politics and political philosophy one begins from a principle that underlies practical politics, constitutional forms and the modes by which states function. For example, the law, which would be embodied in the action of a political power, in the organisation of the state, and in constitutional texts, as well as

172

in what we might call the philosophical base supporting the whole. But what I try to show is precisely that this homogeneity is illusory. There is no principle of politics that could incarnate itself in all the places where it is a question of the community, of its organisation, and of the state. It is clear that the modern parliamentary state is responsible for this confusion. And this way of thinking of the political field as unified is responsible for a sort of unthinking parallel between a discourse of political philosophy on the one hand, and state practices on the other. It is my idea that the two must be separated if politics is to have any meaning and, in particular, we must stop seeing it as the incarnation of a principle of community.

I try, therefore, to think the political as an encounter between two heterogeneous processes. As a process, a general law of the distribution of bodies in places and functions, a system of relations between parts which organises every social order; and I reserve the term 'police' for all the activities which create order by distributing places, names, functions etc. This means separating the idea of police from that which usually accompanies it, that is to say, the idea of forces of order, repression, the political police and so forth, and returning it to its original sense: the police is the division of the perceptible, which in itself defines the constitution of parties and their parts, from the ancient distribution of the three orders up to the relationship between our governments and the totality of 'opinions' classified by opinion polls. Politics is the singular apparatus [*dispositif*] which subverts this division by the simple introduction of a presupposition which is heterogeneous to it: that of the equality of anybody with anybody. This presupposition translates into subjects like 'the people' or 'the proletariat' which are not social entities but operators of

the logic of the political: the manifestation of a singular 'part' of the part that has no parts. More precisely, the political, understood as the place of practical politics, would be the meeting place of two heterogeneous logics: the logic of the police, as I understand it, that of distribution and its legitimations, and the logic of the verification of equality.

This way of thinking came to me by a detour. When I was working on the theory of intellectual emancipation elaborated by Joseph Jactot, a Frenchman who was completely marginalised at the beginning of the nineteenth century, I was struck by the way he opposed a logic of what he called 'intellectual emancipation', founded on the presupposition of the equality of anybody with anybody, to all forms of social logic. For him, the equality of minds was ultimately presupposed by any order, even the most inegalitarian. It was possible to disengage that presupposition and to make it work. That is what 'emancipation' means, to make equality effective. But this effectiveness of equality could not become collective, could not govern the logic of social bodies, which is a logic of weights and counterweights. It was possible to imagine that all the individuals of a society were emancipated, but not that society was equal. No society could be egalitarian.

It is a kind of challenge thrown down to all problematics that are progressive, socialist or simply democratic in the modern sense. And I was interested in the way one could try to force this opposition. My endeavour to force this opposition, or this logic of opposition, led me to think more specifically about the role of politics as the constitution of apparatuses of subjectivation, which allow the law of equality to produce an effect in the social order. My idea was that there are meeting points. It is true

173

that the logic of equality, of the verification of equality, and the logic of distribution, of social arrangement, are two heterogeneous logics, but it is nevertheless possible to produce an effect of equality in the social order. That is, this logic can only be produced in the social order by means of something we can call 'place-holders'. This supposes that specific apparatuses constitute themselves to put into play what I call additional or surplus unities which superimpose themselves on those unities which are part of society. Political 'subjects' combine, in the name of a party or identity, with the empty name of the simple equality of anybody with anybody. My idea is that if democracy has any meaning, it is as a mode of political subjectivation where the people, or indeed any other subjective figure, is something other than the population, the race or any other embodied entity.

Among the place-holders of the logic of equality there is a privileged figure, a singular subjective figure called 'the people'. The long history of this figure, which has been present from the beginning of political philosophy, poses the question of its meaning in this role as a political subject and, more generally, how to construct and think these meeting points between the two heterogeneous logics which constitute any social order.

J.R.: What I am trying to do is to link what we can call original questions, which were posed at the beginning of politics, and those which are posed today. The original question is the one a philosopher like Plato may have asked faced with this entity called the people, the *demos*, which identifies with the community without, however, being the whole of it and even, rather, naming a division at the heart of it.

The *demos* is identified with the whole community by the fact of incarnating the part which has no parts. I try to think the relation between this original difference from itself of the democratic people and the modern phenomena of the masking of this difference: the recent embodiments of the people in race or the glorious worker or its current transformation into a collection of communities of race, sex, culture, and so forth. The regression of democracy is always tied to the loss of this difference from itself.

So it is from this point that I try to think politics as processes of subjectivation which differentiate themselves from all action in the name of a social group identifiable as a part of the society. There are subjectivations when there are named subjects. Thus, for politics to exist there must first be a subject of enunciation, a 'we'. Politics begins when it is possible to say 'we'. It may be 'we citizens', 'we workers', 'we proletarians', 'we women', and so on. Politics begins when a 'we' can be enunciated and I would say that a 'we' puts in place an apparatus of subjectivation which names subjects in their difference from themselves. If it is said 'we proletarians', this we appeals to a community which is not realised and which does not exist already, such that it could not just be represented.

So, a subject of enunciation creates an apparatus where a subject is named precisely to expose a particular wrong, to create a community around a particular dispute. That is to say, there is politics precisely when one reveals as false the evidence that the community exists already and everyone is already included. Political subjectivation is always attached to the name of a subject, to the figure of a subject, to the extent that this name, this figure, is problematic. There is politics when the 'we's arrange by their words and acts the visible sphere of subjects who are not collective bodies or social groups, but operators who, under diverse names (citizens, patriots, workers, women), make visible and dispute the relation between inclusion and exclusion.

Different modes of subjectivation put into question, one might say, the relation between universal and particular. So the question then becomes, how to uncover, in the domain of the political, the specific logic according to which the relation between the two is ordered.

J.R.: I would say that in politics every universal is singularised. There are two ways of conceiving politics. At the present time there are the partisans of universality who say: there is the law of the universal and all politics is organized from there. Then there are those who hold to particularity, who think political society as a grouping of a certain number of identities or groups and the universal as nothing more than a pact made by those parties. I try to show that there is politics when there are forms of singularisation of the universal which raises the question of knowing in what the universal is universal, and in what it is power. Politics makes the concept of the universal work in some way.

There are two forms by which politics is denied: that which says the universal is the concern of the state; and that which says, the universal is the lie behind which there are particular interests. Politics is the practice by which the universal is put to the test, in singularising it, in demanding what follows from the idea of citizenship, of equality before the law, of the undecided relation between man and citizen in this or that case; the worker and his employer: are they two citizens linked by the universality of citizenship? The rights of man: are they the rights of women? Politics constructs cases, polemic apparatuses of verification of the universal. The mod-

ern democratic movement has consisted entirely of bringing into play the universal, citizenship, equality before the law, by constructing a relation between their affirmation and their negation, by showing how it is denied in certain cases, at work, for example. That is to say, by applying it in a polemical construction. The universal of politics is not equality before the law, it is its logic that puts equality into question in apparatuses which confront it with its own negation, in argumentations which are at the same time manifestations constructing the perceptible space of the argumentation. Political demonstration makes visible two worlds in one. And by this fact it is always child's play for philosophy to prove that its singular universal is not the real universal or that it is nothing more than ideological mystification.

One of the virtues of democratic politics is the way it deals with a wrong. Nevertheless we must first ask a very naive question. What, for you, is 'a wrong'? Or rather, how does it arise and how should it be dealt with?

J.R.: A wrong (*le tort*) is first of all something like a torsion, a wringing (*une torsion*). This is not a play on words. A wrong is in the very constitution of the political scene. It is the encounter between logics which could never meet. I try to show that when one wants to define political justice, or to deduce political justice from a discussion on the useful and the harmful etc., there is something which escapes and I try to delimit it in the founding texts of political science, notably Aristotle's, around such concepts as injury, harm and so forth. It is the same problem as that of the relation between arithmetic and geometric equality. There is another equality, which is neither one nor the other, and similarly there is a torsion which is somewhere between the harmful and the unjust, an absence of passage from one equality to another, an absence of deduction from one level, that of rational individuals, to another, that of political justice. So a wrong in the first sense is nothing but the constitution of politics, the encounter between the logic of the police and the logic of the verification of equality. Thus, for Aristotle, to pass from the order of the useful to the order of the just which defines the political community, it is necessary to pass through an adding up of the parties of the city and the claims they try to uphold in the community. Now, the only claim, the only property the *demos* has, is that of its liberty. But it's an empty claim, it appears to be a given fact rather than a principle incarnated in a body. I would say that this liberty is the place-holder of equality by means of which it has the effect of pure interruption in the supposedly natural order of domination insofar as it reaffirms the paradoxical, and yet foundational, truth that inequality itself is ultimately possible and thinkable only because of equality.

A wrong is the encounter of heterogenes, the measure of incommensurables. Political philosophy is, in one sense, the refusal of this encounter, the request that politics should have its 'own' foundation, the refusal of the equality that blocks at one and the same time, the logic of arithmetic exchanges and the calculation of geometric proportions, of the exhibition of a wrong which comes before the definition of the just. The political scene is biased from the point of view of philosophy.

This can be seen also in the Aristotelian definition of the political animal: man is 'naturally' political because he has at his disposal the *logos* which argues and not only the *phone* which expresses pleasure or pain. Now this division of principle is in fact the stake of a permanent dispute. Because, in fact, the *logos* doubles itself: it is the linguistic capac-

ity but also the account that is given of it. The order of police divides men, and the places of the *logos* and men, and the places of noise. The political intervention is that which designates as the manifestation of a *logos* what in the police order is seen only as noise. A worker's strike, a demonstration in the street, show themselves as belonging to a *logos* and defining a community which is only audible as the noise of a group belonging to a particular type of animal society.

Wrong consists in the fact that the political scene is always asymmetrical and it can be thought in both directions. There are philosophers who want to found politics in right, so that for them injustice arises because equality already exists, and exists badly, in a contingent fictitious way, without responding to an *arche* of the community. And on the other side there is politics as the scene of constant dispute concerning whether the community exists. There is a community because it is always contested: there is dispute concerning who is included, which statement is a *logos* constituting the community and which is a noise. That is how an apparatus of political subjectivation creates a community, by making evident a non-community. The political community is that which is deployed in a dispute against the community.

The founding wrong of politics must be distinguished from two things: judicial rulings on the one hand, and infinite wrong or inexpiable debt on the other. If there is an inexpiable debt, is there politics? And it is the same if the treatment of wrongs is replaced by a scene in which there is right, the universal and people who discuss in order to try to universalise their interests and the validity of their norms. This is the Habermasian problem, maintaining that there is a rationality of politics once one comes to conclude that arguments can be judged on the basis of universal norms. Now, if there is politics it is because one party does not recognise the other as such, or considers that there is no object of dispute, or that the subjects of the discussion are not constituted. Political argumentation must polemically construct the scene of its validity.

To the extent that wrong is always singular can one speak of dealing with a wrong? Is it not always blocked in advance?

J.R.: For me a wrong is not always unmanageable. It cannot be ruled, it can however be treated and is constantly treated. Political discourse and action constantly deal with heterogeneity so it doesn't mean intractability. I think there is a whole series of forms that deal with wrongs. But they are, nevertheless, always singular, they are singularisations of the universal. The problem of politics today is that there are no longer any means of singularising the universal. There is the universal and then there are identities.

How, then, should we think the singular of the universal today, given that there are no more examples? And what does modern racism mean, what impact might it have on democracy? Is it a phenomenon that is inherent to democracy itself or rather something that is quite foreign to it?

J.R.: Concerning the phenomena of political catastrophes, I don't think they require a great effort of thought. Every form of polit-ical catastrophe, like all forms of abjection, individual and collective, are so ordinary and simply, always brutally, there that, in my opinion, arguments which suggest that they are very complicated and that we need a specific theory for

them, are unconvincing. No, I think racism, hatred, fear of the other, and so on, are always there, close by.

The point is that when there is democratic politics, there are heterologous forms of subjectivation which traverse this domain. If there is democracy, that means there are figures of subjectivation which are figures of a difference. The people is something which is not the population, race, blood, and so forth. The proletariat is not a social group. The political forms of democracy have a virtue against all forms of xenophobia, racism, hatred of the other because they constitute the sphere in which non-identical subjects are able to appear.

Racism is not therefore inherent in democracy but in the fact that democracy always functions on the edge of its abyss. Its subjectivations are the differences between identities, identities different from themselves, but homonymous with 'real' identities. The people is the part without parts manifested in apparatuses of subjectivation that make up all of 'reality', but it is also the name of a real population, an *ethnie*, the support of a certain number of supposedly natural qualities. Racism can, therefore, always appear and it appears where there is a striving to remove from the people its character of *appearance*, either in the name of an organicism of the community, or of a realistic calculation of the parties involved and their social interests. When the 'appearance' collapses, what's left is the naked reality of identities and their alterities. That is what is happening in what I call post-democracy. Post-democracy is a system in which democracy is thought of as a simple conjunction between a state of the social (democratic 'individualism', and so forth) and constitutional forms. But democracy is neither one nor the other. It is a mode of subjectivation of politics. There is democracy, if there is a sphere in which the people appears as a manifestation of a wrong, if there are subjects that are not social groups. It is claimed that today there is a politics without the people, where 'people' no longer designates an instance of enunciation, but is identified with a real group divided up into social groups. But to think of politics in this way, is to identify it with the police in the sense in which I understand it. The ideal of so-called 'realist' politics is to identify subjects with real groups. In this way the 'realist' wisdom prepares the ground for an identitary ethnic and racist madness. Subjects, different from themselves, which characterise democracy, are not wanted. Its people are dismissed as a phantom. As a consequence, we see the return of the 'real' people: that which is defined by race, blood, and so forth. The 'old' racism – which still has many good days left in it – is derived from the organicist vision of the nineteenth century. The new takes root in liberal 'realism'. Our present is the conjunction of both.

interviewers: jelica sumic and rado riha
translator: kate nash

DEBATE

Readers are invited to submit responses to pieces published in the journal to be considered for publication in the debate section. Responses should be no more than 3,000 words, and should be sent in duplicate, double-spaced.

The first issue of this journal included an article by David Howarth defending some of Ernesto Laclau's statements about the sort of categories needed to articulate a suitably radical political practice (Howarth, 1993). The crux of the article involved a clarification of the status of the categories of space and time Laclau was using – a clarification successfully deflecting some of the criticisms levelled against Laclau's thesis. However, in passing, Howarth made some claims about what being radical involves, and it is these that I feel I must take issue with. They raise deep questions about the ground and the aim of our critical practice.

Towards the end of his article Howarth lent his support to a politics of disruption and discontinuity – a notion thought through a category of time. He contrasted this radical attitude with a conservative one aiming to fix a particular set of identities – a concern for patterns of repetition thought through a category of space. The conservative attitude was said to involve 'the valorisation of tradition, particularism and the privileging of the provincial over the cosmopolitan' (53). Referring more specifically to parochial concerns with particular spaces and places he stated that these concerns tend:

> [T]owards inherently conservative and reactionary positions. In other words, though this type of opposition to modernity may provide a bulwark against processes bound up with the omnivorousness of globalisation and universalisation, new forms of particularity articulated around the preservation of space, territoriality and place cannot offer meaningful or proactive alternatives to these dominant global logics. (53)

Howarth is surely right to criticise those who seek to hide from modernity in a cosy hamlet, leaving the political and economic

michael reid

THE AIMS OF RADICALISM
a reply to david howarth

forces to do their worst. He is also right to criticise the sort of xenophobic defence of particularity that supports policies of ethnic cleansing. But in our concern to distance ourselves from reactionary and paranoid attitudes we need to be careful not to forget the way in which a concern for the parochial, the particular and the concrete can radicalise us. In setting ourselves against the pernicious conservatism Howarth highlights, we need to be careful not to overlook a radical concern for particularity.

The discourse he employs sets up an opposition between a radical and a conservative attitude that risks being complicit with the worst excesses of modernity. It risks manifesting a rage against the particular and the concrete. Although this is certainly not true of Howarth personally, it may be true of the discourse he uses.

Conservatism, according to this discourse, seeks to preserve a particular way of identifying the world. I can only tolerate one set of identities. This can either be a benign insistence upon a narrow horizon or it can be violently exclusive. Ethnic cleansing marks an extreme form of this attitude.

We cannot stomach this conservatism, partly because we are conscious of the constructed character of all discourses. We cannot take anything as given any longer. Hence the need for a radical political discourse that thematises the historicity, the impurity and the openness of our practices. To a great extent the consciousness articulated through this discourse will have been inspired and informed by theoretical works.

Radicalism privileges disruption and discontinuity, valuing whatever breaks with established patterns of identification. Now, without wishing to give a reactionary defence of a particular set of identities, we can ask the following question: is disruption and discontinuity an end in itself? When we are concerned with the openness of our practices, is there not something more at stake than mere disruption and discontinuity? If there were not something more at stake we, as radicals, would surely soon become weary and apathetic.

The only notion of radicality that does justice to our actual concerns and can sustain our motivation is one guided by a hope that the things we now see degraded, polluted and abused, and the people we now see marginalised, debased and impoverished will be able to flourish in the future. When we thematise the openness of our practices what surely matters is an openness that will allow that flourishing to occur. The concern for the fate of those particulars helps to guide our critical practice. Without it we empty the future of anything that could matter to us.

What calls conservatism into question is not just a set of theories about the logic of

identity and the role of the constitutive other. These are important but they will be almost meaningless unless we are moved by the suffering and havoc wreaked by contemporary practices. It is the degradation and the suffering of those particulars that, for us, indicates the untruth of the prevailing practices and the untruth of the sort of thinking that governs them.

It is through responses like these that we see beyond the circuit of identities the conservative insists upon. We are prompted to see beyond that circuit insofar as we see the necessity for a different set of practices – ones giving room for those who are now unable to flourish. When we try to engage with a pernicious conservatism theoretically, we need to remember the importance for our political orientation and our theoretical practice of this response to suffering particulars. When Howarth dismisses 'the valorisation of … particularism and the privileging of the provincial over the cosmopolitan' (53) he risks forgetting the importance of this.

In a sense, there is something conservative about this response. It is conservative insofar as it recognises something worth conserving. But what is to be conserved is not a set of identitarian practices but the possibilities of the thing itself. We are concerned that the other (a habitat, an animal, individual person or cultural group) be able to flourish and develop. We are concerned to keep our practices open to accommodate and facilitate a development we cannot predict.

Talk of a conservatism concerned with an open-ended development is incongruous, but I will leave this as it stands. The attempt to appropriate the category 'conservative' to a fuller understanding of a radical politics is made because conservatism has been associated in the discourse Howarth uses with a concern for the particular. How that concern is labelled is not as important as acknowledging its grounding and guiding role in our critical theory and practice.

I have said very little here about the concerns for place Howarth thematises after dealing with 'space' as an ontological category. These, it is said, 'cannot offer meaningful or proactive alternatives to [the] dominant global logics' (53). It is easy to see how these parochial concerns could lack any deeper engagement with wider economic and political processes. But the concern for the ways in which places become homogenised or degraded and polluted, and the way in which communities giving a cultural life to them become atomised and silenced by forms of instrumental reason – these are concerns we have to hold on to. The developing habitats and the flourishing public spaces are among the most important goods that a radical politics will secure. In themselves they may not be an alternative global logic. But perhaps we should not be trying to construct a wholesale alternative. Perhaps we should be concentrating on the sorts of interventions in prevailing practices needed to secure the very parochial goods that motivate our critical practice.

references

Howarth, David, 'Reflections on the Politics of Space and Time', *Angelaki*, vol. 1, 1 (*The Uses of Theory*) (1993) 43-56.

notes on the contributors

benjamin arditi

is completing his doctoral thesis on post-liberal politics in the Department of Government at the University of Essex. He has published several articles on political theory and the transition to democracy in Paraguay.

david bensusan

is Lecturer in Philosophy of Education in the Department of Education at the University of the Witwatersrand, South Africa. He has published on theoretical issues concerning subjectivity, including a contribution to *Perspectives in Education* (1982).

michael cholewa-madsen

completed an MA in Ideology and Discourse Analysis in the Department of Government at the University of Essex. He is currently writing a thesis on postmodern radical political praxis at the Institute of Political Science, University of Copenhagen.

sue golding

is a Lecturer in Political Philosophy at Greenwich University. Her work centres on democracy, feminism, sexualities and the journeying of identity itself, in all their impossible perverse pleasures and risks. Her first book *Gramsci's Democratic Theory* (1992) is being followed by a new work which steps into the virtual realities of a Nietzschean / Wittgensteinian / Foucauldian blend to explore, as it is entitled, *The Cunning of Democracy* (Phronesis Series, Verso: forthcoming).

david howarth

is a doctoral student at the University of Essex in the Ideology and Discourse Theory Programme, and teaches politics at the University of Essex.

timothy s. murphy

is a doctoral candidate in literature at the University of California, Los Angeles; he also teaches at the University of Pepperdine in Malibu. He is currently completing his dissertation, *Wising up the Marks: Amodernism in the Work of William S. Burroughs and Gilles Deleuze*, a study of aesthetic, political and philosophical alternatives to postmodernism.

aletta j. norval

is a Lecturer in the Department of Government at the University of Essex, and is Director of the MA in Ideology and Discourse Analysis. She has published several articles on South African politics and post-structuralism, and her book on apartheid is to be published by Verso in spring 1995.

david owen

is a Lecturer in Political Theory at the University of Central Lancashire. He is author of *Maturity and Modernity: Nietzsche, Weber, Foucault and the Ambivalence of Reason* (Routledge, 1994) and a contributor to *The Fate of the New Nietzsche* (Avebury, 1993) and *Politics and Modernity* (Sage, 1993). He is editor of the *Journal of Nietzsche Studies* and is writing a book on Nietzsche and the critique of liberal reason, while also co-authoring a text on Foucault and Habermas.

michael reid

completed a PhD in philosophy at the University of Essex and is a contributor to *Radical Philosophy* (summer 1993). He is now teaching English in Nottingham.

rado riha

is a Senior Research Fellow of the Institute of Philosophy, Centre for Scientific Research at the Slovene Academy of Sciences and Arts, Ljubljana. He has published extensively in German, Austrian and Slovene journals and collections on Kantian philosophy, Althusser and French structuralism, epistemology and political theory. His books include *Law and Kant's Critique of Practical Reason* (Urt, Ljubljana), co-authored with Jelica Sumic, and a Lacanian interpretation of Kant's political philosophy *Zur Kritik der Urteilskraft im Lacanscher Absicht* (Hora Verlag, Vienna).

yael shalem

is a Lecturer in Sociology of Education in the Department of Education at the University of the Witwatersrand, South Africa. She has published widely in the field of education and has contributed to the *British Journal of Sociology of Education* (1992).

jelica sumic

is a Research Fellow of the Institute of Philosophy, Centre for Scientific Research, at the Slovene Academy of Sciences and Arts, Ljubljana. She has published several articles and two books on philosophy of language and of law. She is currently, together with Rado Riha, working on a book on discourse and hegemony to be published by Verso.

rudi visker

studied economics and sociology in Leuven (Belgium) and philosophy in Leuven and Bochum. He did his PhD in philosophy on 'A Postface to Transgression. The Status of Foucault's Critique' (1989). He is presently a Postdoctoral Researcher of the Belgian National Fund for Scientific Research, affiliated to the Institute of Philosophy (Katholieke Universiteit Leuven), where he teaches phenomenology and contemporary philosophy. He is also a Fellow of the University of Essex and his book on Foucault will appear in English from Verso in summer 1995.

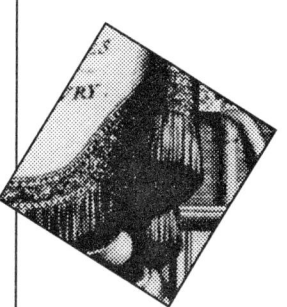

ANGELAKI

Angelaki is a new triannual journal edited by researchers in philosophical, literary and social theory. The journal seeks to publish challenging work from contributors in different centres in the UK and overseas, and to foster a spirit of vigorous debate within and between disciplines.

Angelaki encourages a critical engagement with theory in terms of disciplinary development and intellectual and political usefulness; the inquiry into and articulation of culture, and the complex determination of change and its relation to history.

The journal especially strives to foster the theory of minor movements, recognising their significant impact on and dynamic relation to the development of cultures, political spaces and academic disciplines, and emphasising their formative power, rather than their oppositional entrenchment.

Angelaki provides a forum for the inquiry into questions of existential and political definition and agency, on the personal, collective, institutional and policy-oriented levels, and promotes the work of spirited and experimental theoretical writing in all areas of value-production.

The journal publishes thematic issues.

call for papers / issue proposals

Angelaki invites the submission of original articles of 2-10,000 words, reviews and review articles, and proposals for translations and interviews. Typescripts should be in duplicate, double-spaced. The editors also encourage the submission of publishing proposals from individuals prepared to assume responsibility for producing an issue of the journal. Issue proposals should be at least 500 words, and should make clear the kind of publication envisaged, and the way in which it will contribute to *Angelaki*'s project.

debate

Readers are invited to submit responses to pieces published in the journal to be considered for publication in the debate section. Responses should be no more than 3,000 words, and should be sent in duplicate, double-spaced.

Angelaki
44 Abbey Rd
Oxford OX2 0AE UK

Angelaki is a refereed serial.

back issues

vol. I, no. I
the uses of theory

Publication: September 1993. Pages: 144.

Editors: Pelagia Goulimari
and Gerard Greenway

Contents
On the Line of Flight: How to be a Realist?, *Pelagia Goulimari*. Crisis in Politics, *Barry Stocker*. Reflections on the Politics of Time and Space, *David Howarth*. Surprise in Literature, *Sarah Wood*. Title without Colon, *Robert Smith*. Yuli's Birthday Party: A Philosophical Short Story, *Mozaffar Qizilbash*. Never Mind the Ballads, Here's Thomas Percy, *Nick Groom*. Interview with Félix Guattari. Félix Guattari: Towards a Queer Chaosmosis, *Josep-Anton Fernández*. William Burroughs Between Indifference and Revalorisation: Notes Towards a Political Reading, *Timothy S. Murphy*. In the Shadow of Cybernetic Minorities: Life, Death and Delirium in the Capitalist Imaginary, *Charlie Blake*.

vol. I, no. 2
narratives of forgery

Publication: April 1994. Pages: 176.

Editor: Nick Groom

Contents
Rewriting Plagiarism, *Don Nichol*. The Isle of Pines and the Problem of Genre, *Daniel Carey*. Forgery or Plagiarism?, *Nick Groom*. Chatterton in Bristol, *Jonathan Barry*. What Thomas Knew, *Michael F. Suarez S.J.* The Macaroni Parson and the Marvellous Boy, *Paul Baines*. Forgery Discovered, *Randall McGowen*. Identity, Authenticity, Class, *John Goodridge*. Arthur as Artefact, *Inga Bryden*. Thomas Chatterton: Early Sources and Responses, *Review Article*.

forthcoming issues

vol. 2, no. 1
home and family

Publication: spring 1995.

Editor: Sarah Wood

Theory can do more than simply extend the topography of the *oikia* (household) into unfamiliar spaces. The lexical itinerary of *oikia* incorporates interminable detours. How choose between one's literal and figurative home, one's romanticised families? How to move between establishments? Are big theories the place for these considerations? Marx established a new set of proprieties; but what has kept Marx in circulation is unfamiliar material practices (reading, substitution, exchange). Can household names take on the attributes of Kafka's 'assistants': 'neither members of, nor strangers to ... but, rather, messengers from the one to the other' (Benjamin)? When psychoanalytic theory displaces topography with toponymy, the reassessment of establishments through cryptic disturbances and unplaced silences might occasion unprecedented articulations.

Provisional Contents
Introduction, *Sarah Wood.* This is not a Book Review, *Nicholas Royle.* Theory on the Toilet: A Manifesto for Dreckology, *Roy Sellars.* Fourier's 'Famillism' versus Couples, *René Schérer.* Notes on 'Famillism', *René Schérer.* Privatising Culture: Reflections on Jean-François Lyotard's 'oikos', *Bill Readings.* Rhetoric and Political Economy, *Forbes Morlock.* The Art of Doing Nothing, *Fran Sendbuehler.* Luce Irigary – at Home with Martin Heidegger?, *Alison Ainley.* Rat Man's Crypt, *Robert White.*Traversing Identity: Home Movies and Road Movies in *Paris Texas,* Roger Bromley. Imaginary Homelands: Notes on *Heimat* and *Heimlich, Stephen Keane.* Homes Without *Heimats*: Jean Améry at the Limits, *Dan Stone.*

vol. 2, no. 2
authorizing culture

Publication: summer 1995.

Editors: Gary Hall and Simon Wortham

For many, criticism is currently trapped in a struggle whereby the representation of popular culture is restricted to a choice between what appear to be two equally unacceptable positions: between, on the one hand, a traditional position of cultural critique and critical distance; and, on the other, a denial of distance and difference in favour of a simple celebration of cultural forms. It is this impasse, between the reactionary repudiation of popular culture, and its unequivocal and complacent celebration, that *Authorizing Culture* will explore. In what ways does this problem affect contemporary forms of cultural criticism (cultural studies, cultural materialism, new historicism, post-structuralism, psychoanalysis, post-colonial discourse, et al.)? Can cultural criticism really take no other form than an opposition between optimism and pessimism, inside and outside, critical objectivity and populist celebration? And is a change in attitude needed toward those commonly considered to be the modern masters?

Provisional Contents
Rethinking Authority, Interview with *Homi K. Bhabha.* It's a Thin Line Between Love and Hate: Why Cultural Studies is so 'Naff', *Gary Hall.* The Glasse of Majesty: Reflections on New Historicism and Cultural Materialism, *Simon Wortham.* Saint Raymond, *Robert Young.* Towards an Ethics of Discipleship, *Jonathan Darbyshire.* 'Something Still More Exact': T.S. Eliot's 'Traditional Claims', *Elizabeth Beaumont Bissell. Plus* review articles on recent publications by Derrida; on Nietzsche; in Cultural Studies.

vol. 2, no. 3
intellectuals and global culture

Publication: autumn 1995.

Editors: Charlie Blake and Linnie Blake

Whether the issue is institutionalisation or degeneration (Jacoby, Bloom), genealogy or delegitimation (Turner, Baumann), specificity or universality (Spivak, Said), or redundancy (Johnson, Carey), the intellectual is now a species under anxious, largely autolectic, scrutiny. This number will consider the broad issue of the intellectual as both regional and global phenomenon – as visualiser of the *world* as much as the *locality*, the *universal* as much as the *specific*. The issue will examine the mutable status of the intellectual in different periods and, importantly, in different parts of the world; in the corporation and the revolutionary cell; in the imagination of artists and dreamers.

The editors invite papers and proposals from all points of view (nation, gender, sexuality, class, cultural identity in general) on themes relating to intellectuals and global or local culture.

Provisional Contents
Falling Down, *Tim Shakesby*. And Now Here Comes a Book that Makes Everything Easy: Intellectual History and the Field of Intellectual Production, *John Beasley-Murray*. Critical Mass: Intellectual Politics and the Mode of Complexity, *Charlie Blake*. The Jew, the Red, the Whore and the Bomber, *Linnie Blake*. The African-American Intellectual Abroad, *James Wilie*. The Impertinence of Intellectuals: Democracy and Post-Modernity in Latin America, *Joanildo N. Burity*. Soyinka and Cultural Politics: The Politics of Culture, *Caroline Ukoumunne*. On Bulgarian Intellectuals, *Yanna Popova*. Bugger Bentham: Sodomy and the Panoptic Intellectual, *Elaine Brown*.

vol. 3, no. 1
the love of music

Publication: spring 1996.

Editors: Timothy S. Murphy, Roy Sellars and Robert Smith

Music surrounds us today. But as our range of choice in musics has widened, our power to choose to hear or not and our ability to listen have narrowed. In moving out of the concert hall and the shrine into the home, the workplace and the market, music has taken on a series of contradictory and unstable determinations: soundtrack to everyday life, assertion of ethnic or social identity, testament to taste, 'pure' aesthetic, Edenic language, commodity, and so on. The difference between music and noise is no longer clear.

In the midst of this polyphony or cacophony, what can it mean to love music? What is the place and time and voice of music, and how does music find its way into our domestic lives and intellectual work? How do we use music, whether as alibi, idea, marker of status, ur-language, or Other? Is the appropriation of music inevitable, impossible, or both?

The editors invite contributions from all critical perspectives (musicological, philosophical, psychoanalytic, literary, social) addressing any field of music. Submissions should be sent to one of the following:

Timothy S. Murphy, 3614 Faris Drive #31, Los Angeles, CA 90034-7544, USA.
(e-mail: IZZYZR8@MVS.OAC.UCLA.edu)

Roy Sellars, Dépt. d'anglais, Univ. de Genève, CH-1211 Genève 4, Switzerland.
(e-mail: SELLARS@uni2a.unige.ch)

Robert Smith, All Souls College, Oxford OX1 4AL, UK.

THINKING *the* POLITICAL

NEW SERIES

General Editors, **Keith Ansell-Pearson,**
University of Warwick,
and **Simon Critchley,** *University of Essex*

The work of Continental thinkers presents a major challenge to philosophers and political theorists alike. *Thinking the Political* will present the major continental thinkers of our time, and the debates their work have generated, to a wider audience by revealing how their ideas on society, the human being, sexuality, time, metaphysics and revolution, open up new realms for re-thinking the political.

First title in the series . . .

Foucault and the Political
Jonathan Simons

". . . unquestionably the work of a first rate scholar . . ."
– N.J. Rengger, University of Bristol

The first major introductory study of Foucault as a political thinker, Simons relates Foucault's work to contemporary political thinkers and challenges conventional political categories, especially within feminist and gay studies.

November 1994: 234x156: 208pp
Hb: 0-415-10065-8: £35.00 Pb: 0-415-10066-6: £10.99

Future volumes will consider the work of
***Gilles Deleuze, Jacques Derrida, Luce Irigaray,
Martin Heidegger, Julia Kristeva, Ernesto Laclau***
and ***Chantel Mouffe, Emmanuel Levinas***
and ***Friedrich Nietzsche.***

ROUTLEDGE

ACTA PHILOSOPHICA
FILOZOFSKI VESTNIK

Acta Philosophica/Filozofski vestnik is a journal of philosophy with a distinct interdisciplinary and international character. It is published and edited by the Institute of Philosophy in the Centre for the Scientific Research of the Slovenian Academy of Sciences and Arts. *Acta Philosophica/Filozofski vestnik* provides a forum for the discussion focusing on a wide range of currently relevant problems in contemporary political philosophy, philosophy of law, social philosophy, epistemology and philosophy of science, cultural critique and aesthetics. *Acta Philosophica/Filozofski vestnik* encourages a dialogue between philosophy, history, literary theory, aesthetics sociology, feminist studies, and jurisprudence; and promotes a cultural interchange within the Slovenian, Anglo-American, French, and German world.

Acta Philosophica/Filozofski vestnik appears twice a year, in Spring and Fall. The Spring issue is published in Slovenian language, while the Fall issue, international in character and dealing with a chosen topic, brings contributions in English, French, and German. Among its recent contributors are A. Berten, H. Brunkhorst, P. Crowther, M. Frank, M. Jay, J. Keane, E. Laclau, Ch. Mouffe, A. Norval, J. G. A. Pocock, F. Proust, E. Vollrath, S. Žižek.

Recent special issues:
Vol. XII, No. 1 (Spring 1991) *Form in Art and in Other Theoretical Discourses*
Vol. XIII, No. 2 (Fall 1992) *The Actuality of Kant*
Vol. XIV, No. 2 (Fall 1993) *Questioning Europe*
Vol. XV, No. 2 (Fall 1994) *Fictions* (forthcoming)

All communications should be addressed to the Editor *Acta Philosophica/Filozofski vestnik*, Institute of Philosophy, ZRC SAZU, Gosposka 13, 61000 Ljubljana, Slovenia (Fax: +386 61 125 5253).
ISSN 0353-4510; Annual Subscription: 18 $ for Individuals, 36 $ for Institutions. Single issue: 10 $ for Individuals, 20 $ for Institutions. Back Issues Available. Send cheques payable to: ZRC SAZU, Ljubljana.

OLR

Frontiers
Edited by **Geoffrey Bennington** and **Barry Stocker**
Volume 14

240pp

Experiencing the Impossible
Edited by **Timothy Clark** and **Nicholas Royle**
Volume 15

260pp

Prices: £7.95 (UK); £10.50 or US $19.00 (foreign) per volume
Make cheques payable to *Oxford Literary Review*.

Send to:
OXFORD LITERARY REVIEW
DEPARTMENT OF ENGLISH STUDIES
UNIVERSITY OF STIRLING
STIRLING, FK9 4LA
SCOTLAND

TELOS

A Quarterly Journal of Critical Thought

Since its appearance in May 1968, *Telos* has introduced into the English-speaking world the best of continental thought and tackled major international issues. Committed to the development of an *American* Critical Theory, *Telos* analyzes American and international questions from a broad geopolitical perspective.

Issue No. 96   *Summer 1993*

Special Section On Russia

Subscriptions cost $32 per year (four issues) for individuals; $80 for institutions. Foreign and Canadian orders add 15%. Checks must be in US funds drawn on US banks. No Canadian checks will be accepted. Back issues are $9.50 each (institutions pay $25). Back issues available: 13, 17-18, 20-51, 53-95. For subscription, back issues or information, write:

Telos Press Ltd., 431 E. 12th Street, New York NY 10009

ordering information

Angelaki, Volume I (1993/94)
(3 Issues) ISSN: 0969-725X

Subscription rates per volume (inc. p+p)

	UK	Overseas*
Individuals:	£12.00	£14.00/US$24.00
Institutions:	£18.00	£20.00/US$33.00

Single issue/sample copy rates (inc. p+p)

	UK	Overseas*
Individuals:	£4.50	£4.50/US$9.00
Institutions:	£7.50	£7.50/US$12.50

Please make cheques payable to **Angelaki**.
Send your order with payment to:
**Angelaki 44 Abbey Rd
Oxford OX2 0AE UK**

Please ensure that you provide us with your full address.

If you have bought *reconsidering the political* and you would like to subscribe to the remaining issues in the current volume, *the uses of theory* and *narratives of forgery*, individuals can do so at a cost of: £8.00 / £9.50 (overseas*); US$16.00* – inc. p+p. Send your order, with payment, to the above address.

*Overseas prices subject to change. Other nationalities please apply for own currency prices.